WHO WAS JACK THE RIPPER?

ALL THE SUSPECTS REVEALED

Dedicated to
the eternal memory of Martin Fido

WHO WAS JACK THE RIPPER?

ALL THE SUSPECTS REVEALED

By Members of H: Division Crime Club

PEN & SWORD HISTORY

AN IMPRINT OF PEN & SWORD BOOKS LTD.
YORKSHIRE – PHILADELPHIA

First published in Great Britain in 2019 and republished in this format in 2025 by
PEN AND SWORD HISTORY
An imprint of
Pen & Sword Books Ltd
Yorkshire – Philadelphia

ISBN 978 1 39901 943 9

A CIP catalogue record for this book is available from the British Library.

Typeset in Times New Roman 11.5/14 by
SJmagic DESIGN SERVICES, India.
Printed in the UK by CPI Group (UK) Ltd, Croydon, CR0 4YY.

The Publisher's authorised representative in the EU for product safety is Authorised Rep Compliance Ltd., Ground Floor, 71 Lower Baggot Street, Dublin D02 P593, Ireland.
www.arccompliance.com

For a complete list of Pen & Sword titles please contact
PEN & SWORD BOOKS LIMITED
George House, Units 12 & 13, Beevor Street, Off Pontefract Road,
Barnsley, South Yorkshire, S71 1HN, England
E-mail: enquiries@pen-and-sword.co.uk
Website: www.pen-and-sword.co.uk
or
PEN AND SWORD BOOKS
1950 Lawrence Rd, Havertown, PA 19083, USA
E-mail: uspen-and-sword@casematepublishers.com
Website: www.penandswordbooks.com

MIX
Paper | Supporting responsible forestry
FSC® C013604

Contents

What is H:Division?

The H:Division Crime Club originally started as a small group of enthusiasts studying the crimes of Jack the Ripper and the East End of London but over time soon grew to cover all aspects of true crime across the world. H:Division comprises some of the most respected researchers and authors in the field of Ripper studies and true crime. All experts under one roof.

As we originally formed searching for the identity of Jack the Ripper we decided to name ourselves after the original police unit that hunted the Ripper back in 1888 – a homage to where we started and a reference to the ultimate crime mystery. Thus H:Division True Crime Club UK was born.

All our members share a wide range of crime interests, from the classic criminal cases of the Victorian era right the way through the twentieth century up to and including modern day crime investigations. We also have a deep interest in the historical aspects associated with each unique case and our members also include experts in the scientific and psychological aspects of crime investigation.

Our members include police officers, crime scene investigators, criminal psychologists, researchers, authors, true crime enthusiasts and armchair detectives.

The Crime Club is also a valuable research tool and helpline when investigating a new project, writing a book or studying. Our connections in the field have a wealth of knowledge and expertise to help any enthusiast.

We hold regular meetings and crime events across the UK. These meetings vary and include expert talks and tours and visits to locations relating to the history of UK crime.

For anyone interested in learning more about H:Division please visit the website www.richardcharlescobb.com

Foreword

The Prime Suspects

By Professor David Canter

When asked to provide an introductory overview to a book of contributions proposing suspects for the Whitechapel murders I was surprised by what these accounts revealed. Perhaps the most salutary was the repeated revelations about the life and times of those living in the East End of London in the 1880s. These conditions are not just of historical interest. Not only do they provide the crucial backdrop for understanding the investigations into the horrific murders and the suspects who emerge, they also speak to us across the century with relevance today. This is a relevance both for understanding modern detective work as well as the consequences of desperate poverty and the degradation that often comes with it.

Again and again throughout these chapters we are reminded of the despairing conditions that drive women to dangerously sell sex on the street. This has echoes in the present day. Not long ago I studied the experiences of present-day street sex workers. Violence was accepted as part of their trade. Legal controls and police disdain only made this something they had to live with. In a subsequent study in the Netherlands, a country we mistakenly think of as liberal and facilitative towards prostitution, with the consequent assumption that these women's lives would not be so dangerous, I actually studied 120 murders of prostitutes, a great many of which had gone unsolved.

The murders in the East End of London in 1888 are therefore one more illustration of how predatory men will find vulnerable victims on whom to act out their predilections. Serial killers become skilled in knowing where to find women (usually) who are defenceless and in situations where they can attack and abuse them without being disturbed. This skill poses particular problems for any police investigation. Often the only thing the victims have in common is their vulnerability and location. They have no link to the killer. Consequently, there is no trail to follow of contacts and associations that will lead to the culprit.

In present day murder inquiries in the UK, in which there is no apparent link between the criminal and the victim, huge teams of police officers are put onto the task. One estimate is that it costs the taxpayer as much as a million pounds for these inquiries. When carried out systematically the process is to generate a comprehensive list of possible suspects, from police records, house-to-house enquiries and intelligence sources including informants. The process is then to trace each suspect, check his (typically) identity is correct and then eliminate him through availability, alibi or any other appropriate criteria. Those who survive this trawl then become key suspects who are examined very closely.

If there is any fibre or other forensic evidence, preferably fingerprints or DNA, this can be used to focus the trawl. Of course, if the culprit's identifier is in police records, or comes into the searches of investigators that greatly speeds up the process. But none of this was available to the police in 1888.

Have you noticed that there have been no reports of serial killers in the UK in the last few years? This is the case, although the frequency of violent crime, notably knife and gun crime, has not decreased to a very great degree over that period. I put the lack of serial killers down, at least in part, to the improved effectiveness of the boys in blue. If a person kills a stranger, and gets away with it, that person is more dangerous. Whatever psychological processes gave rise to the killing they are not likely to have faded away. But now the murderer has determined the risks and how to avoid them. He may even believe his success is a sign from the fates that he ought to be doing what he is doing. In other words, incompetent policing facilitates serial killing.

It is almost axiomatic that where a murder, or even more so a series of linked murders, go unsolved that the initial investigation was flawed in a number of different ways. The search for Jack the Ripper fits this process, perhaps not because of bungling by the police – I'm not enough of an historian to comment on that, although there are rebukes recorded by a coroner telling the police they had not interviewed everyone they ought to – but because they did not have the personnel resources or those of modern forensic science to make their investigation more effective. It is doubtful if they had thorough systematic records of known criminals (even today police records are not as accurate or complete as crime fiction often implies). The records of who lived where in the Whitechapel area were also likely to be incomplete. Today, the various spellings and alternative names of immigrants and many others can cause havoc in computer searches. In late Victorian London, seeing waves of migrants passing through was doubtless even more problematic. Martin Fido demonstrates this problem in his discussion of Kosminski and Cohen, both of whom are difficult to identify with any certainty against the range of misspellings, mistaken records and general confusion of the time.

A further challenge in the obstacle course which was the East End of London, where unsolved, stranger murder was not uncommon, is determining which murders are committed by the same person – crime linkage. This is not as established an art as TV dramas would have us believe. There are many reasons why a killer may change his actions from one crime to the next. He may learn 'on the job' so to speak about how to control and kill his victims. He may wish to push his experiences further and try new things that excite him. Also, of course, there is the possibility of being disturbed and his actions therefore being very different.

The other challenge of linking, in the absence of forensic material to tie different crimes together, is that the information about what happened in the crime has to be gleaned from information recorded about the crime scene. Obtaining such records is notoriously open to confusion. In addition, the record has to be interpreted. Even with videos and photographs, the crime scene may have been disturbed by intruders and actions subsequent to the murder. The presence of a 'signature' that defines unique aspects of the crime is extremely rare.

The sobriquet that came to define the Whitechapel murders implies that some form of vicious mutilation was characteristic of all the linked crimes. However, the record of these attacks on the victims' bodies are not as reliable as we would hope and they are certainly not all the same. Nonetheless, the immolation, in any form, of a victim is, happily, extremely rare. Therefore, the linking of murders by the 'ripper' knife wounds is as good a start to considering them the work of one man as anything else available.

We can therefore understand the challenges facing the police investigations in 1888 and the inevitable plethora of suspects that emerged and keep emerging today. But even now we can only TIE (trace, identify and eliminate) suspects generated from available records. Yet in the absence of any forensic evidence, bloodstained coat, body part hidden in a fridge or suspect hair found on the victim's body, how are we to generate suspects and evaluate their likely culpability?

Any crime fiction writer, from Edgar Allen Poe, Conan Doyle and on to the perpetrators of Nordic noir and beyond, will tell you that the narrative can be driven on, in the absence of anything substantial, by speculating about the characteristics of the perpetrator. Thomas Harris, with his invention of Hannibal Lecter, introduced into popular culture the notion of an 'offender profile'. This also generated the mythology that such 'profiles' were somehow the exclusive domain of Special Agents of the FBI. However, although people have been helping investigations by speculating about crucial features of the culprits since biblical times, those Special Agents made an important contribution by showing the value of focusing on the details of what actually happened, when and where, as the basis for any proposals about the offender.

Following the surprisingly profound idea that what a person does and how he does it, when committing a crime, is indicative of who that person is, attention is inevitably drawn to the distinguishing features inherent in the self-proclaimed *nom de guerre* of Jack the Ripper (JtR). It was on the basis of the mutilations of the victims' bodies that the crimes were linked to the same offender.

These links, though, drew attention to another aspect of the crimes. They were all in walking distance of each other. Police records were not collected in a coherent way across London or the country in the 1880s and 1890s so it is possible there were other similar murders. But none have emerged that have an incontrovertibly similar pattern. There are some which may be linked by one feature or another, but the consensus seems to be that we are indeed considering murders that occurred in the Whitechapel area of East London in the autumn of 1888.

This conclusion opens up a further inference. If the murders were in walking distance of each other, over a relatively short period of time, then the killer was very likely to be based in the same area. In a large-scale study I've conducted into serial killers in various countries, it does emerge that as many as three out of every four live within an area circumscribed by where their victims' bodies were found. So, JtR could have been travelling into the area in order to find vulnerable women on the streets, but the highest probability is that he had a base in that area.

Person(s) Unknown

Beyond these possibilities, assumptions about the character of JtR is even more speculative. In her essay in this volume, Katherine Ramsland draws on extensive consideration of serial killers in the USA. Most of these people carried out their crimes in the last half century. There have to be questions, therefore, about how relevant those results are to a Victorian murderer. Yet the plausible description she derives is not that far removed from the proposal put forward by the physician Dr Thomas Bond not long after the murders.

Interestingly she labels JtR as an angry 'lust killer'. He does indeed mutilate and in some cases deliberately leave his victims in a way that degrades them. It seems unlikely he was an amateur anatomist exploring bodies that were available, so anger is an interesting reason for the mutilations. The fact that they were women offering sexual services on the street and that some of the physical attacks were on areas of their bodies usually considered erotic, does open up the idea that sexual gratification, or 'lust', was at base of the killer's actions. The lack of any overt sexual penetration would then need a further explanation. However, the details of the post mortem and records of the victims' bodies are such that it is difficult to be certain that this did not happen.

My own studies of serial killers take a more mundane approach to the actions that distinguish them. My work draws attention to the rarity of mutilation of the victim in the absence of sexual activity. This seems to be linked to a great deal of mental disturbance. These very unusual killers are typically known to be seriously out of contact with day-to-day reality – they are psychotic in some way.

The important point about Katherine Ramsland's or my proposals about JtR are how, or indeed if, they can be used to evaluate the claims about various suspects. The suspects brought together in this volume are limited to those that were known, or assumed, to be in the area of the murders during that autumn in 1888. There are other suspects who appear in various police documents and – again it is a big assumption – those investigating the crimes at the time had good reason to believe the culprit was among them.

Joseph Barnett – The Live-in Lover

The great majority of murders are solved very quickly because the culprits are known to the victims. They either give themselves up or are quickly identified by detectives following links that people have to the deceased. Keith Stride nominates Mary Kelly's lover as a plausible killer of her and the other women who suffered a similar fate. The circumstantial evidence that Keith amasses is interesting, but unlikely to survive a decent defence barrister in court.

In the absence of detailed scientific study of the very rare occurrence of serial killing (the FBI in their often quoted 'study' only got access to a couple of dozen across the US) one-off examples have to be drawn on. It is intriguing, as Stride points out, that there could be parallels between the Ripper of 1888 and the Yorkshire Ripper a century later. Human beings have probably not changed in their fundamentals for at least 40,000 years, so what is a century of apparent progress in that timescale?

William Bury – The Dundee Connection

One particularly interesting suspect apparently fingered by detectives is offered by Bill Beadle. He quotes a hangman as saying that detectives told him when he hanged William Bury 'we are quite satisfied you have hanged Jack the Ripper.' So, there we are (as we say in the area of Wales where I live) all sorted.

Bury was the last man hanged in Dundee. Claims that Bury could have been the Ripper began to appear in newspapers shortly after his arrest. Like Bury, the Ripper had inflicted abdominal wounds on his victims immediately after their deaths, and Bury lived in Bow, near Whitechapel, from October 1887 to January 1889, which placed him fairly near the Whitechapel murders at the appropriate time.

William Bury was known to be a nasty, manipulative man who was hanged for strangling his wife, whom he had mutilated in a not dissimilar way to Jack's ripping. He had left the East End of London not long after the JtR murders there ceased. Bill Beadle draws parallels to the recent serially violent killer Levi Bellfield on the plausible basis that a man who kills women he has no acquaintance with is also likely to have a known history of violence.

In the best crime fiction traditions, Beadle reaches for a motive for Bury killing women on the streets of London. He draws on the delights of psychological interpretations and the vagaries of FBI 'offender profiles'. Interestingly, whereas Ramsland creates a profile of a 'lust murderer', Beadle implies that it is low self-esteem and some sort of fantasy-led desire to mutilate women. That's the great thing about 'offender profiles', there's always one available to suit the culprit you first thought of.

The real problem with FBI profiles is that only a very small proportion of those with the characteristics described in the profile kill anyone, let alone a number of prostitutes. Thus, once again, in the absence of any direct evidence we have to take hearsay and plausible indications of the culprit with the salt that is so readily spread around debate about the 1888 murders.

A different set of suspects from those indicated by investigators are those who are recorded as witnesses in the various enquiries and inquests around the time of the murders.

George Hutchinson – A Person of Interest

A curious figure to emerge as one of the witnesses is proposed by Bob Hinton. He focuses on a forensic examination of a statement made to the police by George Hutchinson. The statement gives a detailed description of a person who could have been JtR. Yet Bob's clinical analysis punches holes in the possibility of Hutchinson having seen what he claims. This opens up the possibility that Hutchinson was trying to mislead the investigation by giving a description that could not possibly have been himself. Curiously, of course, if that description is misleading it throws doubt on other suspects who fit that description.

This does draw attention to another problem faced by investigations in the public eye – all the people who seem to crawl into the light to contribute to the inquiry. Indeed, many of them may even falsely confess to the crime. There were at least fifty people who confessed to killing Olof Palme, the Swedish prime minister. None of whom could have done it.

Some of the witnesses who emerge just want to be part of the excitement. One senior police officer in Israel told me he would never ask the public for help in an investigation because the police would then be inundated with people offering guesses and instructions about what the police should do. Dealing with these would just clog their activities. However, there is another possibility promulgated by FBI Special Agents: that criminals, especially serial killers, will insinuate themselves into an inquiry. There are certainly examples of this when the culprit wishes to use his intervention as a way of finding out what information the police have and how close they are to discovering his identity.

Is that what George Hutchinson was doing? Or was he seriously trying to mislead the investigation. Or was he excited by the furore that was unfolding around the murders and wanted some part of the action?

David Cohen – Mistaken Identity

Martin Fido's explorations for possible suspects also rely heavily on an evaluation of the witnesses who offered up suspects, either in autobiographies or marginalia. These had offered one Kosminski as the most likely culprit. But in the course of the dogged investigation for which Martin has become renowned, he began to believe that the person meant was actually called Cohen, probably David Cohen.

As so often happens in the world of Ripperology, Martin Fido's search for the truth has all the hallmarks of a police procedural about it, with red herrings and false trails there to trip up the unwary. He sidestepped these by going back to the initial source, Chief Inspector Swanson, who had also claimed that his suspect had died in an asylum. According to Martin, David Cohen was the only overtly aggressive patient who had died in Colney Hatch Asylum, being also Jewish, which was assumed to be a characteristic of JtR.

Robert Mann – The Mortuary Assistant

Mei Trow is another contributor who draws on the idea of a 'profile' of the murderer to make his claim for Robert Mann as the killer. Like

Katherine Ramsland, he draws on what is known about twentieth-century US serial killers to draw up, as he calls them, 'ground rules' to characterize JtR.

Robert Mann was a witness at the inquest, like so many other suspects, opening the way into Victorian archives to find out who he was. This revealed a man who seemed to live on his own and may well have had some form of epilepsy. There are no obvious indications why this man in his early 50s would stalk and kill street prostitutes, but in the world of folk looking for suspects, his very plausible harmlessness is a cause for concern.

Jacob Levy – A Syphilitic Butcher

In the pantheon of mentally disturbed Jews living in the area of the murders, Jacob Levy has a claim to significance because of his occupation as a butcher. The traumas in his life included his brother committing suicide by cutting his own throat. Tracy I'anson thus puts her (metaphorical) money on mental disturbance as support for her fingering of Jacob Levy.

The delight of Tracy's explorations is that she has uncovered the clinical file describing Jacob and recorded in The City of London Asylum. I suppose it is reassuring that a qualified doctor was required to diagnose Jacob as mentally disturbed enough to be banished to the lunatic asylum and that he apparently was able to adjust to his life there sleeping and eating well.

Intriguingly Jacob Levy had lived in Middlesex Street, that same street and only location mentioned in the *Diary of Jack the Ripper* as a place where the putative author had 'taken rooms'. (The diary is a journal supposedly written by Liverpool cotton merchant James Maybrick who was murdered by his wife in 1889. It only came to light in 1992 thanks to a Liverpudlian called Mike Barrett who later confessed to it being a hoax.) My own geographical profiling studies show that this street is a reasonable location for a person to walk from to carry out the murders. This combines with the circumstantial evidence amassed by Tracy I'anson to show that he had the capability and knowledge to commit the murders. The trauma and mental disturbance, she claims, would be enough to trigger his killing and mutilation spree.

Charles Lechmere – Hidden in Plain Sight

People who interact suspiciously with the police can quickly become suspects. Colin Stagg found this when he lied about being on Wimbledon Common around the time that Rachel Nickel was murdered. He was eventually fully exonerated. This is perhaps a salutary thought when considering Charles Lechmere who Edward Stow offers as the culprit.

Charles Lechmere came into the investigation as a witness. Edward Stow shows that he had the opportunity to commit the murders linked to JtR but also possibly many other murders around the area, before and after the autumn of 1888. This opens up the sort of can of worms that would have Inspector Abberline and the others central to the detective work spinning in their graves.

The problem for Edward Stow is that Lechmere is not recorded as having any disturbing characteristics other than a delay in coming forward, and some confusion over what he called himself. But, as we know, such details do not limit the serious Ripperologist. Edward Stow reaches for psychological inferences: resentment at falling from his affluent origins and anger at his powerful mother who bigamously married, leading to the projection of this anger onto his victims. It's an interpretation that Sigmund himself might be proud of.

Francis Tumblety – The Man in the Slouch Hat

A quack doctor with homosexual leanings seems an unlikely candidate to be JtR but, as Michael Hawley points out, he is one of the few suspects who was taken to court by the police. He is even quoted as having said that if he had his way he would disembowel street workers. Hawley claims that this apparently was because 'they lured impressionable young men away from a life of homosexuality.' The respectable gay life was being undermined by these disgusting, degraded prostitutes. Certainly, a novel explanation for becoming a serial killer.

However, in the rich world of speculation and the ready availability of a 'profile' to fit the suspect first thought of, Michael Hawley turns not to FBI Special Agents, who have tried to corner the market in 'offender profiling', but to the enigmatic figure of Brent Turvey, whose PhD was awarded for a deeply critical examination of forensic scientists. Michael cites Turvey's recycling of the work of established forensic psychologists Knight and Prentky. They studied rapists in their care and identified a subset of anger-retaliatory and reassurance-oriented rapists. Turvey applies both these epithets to JtR on the basis of details of the crimes. Apparently, this is distinct from a sadistic sexual serial killer, although the evidence for this distinction is hard to find.

Nonetheless this allows the claim that JtR had extreme and bitter feelings towards women to be used to reflect on Tumblety's declared antipathy to prostitutes. The lack of self-esteem, which is required to be diagnosed as needing reassurance, is drawn from his bragging in his autobiography and the fact that JtR seemed to have taken two rings from Annie Chapman. The claim being that the taking of 'trophies', in this case including body parts, is characteristic of those who feel inadequate.

Besides these incriminating pointers, Tumblety also had knives not dissimilar to those used in mutilating the victims. He even had in his possession organs like those taken from the victims. He therefore, in classic crime fiction style, had the motive and means and, as far as can be determined, the opportunity to carry out the 1888 murders. The question therefore has to be asked as to why he was not convicted of the murders. He absconded.

Albert Bachert – Where Did He Go?

Mick Priestley has dug out another person who became of note because he argued with a coroner and was a member of the Whitechapel Vigilance Committee. Thus, he was part of the events surrounding the murders, opening himself up (historically speaking) to having inserted himself into the investigation. Once identified by Priestley, there is then the task of exploring whether he has any of the features that would be associated with a serial killer.

Once again, the flawed study by FBI Special Agents of those couple of dozen serial killers in the US who were willing to talk to them, is drawn on to generate statistics that can provide a template for the killer. Bachert was certainly a nasty piece of goods. Often drunk and frequently disorderly. Involved in many forms of petty crime. However, Mick Priestley notes that only about one in ten of the serial killers studied by the FBI (therefore, a couple) stated conflict with another male was a factor, and only about one in four claimed legal issues had influenced their actions. So, although Bachert suffered from these prerequisites the probabilities are not strongly in his favour.

But if a chronic liar, who had many altercations with the police, was known to be violent on occasion, was involved in a range of crimes, kept on being part of the search for Jack the Ripper and lived in the area of the murders, had been looked at more closely before he disappeared from view, he may have emerged as a likely suspect.

Kosminski – Prime (Unknown) Suspect

The name Kosminski occurs in a number of police documents and autobiographies as a plausible suspect. This makes him a favoured villain as JtR. But this tidy solution, which of course would have killed the Ripper industry stone dead, is happily fraught with problems. As Steve Blomer argues there are two problems with this. One is the reliability of the claims by the police of the time. The inconsistency in their reports and the ambiguity of their statements raise doubts about the validity of their claims.

The second challenge to Kosminski being the first and most well-known, unknown killer of modern times is that, as Martin Fido also points out, it is not at all clear who he is. He may not be Kosminski but someone else of the same name, or possibly a different name. In the hall of mirrors that is the search for JtR, people who may or may not have been Kosminski, who may or may not have been nominated by investigators for the starring role, feature as an enduring monument to the power of human endeavour in the search for the truth.

Montague Druitt – Homicidal Suicide

Apparently, the body of Montague Druitt was fished out the Thames seven weeks after the Miller's Court murder, the most vicious killing attributed to JtR. This fact becomes the cornerstone of David Andersen's proposal that various references by the police at the time of JtR being at the bottom of the Thames makes Druitt a prime suspect. It is not often that a dead body is taken as crucial evidence that it's that of a serial killer, but as Andersen builds his network of hints and links, with Druitt being named in one or two places as a key suspect by detectives, the case is made that he was likely to have been in the right places at the appropriate time for suspicion of his guilt to be convincing.

Here again, the suspect comes into the frame because of what was in the Macnaghten notes for the Home Secretary, when Sir Melville Macnaghten was assistant chief constable for crime. An intriguing aspect of these notes and the surrounding discussion is the general reference to Druitt and other suspects of being 'insane'. He was found with stones in his pockets and a reasonable assumption was that he threw himself in the river. This was put down to his extreme 'insanity' possibly as part of his 'homicidal insanity'.

There are two aspects of this that are worth noting. One is that the police, not infrequently, are convinced who the villain is and have it wrong. The case of Colin Stagg accused of the murder of Rachel Nickell is a recent example. Indeed, Macnaghten is heralded for getting a wrongly convicted man freed and thus contributing to the development of the Court of Criminal Appeal.

The other aspect is the naïve assignment of the general term 'insane' to what today would be regarded as a host of different forms of mental illness. Although it is true that many UK murderers do commit suicide from remorse, that would be unusual for a serial killer. Deep depression – leading to suicide – may have been regarded as a form of 'insanity' in the late nineteenth century, but it is very different from being a 'homicidal maniac'. Even the much-misunderstood term 'schizophrenia' can take many different forms and is often challenged as not being a coherent diagnosis at all.

The suspects thrown up by these intrepid searchers for the identity of JtR reveal a motley crew of syphilitics, ne'er-do-wells and snake-oil merchants, as well as immigrants or the children of immigrants who ended up in lunatic asylums, often with serious, totally untreated, mental illnesses. They've been selected in part because they lived in, or at least knew well, London's Whitechapel. Often, they've come to notice because they played a role as witnesses in the inquests that followed the murders. The recurring problem, though, as I found when I was giving advice to police investigations, is that there is always a person who is thrown up by the inquiry who seems like the perfect suspect, but turns out in the end to be completely innocent.

David Canter, is Emeritus Professor at The University of Liverpool. His most recent book is *Criminal Psychology* published by Routledge.

Introduction

The H:Division Memorandum

Did anyone see the Whitechapel murderer? This has never really been ascertained. Many homicidal maniacs were suspected at the time, and have been for the last 130 years. But no conclusive proof could be thrown on any one of them. We may mention the cases of eleven men whom we feel are the most likely, or best suited, to have been in the position to have committed the Jack the Ripper murders. Some of them were in and around the area at the time and others were mentioned by police officials involved in the case. We have also included and acknowledged a twelfth suspect who embodies the very real possibility that the killer never came under the attention of the police and thus must, and always will, remain a person(s) unknown.

We have listed the following alphabetically so as not to suggest a particular personal preference.

1. Albert Bachert – a resident of the Whitechapel area and a man who injected himself into the murder inquiry. His mannerisms and characteristics aroused much suspicion and make him a person of interest. Mystery still remains as to what actually happened to him. It has been suggested his background and actions are similar to the profile of some serial killers.
2. Joseph Barnett – the only suspect with a direct link to one of the Ripper victims. This man was the one-time lover of Mary Jane Kelly and knew the area well. His appearance matched some eyewitness descriptions and some of his characteristics match the profile put forward by the FBI in the 1980s as the type of person the Ripper would have been. There is also circumstantial evidence which makes him a strong suspect.
3. William Bury – resident of the East End during the canonical five murders and a proven killer whose later crimes bore a striking similarity to the Whitechapel murders. He was hanged for the

murder of his wife in 1889 and remains the last man to be hanged in the city of Dundee, Scotland. There were many circumstances in this individual's life which suggests he could have been the man known as Jack the Ripper.

4. David Cohen – a Polish Jew, living in Whitechapel, who had homicidal tendencies and was confined to a lunatic asylum shortly after the last of the canonical five murders. There is great confusion surrounding the identity of this individual which may involve a possible mix up with the details surrounding the suspect known as Kosminski.
5. Montague John Druitt – a teacher and barrister from a good family who disappeared within weeks of the Miller's Court murder and whose body (which was said to have been upwards of a month in the water) was found in the Thames on 31 December, about seven weeks after that murder. There were several suspicious circumstances surrounding this man, including a suggestion that he was sexually insane. According to one senior officer, there was little doubt that his own family believed him to have been the murderer.
6. George Hutchinson – came late to the party as his first appearance was after the inquest of Mary Kelly when he went to the police with a statement about meeting her on the morning of her death. It was the very detailed nature of this statement which led later researchers to look at him more closely, and he was first named as the killer in 1998. Since then many have considered him to be a very strong suspect.
7. Kosminski – regarded by many to be Aaron Kosminski, a low-classed Polish Jew and resident of Whitechapel. There is great debate regarding this individual and some senior police sources suggest that he may have been positively identified as the killer. There are also many circumstances connected with this man that make him a strong suspect.
8. Charles Lechmere (also known as Cross) – this person was originally brought to the attention of the police as a witness who claimed to have discovered the body of the woman murdered in Buck's Row. There is evidence to suggest this man not only lied about his true identity, but may have also lied about whether he discovered the body. His time alone with the victim also raises much suspicion.

9. Jacob Levy – a man who knew the local area well. Jacob had a history of violence, criminal behaviour and mental instability. Being a butcher, he was skilled with a knife and also possessed the anatomical knowledge necessary to commit the mutilations that were seen on the victims. There is evidence to suggest police strongly suspected a man who worked on the same street as Levy.
10. Robert Mann – a mortuary attendant who came to the attention of the police through Inspector Helson and Sergeant Enright. The officers found him difficult whilst handling the bodies of four of the victims. His workplace, located in the heart of the Ripper's killing ground, provided the suspect with a solitary environment in which to come and go undetected. He had access to surgeons' scalpels and was experienced in watching post mortems being carried out. There were also close similarities between the suspect and Dr Bond's psychological profile of the killer.
11. Dr Francis Tumblety – an Irish-American self-styled quack and a compulsive slummer of the East End. He had a public hatred of women and may have matched a couple of eyewitness descriptions of the killer. He was charged with certain 'vices' but jumped his bail and fled the country. Some sources suggest he may have been the same vile fellow who was pestering pathological museums for any spare body parts. A faction at Scotland Yard, including the Irish Branch, took him very seriously as the likely Whitechapel fiend.
12. Person(s) unknown – the Whitechapel murderer may never have come to the attention of the police and thus positive proof of the Ripper's identity will always remain a mystery. However, with modern criminal profiling and the study of similar killers, it may be possible to pinpoint the type of individual he was.

Chapter 1

Jack the Ripper and the Whitechapel Murders 1888-1891

By Richard C. Cobb

Let's start by acknowledging the fact that we will probably never know the identity of history's most elusive serial killer. Well, not to everyone's satisfaction at least. The police did not catch him. They have variously been called incompetent or party to a conspiracy or cover-up. It's even claimed the police knew who it was but it was someone so important that they could not reveal it to the public.

Thus is the fantasy and romance that surrounds the most infamous murder mystery in the world. But in truth, the reason they never caught Jack the Ripper is because they lacked the experience. They were dealing with a new type of killer, the first of his kind, the world's first modern serial killer. The police were simply not equipped to hunt him down and they closed the investigation down after four years, leaving the case unsolved. There were no forensic examinations, DNA or fingerprints that could be used in an 1888 police investigation.

So much has been written about the Whitechapel murders that it would be impossible to condense all the information collected into one chapter of a book. So, for now, it's best to give a brief rundown of the murders and the world in which Jack the Ripper and his unfortunate victims lived. There have been far more in-depth studies conducted by some of the best names in the field and I would encourage anyone wanting to learn more about the police investigation into the Ripper murders to read the excellent work undertaken by authors and researchers such as Paul Begg, Stewart Evans, Martin Fido, Keith Skinner and Philip Sugden.

So where do I start today? Perhaps it's best to describe the world in which Jack the Ripper lived.

By 1888, London was the largest capital in the world and the centre of the ever-increasing British Empire. Queen Victoria had been on the throne for over fifty years and the public face of Britain reflected Victoria's lifestyle; proud, dignified and above all, distinguished.

It was the centre of empire, culture, finance, communication and transportation, with an emerging mass media called the new journalism, later to be dubbed the tabloids.

However, right on its doorstep in the East End lay the district of Whitechapel. Seedy by any standards, it was a crime-ridden sordid quarter where 78,000 residents lived in abject poverty. It was an area of doss houses, sweatshops, abattoirs, overcrowded slums, pubs and a few shops and warehouses, leavened with a row or two of respectably kept cottages.

Whitechapel housed London's worst slums and the poverty of its inhabitants was appalling. Malnutrition and disease were so widespread that its inhabitants had about a fifty per cent chance of living past the age of 5 years old.

Here, three classes existed:

- The poor (builders, labourers, shopkeepers, dock workers and tailors).
- The very poor (women who were usually seamstresses, weavers or launderers, and children).
- The homeless (who lived in a permanent state of deprivation).

Whitechapel was also the immigrant district due, in part, to the large influx of Jewish, Irish and Russian transport ships docking nearby in Limehouse. The potato famine had seen a deluge of Irish immigrants in the mid 1800s, along with the Jewish population who arrived in their thousands whilst fleeing persecution in Russia, Germany and Poland. In just a single decade, the Jewish population had risen to over 50,000.

All these different nationalities had one thing in common: every day was a struggle for survival.

The West End of London was undergoing massive renovation and prosperity, opening up new concert halls, music halls, restaurants and hotels. As the city expanded, cheap housing was being demolished to make way for warehouses and business offices, which forced more people into smaller areas.

Overcrowding and a shortage of housing created the abyss of Whitechapel. For most of the population in the East End, one lived and died in the neighbourhood in which they were born. Hope was in short supply.

A maze of entries, alleyways and courtyards were lit by single gas lamps, giving out only about six feet of light, and in between this was a darkness so thick, that you would struggle to see your own hand in front of your face. Sanitation was practically non-existent and people would throw their raw sewage into the street, making the stench of the district unbearable.

For the poor and destitute, common lodging houses offered a bed for the night. Here you would be cramped into a small dormitory with up to eighty others and for four pence you could get a bed, which was practically a coffin lying on the ground. For tuppence you could lean against a rope, which was tied from one end of the wall to the other. Every night 8,500 men, women and children would seek shelter within these walls.

These doss houses lay just off the main roads of Commercial Street. Areas such as Thrawl Street, Flower and Dean and Dorset Street (a street so bad the police, allegedly, wouldn't go down unless they were in teams of four) were run by greedy landlords that had one motto: 'No pay no stay.' No money meant the night in doorways, lavatories or huddled up in the church park.

For men, work could sometimes be obtained down by the docks, offloading ships or as market porters. For women, work was scarce and any work they could find paid very little to be able to survive, so out of sheer desperation many turned to the oldest profession in the world, prostitution.

According to one account, the women of the East End at the time were so destitute that they would sell themselves for as little as three pence, or a stale loaf of bread. In October 1888, the Metropolitan Police estimated there were over 1,200 prostitutes working the streets in Whitechapel alone. This was almost certainly an underestimate, for sheer want drove many more to occasional prostitution.

This was their only means of income and survival. With the little money they earned, most would seek comfort in alcohol as the only refuge from reality. Drink was cheap and drunkenness rife, at any time of day or night, leading to brutality and violence. Brawls were commonplace and, as one Whitechapel inhabitant put it, cries of 'Murder!' were 'nothing unusual in the street'.

The Hollywood interpretation of these fallen women has them portrayed as the showgirl type you would see on a stage in the rich West End, with charming looks and pretty features. The reality was far different. By the age of 20 most would look about 40, due to hard drinking and the East End lifestyle taking its toll. Most had missing teeth and wore the same clothes day in and day out. Bloated and diseased, life would have been short for these women. Dubbed 'unfortunates', these women would ply their trade within brothels and dark alleys.

It was certainly a world in which the Ripper would have no problem finding a victim, but just how many victims he had is still open to debate. Positive proof of the killer's identity is simply not available; there was no trial, no signed confessions and no cold case inquiries, so we do not know for sure just how many fell to the Ripper's knife.

What we do have is a list of eleven unsolved murders in London between 1888 and 1891. These crimes are known as the Whitechapel murders and although it's highly unlikely that they are the work of one single killer, at least three of these murders should be considered the work of the one man known as Jack the Ripper.

In modern culture, it's almost common knowledge that the killer had five victims. This idea bore fruit in the 1950s when researchers uncovered a memo from the chief constable of Scotland Yard, Sir Melville Macnaghten, outlining his own preferred suspects in the case and stating in his opinion that the Ripper had 'five victims and five victims only'. Since then, this memo has formed a solid basis for the majority of historical studies and accounts of the Whitechapel murders.

But is it correct?

Macnaghten was a senior officer, with a keen interest in the murders and he would have been privy to all the information the police received, but he, just like every other officer in Victorian London, would still be hampered by the lack of experience in dealing with a serial killer. In fact, the term 'serial killer' didn't even exist in the 1890s. It would take another eighty years before Robert Ressler of the FBI would coin the term when studying the psychological profile of violent offenders. So, although Macnaghten had access to the files, he would not have had the extensive knowledge of his modern-day counterparts who study crime-scene characteristics and serial-killer signature factors to help them determine whether or not it is the same man committing the crimes. All that aside, the *Macnaghten Memoranda* presents us with five victims who are now known as the canonical five. They are included in the Whitechapel murders file and I have marked them accordingly.

Let's look at the eleven' murders we have on file and briefly outline the circumstances surrounding each case. I will leave it up to you to conduct your own research and decide who may or may not have been killed by the same hand.

The Whitechapel Murders – Victims 1888-1891

Emma Elizabeth Smith – attacked 3 April 1888 (died 4 April)

The Whitechapel murders began on 3 April 1888 with the attack and later the death of a prostitute named Emma Elizabeth Smith. Smith was attacked on Osborn Street in the Whitechapel area during the early hours of the morning. Cut and bleeding, she managed to make her way back to her lodging house, where, on arrival, she was taken, against her will, to hospital. It was here she told the story of how she had been making her way home along Brick Lane when she was chased by a gang of three men. They caught her on the junction of Osborn Street, where they subjected her to a horrific attack and sexual assault. The men beat and raped the poor woman before lifting her skirts and forcing a blunt object, possibly a table leg, into her vagina. Such was the force and brutality it caused internal bleeding and later infection.

The day after being admitted to the hospital, Emma Smith died from her wounds.

Most researchers believe this particular murder was not the work of Jack the Ripper and was down to the gang assault, just as Emma Smith had described. However, other researchers point out that this could have been a cover story to conceal the fact she had been out on the streets as a prostitute. It may be the case that one client alone was responsible for her injuries and this client could have been Jack the Ripper committing his first ever attack. Other theories suggest that the Ripper could have been one of the gang who then developed a taste for the sexual brutality inflicted on Smith and decided to escalate his violent sexual tendencies alone.

Martha Tabram – 7 August 1888

The next victim in the series of Whitechapel murders is the one that researchers have the most difficulty agreeing on. It's very likely she was an early Jack the Ripper victim but she is not included in the canonical five murders.

Martha Tabram was a prostitute in the East End. On the evening before her murder, Tabram and an associate nicknamed 'Pearly Poll' had been in several of the drinking dens around Whitechapel. One of these pubs, The Two Brewers on Brick Lane, is where they met two soldiers, who joined the pair in their night's escapades. Shortly before midnight on 6 August, Tabram and Poll paired off with their clients and went their separate ways. Leaving Whitechapel High Street, Pearly Poll took her client up Angel Alley for the purposes of sex and Martha Tabram headed up an adjacent alleyway known as George Yard Buildings. This would be the last time she would be seen alive.

At 3.30am on 7 August, a resident of George Yard Buildings, Mr George Crow, returned home from work. He noticed a woman lying on the ground in the stairwell. It was dark so his initial reaction was he had stumbled across a drunk who had passed out on the landing. He ignored the body and went about his business.

An hour-and-a-half later, around 5am, the body was once again discovered. This time it was by a local resident called John Reeve, who had been on his way to work. By this time, sufficient light had been cast upon the body and her injuries could be seen clearly. Martha Tabram was lying on her back, her clothes disarranged and she had suffered thirty-nine horrific stab wounds to the throat, chest, trunk and lower abdomen. Later, during the autopsy, it was suggested a pocket knife may have inflicted the majority of the wounds. One of the injuries suggested a longer blade, such as a dagger or even a bayonet, had been used in the attack. This could suggest a killer using two knives or perhaps two killers. Or maybe the doctor had misjudged the length of the wounds.

So was Martha Tabram a victim of Jack the Ripper?

Some researchers feel that because her throat had not been cut open or there was no mutilation of the abdomen, she must have been a victim of another killer. Her wound patterns were different from the later canonical five murders, in that she received only multiple stab wounds as opposed to being slashed open or disembowelled, which is believed to be the modus operandi (MO) of the Ripper.

Others suggest the circumstances of the crime point very clearly to Jack the Ripper because:

- The victim was a prostitute.
- A knife was used in the attack.
- The killer targeted the throat and lower abdomen.
- The body had been positioned. It lay on its back and the clothes had been pushed up.
- The victim had been murdered in the early hours of the morning.
- The location of the crime was in the centre of the Jack the Ripper killing territory.

Whether or not Martha Tabram was a victim of Jack the Ripper remains a mystery. It should be noted that only three weeks following her death the first of the Ripper's canonical five murders began.

The Canonical Five

The following five victims were all prostitutes and their injuries share a similarity to each other. In all the cases their throats were cut and in all but one of the cases, there was mutilation of the lower abdomen. The murders occurred at the start and end of the month and either on the weekend or a day before, as with Tabram. These links are based on the opinions of Chief Constable Sir Melville Macnaghten. It should be pointed out that other officers at the time considered the killer to have had more than five victims.

Mary Ann Nichols – 31 August 1888: first of the canonical five victims

The first of the canonical five murders was that of Mary Ann Nichols, known locally as Polly Nichols. At 3.40am on the morning of 31 August 1888, a cart driver by the name of Charles Lechmere, (sometimes called Cross) stumbled across the body of Polly Nichols in Buck's Row, Whitechapel. At first he wasn't too sure about what he had found, thinking the bundle might be a piece of discarded canvas or tarpaulin. He was joined by a second man, Mr Robert Paul, and both men loomed over the body in the darkness, attempting to see if the woman was drunk, dead or injured. There is evidence to say her clothing had been pushed up, how far is uncertain, but the two men pulled it back down to cover her modesty. It was decided to leave her there as both men were late for work, but they agreed to tell a policeman if they saw one.

As they continued to work, around the corner came Police Constable (PC) John Neil. Having the advantage of carrying a lantern, he could see right away the woman was, in fact, dead. Mary Ann Nichols had received two deep cuts in her throat from left to right, severing her windpipe and almost decapitating her.

A doctor was called and the body was taken to the nearby mortuary, where a full autopsy could begin in the morning. Unknown to the police and doctor, the throat wound was not the only injury inflicted on the body. When her clothing was removed the next morning by the mortuary staff, it was discovered that her abdomen had been viciously attacked. It had been partially ripped open with several deep and jagged wounds and there had been stab wounds to the vagina. Her intestines were protruding from the wound.

Annie Chapman – 8 September 1888: second of the canonical five victims

Annie Chapman was, like Polly Nichols, a penniless prostitute trying to survive in the abyss of Whitechapel. She would be murdered one week after Nichols.

At 5.30am on the morning of 8 September 1888, Mrs Elizabeth Long was making her way along Brick Lane and into Hanbury Street. As she passed the front door of number 29, she saw a man and woman talking. The man had his back to her and she couldn't see his face, but the woman she later recognized as Annie Chapman. The man was described as wearing a long dark coat, a brown deerstalker hat and had a shabby genteel appearance about him. Mrs Long thought he might be a foreigner and heard him ask Chapman, 'Will you?' to which Chapman replied, 'Yes.'

This was the last recorded sighting of Annie Chapman alive. However, it may not have been the last time she was heard.

Shortly after this sighting, Albert Cadosch, who lived next door at 27 Hanbury Street, was stepping out to his backyard to visit the toilet when he heard a woman's voice on the other side of the fence, which divided his yard from that of number 29. The voice appeared to be saying 'No' and this was followed by what sounded like a body falling against the fence.

Around twenty minutes later, the mutilated body of Annie Chapman was discovered by John Davis, the son of a resident, as he stepped into the back yard of 29 Hanbury Street. Her throat had been cut across and back to the spine. Her clothing had been pushed up to expose her red and white stockings and a great gash had ripped open her abdomen. This time the killer had reached in and pulled out her intestines, throwing them over her shoulder in the process. A portion of the stomach wall had been cut out and placed beside her head. It would later be established that the killer had removed her uterus, a portion of the bladder and the top third of the vagina.

The Double Event – 30 September 1888

The next two killings committed in the Whitechapel murders series happened the same night, on 30 September 1888. The murders were committed about a mile apart and took less than forty-five minutes. One of the murders would take place in the City of London (the only murder to be committed in the City) and in effect bring both the Metropolitan and City Police into the case. This would create the largest criminal manhunt in British history, at that time.

Elizabeth Stride – 30 September 1888: third of the canonical five victims

Elizabeth Stride was found murdered at 1am in a yard way called Dutfield's Yard, off Berner Street. The case of Elizabeth Stride raises problems as to her whereabouts the night of her murder. She was apparently seen with a man outside the Bricklayer's Arms pub in Settles Street, on the other side of Commercial Road, not far from the murder site. An elderly fruit merchant called Mathew Packer may have sold grapes to Stride and a male companion in Berner Street only an hour before the murder, but Packer changed his story several times, apparently to please listeners. The police thought his evidence unreliable.

There were other more reliable sightings. At 11.45pm a labourer, William Marshall, was standing at the door of his lodgings at 64 Berner Street. Across the road, a man was talking to a woman whom Marshall later identified as Elizabeth Stride. He heard the man say, 'You would say anything but your prayers.'

At 12.30am, PC William Smith passed along Berner Street on his shift. He too saw a man and a woman. When he was later shown Stride's body in the mortuary, he immediately identified her as the woman he had seen.

At 12.45am Israel Schwartz stated that he saw a man stop and speak to a woman, who was standing by a gateway on Berner Street. The man tried to pull the woman into the street, but he turned her round and threw her down on the footway and the woman screamed three times, but not loudly. On crossing to the opposite side of the street, he saw a second man standing, lighting his pipe. The man who threw the woman down called out, apparently to the man on the opposite side of the road, 'Lipski', and then Schwartz walked away but, finding that he was followed by the second man, he ran as far as the railway arch, although the man did not follow that far. Although the Schwartz statement is considered highly important by some researchers, it is only fair that we point out he was never called to give evidence at the inquest and changed his story at least once when recalling the details. However, English was not his native language and he needed an interpreter.

At 1am Louis Diemschutz made his way down Berner Street with his pony and cart. He turned to go into Dutfield's Yard when his horse shied away from something that was lying on the ground. Diemschutz climbed off the cart and examined the bundle on the ground. He realized it was a body and he went into the working men's club, located through the yard, to alert others.

Stride's body was found with her throat cut, severing her left artery, yet no other slashes or incisions had been made on the body. The absence of abdominal mutilations and the estimation from the doctor about the time of her death have led most researchers to conclude that the Ripper was probably disturbed in the act of killing, by Louis Diemschutz entering the yard. It's highly possible the killer was still in the yard as the body was discovered and then made a hasty retreat once Diemschutz had gone to alert others. It's also possible that the murder was unconnected to the Ripper murders and might never have been included in the canonical five killings if it had not been for another murder less than forty-five minutes later.

Catherine Eddowes – 30 September 1888: fourth of the canonical five victims

At 1.35am, half an hour after the discovery of Elizabeth Stride's body, Joseph Lawende, a commercial traveller, left the Imperial Club in Duke Street, Aldgate, with friends Joseph Levy and Harry Harris. A short alley called Church Passage linked Duke Street to Mitre Square and, as they passed, they saw at the entrance a man talking to a woman whom Lawende would later identify as 43-year-old Catherine Eddowes.

Earlier in the evening, Eddowes had been found drunk in Aldgate High Street and was taken to the police station in Bishopsgate to sober up. She was released shortly before 1am.

At 1.45am, only ten minutes after Lawende and his companions had passed by, PC Edward Watkins of the City Police entered Mitre Square on his beat and found the mutilated corpse of Eddowes. According to the post mortem, death was immediate, caused by 'haemorrhage of the left common carotid artery'. The report added that the throat had been instantly severed so that no noise could have been emitted. Eddowes' face, groin, liver and upper thighs had been hacked and stabbed; the abdomen had been ripped open and disembowelled, a two-foot-long section of the large intestine had been placed between her arm and body, and most of the uterus and a left kidney had been removed.

With this murder the police had an eyewitness because, if the timings were correct and the woman seen by Lawende and his companions was Catherine Eddowes, then the man she was with was almost certainly her killer. However, to the dismay of the investigators, neither Harry Harris nor Joseph Levy could remember seeing the man and woman and although Joseph Lawende was able to identify Catherine Eddowes' clothing and the style of hat the killer wore, he was sure he wouldn't recognize the man again.

Mary Jane Kelly – 9 November 1888: fifth of the canonical five victims

Mary Kelly (also known as Marie Jeanette) was a pretty 25 year old from Ireland, although she had spent most of her life in Wales. Her husband had been killed in a mine explosion and Mary had drifted off into the gutters of Whitechapel and taken up prostitution in an effort to survive. By Easter 1887, she was living with a market worker called Joseph Barnett, and the two of them lodged together in a pokey room at 13 Miller's Court, off Dorset Street. The room was actually the partitioned-off back room of 26 Dorset Street and could only be reached by walking through a narrow, three-foot-wide, arched passage that ran from Dorset Street into Miller's Court.

Shortly before her murder, her relationship with Joseph Barnett had broken down and he had moved out, leaving Mary to return to the streets to earn a living. On the night of her death she was allegedly seen out on Commercial Street, no doubt looking for money or a client, and was then seen by a witness walking back down the street with a strange, well-dressed man. The witness, George Hutchinson, described how he had followed the pair down to Miller's Court and watched as they disappeared up the narrow archway to Kelly's room. He waited around for a while before deciding to leave. This was the last time Kelly was seen alive.

The next morning, the landlord's assistant, Thomas Bowyer, was sent to collect the rent, which Kelly had been six weeks behind in paying. When she didn't answer his knock at the door, Bowyer reach his hand through a crack in the window. He pushed aside a coat being used as makeshift drapery and what he saw inside sent him reeling back in horror. The body of Mary Jane Kelly was lying on the bed, butchered like an animal.

Kelly's throat had been cut from ear to ear, back to the spinal column. Her nose had been cut off and her face was so horribly mutilated it was difficult to identify her body. She had been completely disembowelled and her entrails had been taken out and placed on the table next to her bed. Both her breasts had been cut off and placed on the bed. Her thighs had been stripped to the bone and her groin horrifically mutilated. According to one doctor, it appeared as if the killer had spent a couple of hours with the body.

Other Whitechapel Murders

Rose Mylett – 20 December 1888

Rose Mylett (known to friends and acquaintances in Whitechapel and Spitalfields as 'Drunken Lizzie' Davis) is among the list of Whitechapel murder victims because her death was ruled as a murder. There is, however, debate on whether or not her death was accidental.

At 4.15am on 20 December 1888, Police Sergeant (PS) Robert Golding came across the lifeless body of Rose Mylett in a yard way, between 184 and 186 Poplar High Street in Clarke's Yard. She was lying on her left-hand side and her body was still warm to the touch. Her clothes were not torn or disarranged in any manner, and there was no obvious sign of injury. The fact that she was a known prostitute and, given the area in which she was murdered (the Ripper's stomping ground), rumours were rife that Jack the Ripper had claimed the life of another victim.

At first doctors were confused as to what had actually been the cause of death. It certainly didn't appear to be a Ripper murder; for a start there was no cut throat or any sign of abdominal injuries. A further examination revealed a small mark around her neck which appeared to have been caused by string. Naturally, strangulation was the first thought.

However, Sir Robert Anderson of the Metropolitan Police wasn't convinced that this was a murder. There were no signs of a struggle and the body appeared to have been in a natural position when found. To back up his theory of an accidental or natural death, he called for Dr Thomas Bond, police surgeon for the Metropolitan Police's A Division, to be brought in to re-examine the body.

Before Dr Bond could arrive, two other doctors decided to examine the body and they believed it was an act of murder by strangulation. The matter became even more confusing when Dr Bond finally arrived to conduct his own examination and came back with the belief that Rose Mylett had fallen down while drunk and was choked to death by her stiff, velvet collar. It would now be up to an inquest to get to the bottom of the mystery. The inquest into the death of Rose Mylett was held on 21 December 1888 and in the end the jury decided to go with the first opinion that Rose Mylett was the victim of murder by strangulation. The police were outraged that their conclusions had been dismissed and they refused to volunteer any manpower to solving (in their mind) a non-existent crime.

The death or murder of Rose Mylett continues to be debated among students of the Whitechapel murders and there are mixed feelings regarding who was correct, the doctors or the police.

Alice McKenzie – 17 July 1889

On 17 July 1889, the body of Alice McKenzie was discovered in Castle Alley, Whitechapel. She was found at 12.50am by PC Walter as he walked his beat in the area. Her body was lying on the pavement close to a lamppost. Her throat had been attacked with a knife; there were two deep stabs which joined together into one wound. This had severed off the left carotid artery, causing death. Her clothing had been disarranged and her skirt pushed up. She had received knife wounds to her thigh and abdomen and slice marks from her breast to her navel, but these were not as savage as had been seen in previous Ripper attacks.

Police surgeon, Dr George Philips, arrived on the scene and pronounced life extinct.

Dr Bond was called in to examine the body and concluded: 'I see in this murder evidence of similar design to the former Whitechapel murders. A sudden onslaught on the prostrate woman, the throat skilfully and resolutely cut with subsequent mutilation...I am of the opinion that the murder was performed by the same...person who committed the former Whitechapel murders.'

However, Dr Philips was of a different opinion and after his examination, concluded that the murder of Alice McKenzie was not the work of Jack the Ripper. He said: 'After careful and long deliberation I cannot satisfy myself that the perpetrator of all the "Whitechapel murders" is one man...I am on the contrary impelled to a contrary conclusion.'

Many past researchers dismiss the idea that Alice McKenzie was a victim of Jack the Ripper, but there is enough circumstantial evidence to support the idea that she may have been a Ripper victim:

- Her throat was cut.
- She had abdominal injuries.
- She was a prostitute.
- She was murdered at the right time and in the right area for a Jack the Ripper attack.
- Her clothing was disarranged/pushed up.

- Officers at the scene remarked on the similarity with the positioning of the body to that of earlier Ripper victims.
- An examination showed she had been dead minutes before she was discovered, making it possible the killer was disturbed in the act before he was able to complete his usual ritual.

The Pinchin Street Torso Murder – 10 September 1889

As the name suggests, this was different from the other Whitechapel murders because only the torso of the victim was found. At 5.15am on 10 September 1889, PC William Pennett was on duty around the railway arches of Pinchin Street when he stumbled upon a bundle wrapped in a chemise. As he inspected the bundle he discovered the body of a woman. The victim was missing her head and legs and it became apparent she had been dead for some time as the stench of decomposition was overpowering. The alarm was raised and soon investigations were taking shape. Three homeless men were arrested nearby and brought in for questioning but were later cleared of any wrongdoing.

An examination of the torso revealed the abdominal region of the body was heavily mutilated, reminiscent of the earlier Jack the Ripper murders. Some reports suggest her womb had been ripped out and was missing. It was noted that although there was similarity in the abdominal injuries, there was none of the usual genital mutilation that went with a typical Ripper murder.

As for the identity of the murdered woman, there were suggestions it might be a missing prostitute by the name of Lydia Hart, but this was never proven and to this day her identity remains a mystery, as does the identity of her killer.

Frances Coles – 13 February 1891: the final Whitechapel murder victim

The Whitechapel murders finally came to an end on 13 February 1891, with the murder of prostitute Frances Coles. She was murdered at 2.15am in Swallow Gardens and this time the killer was almost certainly disturbed in the act of murder.

PC Ernest Thompson was on patrol beat along Chamber Street, only minutes away from Leman Street Police Station. A new starter with the police force, he had been in the job about two months and tonight would be the first night he would be out by himself without a superior accompanying him. As he approached Swallow Gardens he heard footsteps moving away from him in the direction of Mansell Street and he quickly went to investigate. A few seconds later he stumbled across the dying body of Frances Coles. She was still alive, her eyes were opening and closing, but blood was oozing out of a wound in her neck. Thompson had two choices – stay with the woman or give chase to the man who had almost certainly attacked her. He decided to follow proper police protocol and stay with the injured victim. It would be a decision that would haunt him for the rest of his life and until the day he died he often wondered if he could have (possibly) caught the man known as Jack the Ripper.

By the time assistance arrived, Frances Coles was dead and all that was left was to examine the body and the scene for clues. According to doctors, it appeared that the victim had been thrown down onto the ground and whilst on the ground her killer had held her head back with the left hand, cutting her throat with the right. It seemed as if she had been stabbed twice in the throat and both cuts ran into each other to create one wound. There were no mutilations on the abdomen.

Investigations showed that she had been in the company of a man called James Sadler hours before the murder and he was duly arrested on suspicion of not only being the killer but, in the minds of some officers, being Jack the Ripper. He was discharged on 3 March 1891 due to lack of evidence. As the months and years went on there were no more murders of this nature that took place in Whitechapel and the story of Jack the Ripper became part of the dark history of London's East End.

Nobody knows why the murders stopped and for decades rumours have been circulated that the killer must have died, or committed suicide. Perhaps his family locked him away in an asylum or maybe he left the country to pursue his bloodlust somewhere else. One thing that is for certain, along with the other killer(s) involved in the Whitechapel murders, his true identity has never been ascertained.

The Ripper case is best described as a great whodunit novel with the back page ripped out. For the last 130 years, generations of armchair detectives, historians and researchers have attempted to fill in that page with their preferred choice of suspect.

As early as the second of the canonical five murders, the game of hunt the Ripper had begun. Local residents of the East End were focused on a shadowy character that went by the nickname 'Leather Apron'. Apparently this man was known to try and extort money from them by pulling out a knife and threatening to 'rip them apart' unless they handed over what cash they had made in the course of their night-time activities. Butchers, doctors and slaughtermen would follow, each taking their place as the new hot favourite to be the killer.

The police at the time put forward their own theories as to who the killer may have been. Some, namely Sir Robert Anderson, who was assistant commissioner of the Metropolitan Police, went so far as to say the killer was identified but could not be prosecuted. Other senior detectives suggested the killer may have fled the country or drowned in the Thames. Some just maintained the killer was never caught. It seems they all had their own story to tell.

By the 1970s the Ripper's story had moved out of the East End, climbed the social ladder and was now dining with royalty or perhaps drawing some grand pieces of art. As the years progressed he was even writing classic novels such as *Alice in Wonderland.* He seemed to be moving further and further away from where the crimes happened.

So maybe now, after 130 years, it's time we brought the Ripper back home.

Let us return to the crime scene and strip down the Ripperology beast to the basic origins of the investigation. From here, let us look at the suspects that present themselves to us and ask some very important questions.

If the murders happened today, who would the police consider a person of interest?

With this in mind, we have taken two key principles of the investigation. Who did the police seriously suspect and who was in the immediate area at the time?

These are the questions all modern researchers should be asking and we hope this book will help you find the answers.

The founding member of H:Division Crime Club, the world's premier society for the study of Jack the Ripper and true crime, Richard is also the co-author of the book Diary of Jack the Ripper, Research and Conclusion *and is currently working on a book about Peter Sutcliffe the Yorkshire Ripper. Richard is the organizer of the annual Jack the Ripper conference in the UK, and runs his own tour company in London.*

Chapter 2

Albert Bachert – Where Did He Go?

By Mick Priestley

It will be no revelation to the reader that an awful lot of suspects have been put forward in the time since the murders took place. A handful of them seem plausible, but, unfortunately, the vast majority seem to have been suggested with no real evidence whatsoever, or as a result of wild conspiracy theories.

I always felt it unlikely that the real killer had ever even been suggested, and so using only the original files, facts and sources, combined with modern murder unit methods, I was determined to uncover, finally, an individual with real evidence against him. And in doing so I unearthed Albert Bachert – a very strange and suspicious man who has largely flown under the radar, despite having immersed himself in the investigation and hidden in plain sight the entire time. For the first part of this article, I'd like to briefly mention a selection of strange events from Albert's life, and then use the second part to explain why, in a modern case, he would be viewed as a prime suspect and with undoubted suspicion by an investigating team today.

Albert William Bachert was born in the fourth quarter of 1860 in Whitechapel, the son of German immigrant Johann (John) and Georgine (Georgina) Bachert. He was baptized in Whitechapel as Wilhelm Albert Bachert on Christmas Day 1860, and had three sisters – a fourth sister had been born in 1867 but died as a baby, and is recorded as being 0 years old at the time of her death.

He grew up in the area, and the 1871 census shows the Bachert family living at 49 Duke Street; inside the city boundary, opposite St Botolph's Church and only seven doors from where Joseph Lawende made his witness sighting on the night of Catherine Eddowes' murder. Lawende, as it happens, had reported seeing a man '27-28 years old, wearing a salt and pepper jacket, a flat cap and a reddish neckerchief.' We'll remember that for later.

A decade later, the 1881 census shows the family living at 13 Newnham Street, around 400 metres south east, on Goodman's Fields.

Albert, now aged 21, was living with his parents, two of his sisters and four male lodgers – two Russian, one Dutch and one German. He is recorded in the 1881 census as working as an engraver by that time, engraving copper plates for banknote printing. His older sister, Augusta, for whatever reason, is not mentioned in the census and may have been living elsewhere. In 1884, she married a man named William Collinson in Lambeth. His younger sister Emily was also married in 1884, in Whitechapel, to a man named Samuel Shillingford.

Now, not many books tend to report a great deal about Albert Bachert. A number of better Ripper accounts seem to find him interesting but largely only report that he argued with coroner Baxter after turning up at Frances Coles' inquest and was a member of the Whitechapel Vigilance Committee. We'll get to that in a bit. Some of the better accounts that do mention him, however, state that he first appeared in the newspaper in 1887. That's wrong. He actually made a great deal of newspaper reports, largely through his long list of court appearances, arrests and strange incidents, of which I'd like to mention a few.

He would first seem to have appeared in the paper in November 1885, while working as a canvasser for Conservative Party politician Phineas Cowan. After some disorder at a meeting at Berkhampstead Town Hall, Bachert had gone to court to claim that he had received 'letters threatening him with death', and that all of his windows had been smashed by 'radicals and socialists'. It would appear that he had not informed the police, however, and the magistrate told him to 'go to the inspector and tell him about it.' He was then back in the paper again on Valentine's Day 1886, after a demonstration in Trafalgar Square on 8 February, appearing as a member of the 'East End Fair Trade Leaguers', who had advertised that they would 'seize' the occasion from The Labourers' League, who had originally arranged the demonstration. The scene had ended in scenes of violent disorder, with a crowd of thousands spilling out of the square and rampaging across the West End, smashing shops and terrorizing pedestrians. Dozens were arrested.

A year-and-a-half later, in August 1887, it was reported that he appeared back at Thames Police Court to complain that police were 'conspiring to bring unfounded charges against him following an altercation in which a female acquaintance had been mistreated by two constables.' He claimed that police had mistaken the woman for a prostitute and that, 'He had intervened, and then been assaulted by police and "dragged along the ground" before they let him go.'

Whoever these officers were, however, he was never able to identify them. He was back in court a month later, on 15 September, to report the disappearance of his father, who had, according to him, gone missing with 'several rings, including one large diamond ring [and] about £400'. He described his father as being '54, but looking ten years younger, 5'7', complexion fair, light hair, blue eyes, and with a heavy sandy moustache'. Albert was described as being a 'respectably dressed young man'. Three months after that, he was back in court again regarding an incident at the Bloody Sunday riot in Trafalgar Square. Violent scenes had taken place on 13 November, amidst a crowd of reportedly 50,000 people. Liberal party MP Robert Cunningham and trade unionist John Burns were on trial for 'disorderly conduct' and 'assaulting the police', and Albert turned up to give evidence. He claimed he had simply happened upon the riot by chance, while heading to visit a friend in nearby Waterloo House, but claimed that he had personally witnessed the pair, amidst the crowds, being assaulted by police, and declared their innocence. He proclaimed in court that he had 'worked hard for Phineas Cowan' and was ridiculed by the opposing solicitor – Cowan had lost his election to Liberal candidate Samuel Montagu. The pair were sentenced to six weeks at Pentonville. When 1888 arrived, Albert was 27, approaching 28 years old. He appeared in the press a surprising number of times, made numerous court appearances, and claimed to receive an unparalleled amount of correspondence from the killer. In September 1888, this period of heavy activity began when he wrote a letter to the press 'on behalf of a number of tradesmen and shopkeepers in Whitechapel', expressing horror at the murders.

Shortly after this, he made his first apparent sighting of the killer, on the night of the double event, in the Three Nuns Hotel on Aldgate High Street. He claimed that the man carried a black shiny bag, stood 5ft 6in to 5ft 7in, and asked him if the prostitutes outside the pub would go with him down nearby Northumberland Alley, off Fenchurch Street. Albert said he didn`t know, but 'supposed they would' and told him that 'he had heard' they usually went with men 'to places in Oxford Street, Whitechapel [around one kilometre/nearly two thirds of a mile from the Three Nuns]; others to some houses in Whitechapel Road, and others to Bishopsgate.' His first contact from 'Jack the Ripper' came when a message was apparently sent to his home, via a postcard. It was written in red ink, addressed to Toby Baskett, and the sender told him 'yer only tried to get yer name in the paper when you thought you had me in the three tuns hotel. I'd like to punch yer bleeding nose.'

On the day of Mary Kelly's funeral, he claimed that someone had written 'dear Boss, I am still about. Look out – Yours, Jack the Ripper' on the side of his house, but that the words were 'obliterated' before police could photograph them.

By 19 June 1889, some seven months had passed without any particular incident since the murder of Mary Kelly. Albert had been lying low too – but on that day he was back in court charged with assaulting a butcher, Tomas Davis, at 4 Whitechapel High Street. He had entered the shop while drunk, and 'shoved' the butcher, who punched him in return. He refused to leave the premises, and was arrested. He created a scene as he was taken away, insisting that Davis should be arrested instead. At his trial, Davis stated that Albert 'often came into the shop when drunk, and was often very drunk, especially on Mondays and Tuesdays.' He was sentenced to '5s [shillings] or five days.'

A few weeks after his sentencing, in July 1889, his next letter from 'Jack the Ripper' arrived, addressed as being from the Eastern Hotel, Poplar, this time warning he would 'recommence his work that month'. Only days later, on 17 July, Alice MacKenzie was found murdered and mutilated in Castle Alley. Two days after that, Albert claimed to have stopped a 'murderous' assault near Aldgate East station on Whitechapel High Street, between the junctions of Castle Alley and Goulston Street, and taken a knife from a man attacking a woman. This report would seem to have produced the only image of him to have survived – in the form of a sketch of the supposed incident. The man later claimed that the woman had tried to rob him, and that he had only drawn a knife in self-defence. Five days after that, he appeared again at Thames Police Court to apply for warrants against two officers whom he believed `guilty of perjury'. Nothing came of it. Seven weeks later, a mutilated torso was discovered on nearby Pinchin Street, close to the murder site of Elizabeth Stride. Albert wrote to the press to say that he had been 'questioned by a number of people about the discovery' and noted that it was 'a curious fact that in all places where these murders have occurred the houses are such that any person can enter by pulling a string, which lifts the latch.' A week later, he wrote to the press again to allege that Leman Street Police Station had received a letter claiming the killer was a woman dressed as a man. On 9 October, he claimed to have received a threatening letter to his home from 'Jack the R' before being arrested, and appeared back in court on 30 November charged with 'uttering counterfeit coins twice on the same day' at two pubs, and 'stealing a pewter pot from another'. He was acquitted but his two co-defendants were given prison sentences. Ten months later he was back at Thames Police Court to ask 'the advice' of Mr Mead, who would oversee the case against James Sadler – who had been arrested on suspicion of being the killer, but was released after the murder of Frances Coles. Albert claimed he had 'been writing to the newspapers' regarding the Kingsland murders – a double murder that had taken place outside a pub in Kingsland, but claimed that a friend of the accused was threatening him. Mead told him that if he was threatened again he could obtain a summons.

His next letter arrived only a week later; the supposed killer this time warning him that he would commit a murder either in Hackney or The Strand. Five days after that, he wrote to the press again, this time to claim that a woman had visited him at his home to report a suspicious lodger at her house on Aldgate High Street. The man, she apparently said, had been writing letters in red ink and sending body parts to George Lusk of the Whitechapel Vigilance Committee. He had had bloodstained clothes, she said, a 'white apron, bloodstained', a number of 'brass rings' in his room, and was in possession of various weapons. The woman was found, however, and denied having said any such thing. When the story made it into the newspaper, Inspector Thomas Arnold disputed it, and claimed that it was 'yet another fantastical story with no basis in fact'. By this point, Albert was also claiming to be the 'chairman of the vigilance committee', but many newspapers were reporting that the members of this supposed committee were 'totally unknown'. Four months passed and on 29 June 1891, he appeared at an inquest into the death of 20-year-old Charles Lawson at the Old Bailey, having claimed to have witnessed the fight that killed him, and standing alone in his belief that the defendant was innocent. Bachert said he had been walking by and randomly witnessed the fight, and indeed the fatal blow.

The next month, on the day following the murder of Frances Coles in February 1891, he claimed to have seen the killer with Frances twice on the night she died – outside Leman Street Police Station, and outside of his home. 'If you don`t go home with me you will never go home with another man,' he heard him say to her.

Albert's statements, though, clashed wildly with those later given at the inquest, by people he would have been unaware of at the time. Next, he received another threatening letter to his home – this time the killer claimed his name was 'G.W.B' and gave his address as George Yard. On 16 November he was back at Thames Police Court, this time charged with being drunk and disorderly. He had been arrested, interestingly, on East India Dock Road, by the Eastern Hotel where he claimed the killer had contacted him in July 1889. The charges were 'a conspiracy got up by the police', he stated, and he 'called many witnesses' to claim the police had assaulted him. The magistrate said he would give him 'the benefit of the doubt' and discharged him. Strangely, three days later, he appeared at St Bartholomew's Hospital, as a witness into the inquest of Charles Puleston, 14, who had apparently been killed when a roof ornament fell from the top of 1 and 2 Poultry, not far from St Paul's Cathedral. Coroner Samuel Langham was presiding, the same man who had presided over Catherine Eddowes' inquest. This was the second time Bachert claimed to witness the untimely death of a stranger in the last four-and-a-half months. He claimed to have gone to the boy's aid, and stated that he had to use a handkerchief to wipe the blood from the boy's face.

In January 1892 another letter arrived at his home; the sender, this time 'threatening to start work again.' Another arrived in March 1892, signed 'A.F.P' and with a coffin and crossed bones drawn on the letter. Bachert went back to court, to appear again before Mr Mead, and told him that he knew 'the author of all the Jack the Ripper letters'. He wanted permission to take this person into custody himself, but Mead declared to the court that Albert was talking 'nonsense' and told him that if he had a complaint he should go to the police. He was back at Thames Police Court before Mr Mead again on 3 September, having been arrested and charged with stealing clothing and money from his father, totalling £358.10s. His father (whom Bachert had earlier reported as missing) stated that Albert had stolen the money while he was in another room, after packing it into a box before he left for Germany.

In November that year, Albert was receiving attention in the press as an 'agitator' through his involvement with numerous groups holding meetings at Tower Hill. He was involved in a number of marches in London that ended in violence, and in December went back to Thames Police Court again to claim that a Mr Henry Waite, arrested after a fight at Tower Hill, had been arrested unreasonably. He appeared again before Mr Mead. By January 1893 he had taken a job with the Tower Hamlets Unemployed Relief Committee, earning 25s a week as a 'secretary and servant' of a man named Harry Wilson. His job was to take all requests for relief to Mr Wilson and, if approved, he would then take the order to 'the tradesmen', and deliver the food relief to the deserving poor. He was described as a good worker and 'valuable to the committee'. On 14 November, however, he submitted a fraudulent order; received food and delivered it to a Mrs Avenall, who ran a beer shop. He was not entitled to do this, had defrauded the committee, and a warrant was issued for his arrest. By this point, however, he had fled to Bristol but wrote a letter to the newspaper there 'stating his intention to rally the unemployed', with his full name and new address included. This was soon discovered by H:Division Police, who sent an officer to arrest him.

At his trial, Albert was reported to have told Mrs Avenall to ignore the police. 'They have come here on the bounce,' he said. 'I have ignored them before, and I will again.' When this statement was read out in court, perhaps strangely, Albert replied, 'Hear, hear!' He was described again as an 'engraver', engraving copper plates for bank notes, and was convicted and sentenced to three months in prison. Upon his release, he went back to court again and complained that he had been unfairly treated, that he had been asked previously to stand for parliament but that the conviction had ruined him, and claimed that a fund had been raised to send him abroad to America. The magistrate wished him his best 'for his life in the new land', but if he did actually go, there doesn't seem to be a surviving record of him having done so. In 1901, however, he is recorded, with his name misspelt, in an obscure census report, living with his sister and her family back in Whitechapel, on Sidney Street. Between those two dates there doesn't seem to be any record of him whatsoever, and aside from the fact that he was back in the East End by 1901, nothing more is known about him.

Jack The Ripper

Now, for the final part of this narrative, I'm going to be referring to a number of profiling studies conducted by a number of sources, including Roy Hazelwood, John Douglas, and a study conducted by FBI agents between 1979 and 1983. Dozens of convicted sex killers were questioned, and the data I'm referring to is from that study. To save time, I'm going to refer to 'the FBI'. Albert Bachert's strange life probably led many that knew him to consider him odd or irritating. His regular drunkenness and occasional violence may also have led some to consider him intimidating. He would appear to have never been considered a suspect by anyone investigating the case, or indeed since, but there are a number of reasons why Albert Bachert's behaviour throughout his life is suspicious, and why he can be reasonably be suspected to be the Whitechapel murderer. The FBI reports that killers who leave disorganized crime scenes typically live close by, and commit their crimes within their own geographic area. Whoever the murderer was, to escape through the dimly lit back streets meant he was familiar with the area. Albert had been born in Whitechapel, grew up in the area, and by the time of the murders knew the area very well.

Living on Newnham Street since 1881, two of his sisters were married and gone by 1884, and when he appeared in court after his father charged him for stealing, it was stated that his parents were living at 40 Whitechapel High Street – leaving only Albert, and perhaps his 24-year-old sister Flora at that address, if she had not moved out too. The 1888 electoral roll lists him as living in a single room on the first floor, lists nobody else at that address, and as such it appears that he was living by himself when the murders took place.

Albert's home on Newnham Street was very close to all of the murder sites. Swallow Gardens, the final apparent offence, was the closest at only 195 metres away. The Buck's Row scene was the furthest away – at around 1,260 metres from his home. After the murder of Martha Tabram, he may have deliberately picked a spot further away to avoid attention. Mitre Square was directly behind the house he grew up in, and the spot where Joseph Lawende had made his sighting was only seven doors away. Interestingly, he lived only eight doors away from a woman named Malvina Haynes who had been discovered unconscious in 'a pool of blood' outside Leman Street Railway Station, on the night of 3 April 1888 – only one street across from where they both lived. His home was also directly between the murder sites of Elizabeth Stride and Catherine Eddowes. The sites are a twelve minute walk apart, but it seemingly took the killer thirty-eight to forty-eight minutes to cover the distance. To avoid witnesses in the street, whoever killed Elizabeth

Stride must have run south into Fairclough Street, and avoided PC Smith on his beat and police on Commercial Road. Witness James Brown had seen a man talking to Stride by the board school in a 'coat nearly to his heels' – a different description than Joseph Lawende gave – but both men described a man of similar height, and signature characteristics at both crime scenes show that the killer was indeed the same man. At the time of the murder, he was also 27 to 28 years old, which is exactly the age Lawende had given of the man he saw standing by the entrance to Church Passage when Catherine Eddowes was murdered. If Bachert had killed Elizabeth Stride and left the scene between 12:46am and 12:56am, by Dr Blackwell's findings, he would easily have made it home within minutes, possibly two minutes, before the body had even been discovered. He would not have been seen by police in the streets when the search for him began. Had he changed his coat, swapped the knife that killed Elizabeth for the one that would kill Catherine and headed back out again, it would have taken him no more than a few minutes to make his way in the opposite direction to Mitre Square. He could have spent up to half an hour at home before heading back out again.

A physical description of him has not emerged, but when he appeared in court to report his missing parent, his father was described as being 5ft 7in, with a fair complexion, light hair and a sandy moustache. Lawende's man had stood 5ft 9in, with a fair complexion and a fair moustache. The son of German immigrants, he would also have fitted the killer's 'somewhat foreign appearance' description and perhaps had the 'Eastern European accent' described by other women who had being attacked by a strange man, in the late hours, in the Whitechapel and Spitalfields area. Two women reported a man offering them coins that later turned out to be fake – 'polished brightly' and 'machined around the edges'. Similar coins were also reported by Edmund Reid at the murder sites of Annie Chapman and Alice MacKenzie. Whoever killed Catherine Eddowes would appear to have run away from Leadenhall Street and Aldgate, as he managed to avoid police who were in both areas. He also missed the nightwatchman, James Blenkinsop, who was on duty in St James' Place. It might seem that running north-west into Mitre Street was the only way he could have done this.

From here, he would have had to run into either Heneage Lane or Bury Street to cross Duke Street and Houndsditch. He would have entered Harrow Alley, crossed Middlesex Street, and arrived on Goulston Street via Wentworth Street. He was now the maximum distance he could be from both crime scenes and the police in those areas. He would have passed the doorway of 108-119, dumped the bloodstained apron and, if he wrote the graffiti, written it on the wall facing him, rather than the one behind him, as would have been the case if he had not entered from Wentworth Street. Bachert would have then run to the south end of Goulston Street, crossed the high street, and run the final 190 metres back to his home, via Half Moon Street. He could have been home by 1:55am at the latest, before most police were even aware of the second murder.

By 29 June 1889, eight months had passed since the death of Mary Kelly, and the killer was lying low. Albert hadn't been up to much either; hadn't been back to court, and hadn't appeared in the newspaper. On that day, however, he was in court charged with drunkenly assaulting Tomas Davis in the butcher's shop on Whitechapel Road and was sentenced to five shillings or five days. He then claimed to have received a letter from the killer threatening to 'recommence his work that month' and in the days following, Alice MacKenzie was murdered and mutilated in Castle Alley. Having had an uneventful year, he may have felt stressed or under pressure that June and July, causing him to act out at the butcher's, commit an assault that saw him arrested and taken to court, and triggering his first murder in two-thirds of a year. FBI studies have noted that twenty-eight per cent of sexual killers cite legal issues as a pre-crime stress factor, and conflict with another male as a factor in eleven per cent of cases. Albert was dealing with both of these issues at the time. He was back in court nine days later, to apply for warrants against two H:Division constables for 'perjury'. He seems to have had something of a preoccupation with the court system and the police, which is another trait common among serial sexual murderers. He claimed on multiple occasions to have been mistreated and assaulted by police, and made a large number of voluntary trips to court, all of which, it would appear, seem to have been unnecessary. On many of his trips, he went to appear specifically before magistrates that had been involved with the Ripper case – specifically Mr Mead, who had overseen the James Sadler case, and coroner Langham, who had overseen the inquest into Catherine Eddowes. Sexual killers who leave disorganized crime scenes are also generally found to be socially and sexually incompetent. Albert was still single in his 40s, continuing to live either by himself or with his family members, and would seem to have never married.

They're also shown to have a poor or sporadic work history. The Whitechapel murderer, for example, would appear not to have had a regular job, as shown by the times he committed his murders. Martha Tabram was killed on Monday night/Tuesday morning, Mary Ann Nichols, Mary Kelly and Frances Coles on Thursday night/Friday morning, and Alice Mackenzie on Tuesday night/Wednesday morning. Only Annie Chapman, Elizabeth Stride and Catherine Eddowes were killed on a weekend – five murders out of eight were on a weekday. When Albert was arrested for his drunken assault in the butcher's shop, the butcher stated that he 'often came into the shop when drunk, and was often very drunk, especially on Mondays and Tuesdays.' He was able to turn up to inquests on weekdays without being invited, regularly wrote of his nightly 'vigilance' patrols, and made numerous unnecessary trips to court on weekdays. As such it would appear he didn't have a regular job to go to either. Around half of all sexual killers have also been shown to cite employment and financial problems as pre-crime stress factors before their murders were committed. Alcohol abuse is a common trait, and over half complain that 'conflict with parents' was a triggering factor too. Albert's father pressed charges against him and took him to court for stealing his money, and his parents moved out and left him on Newnham Street. It would therefore appear that Albert was dealing with all of these issues at the time. One FBI study also found eighty-six per cent of sexual killers to be 'assaultive towards adults' when they are adults themselves, and fifty-six per cent to be thieves prone to stealing. By 1893, Albert had been arrested and charged with both of these offences on multiple occasions – assaulting Tomas Davis in 1889, being drunk and disorderly in 1891, stealing from his father in 1892, and stealing from the vigilance committee in 1893, getting three months in prison as a result.

It's also interesting that a number of women attacked in the area reported having been given fake coins 'machined round the edge to look more valuable'. As a copper-plate engraver with years of experience, Albert would have had the tools to do this, and he was arrested and charged in 1889 with passing counterfeit coins on two separate occasions and stealing from two pubs. At his trial for that offence, Albert had chosen to represent himself, and while on bail, he had made his way to the police headquarters at Scotland Yard, claiming he wished to 'identify a photograph' of one of his fellow defendants to 'help as much as he could'. More than two-thirds of sexual killers are also shown to be chronic liars – something else Bachert was regularly accused of. He had claimed to have witnessed a particular police assault at the Bloody Sunday riots after happening upon the riot by chance amidst a crowd of 50,000 people. Newspapers accused him of lying when he claimed a woman had told him of the strange bloodstained lodger near Aldgate Station. Thomas Arnold had said in the paper that it was nonsense. Mr Mead told him he was talking 'nonsense' when he claimed at a court appearance to know the author of all the Jack the Ripper letters, and he made numerous claims of seeing the killer and/or suspicious events that were contradicted by witnesses at the inquests. He regularly gave different stories of his sightings depending on which reporter he was speaking to – during some of these he has to have been lying, and when he claimed to have met the 'killer' in the Three Nuns, said the man had asked where the prostitutes 'usually went with men'. Albert said that he'd told him he 'had heard' that some went to Oxford Street Whitechapel, others to Whitechapel Road, and others to Bishopsgate. Unless he was making it up, it might also appear that he took more than a passing interest in the prostitutes in the area and how they did their business. When he gave his story of the bloodstained lodger on Aldgate High Street, he had claimed that the woman said he had 'several brass wedding rings' and 'a white apron, bloodstained'. Catherine Eddowes' apron had been white, while Annie Chapman, and possibly Mary Nichols had brass rings stolen from them. He wrote to the press to claim that 'the houses near the murders could be entered by pulling a string which lifts the latch' – this had been the case on Hanbury Street. He either had an excellent memory for details he had learned through his own exhaustive enquiries, or he may have been recalling his own events. Not to mention the large number of letters he claimed to have received or the graffiti on the wall of his home. George Lusk received three letters, John McCarthy's wife received one while Albert claimed to receive at least *eight* – nine including the supposed graffiti on the wall of his home. That's not counting the 'letters threatening him with death' he claimed to have received in 1885 when he was working as a canvasser for the Conservative Party. Despite all of his allegations, he was never called to speak at any inquest. Murderers who inject themselves into the investigation like this are also shown to follow police enquiries and take an interest in the news reports, which Albert clearly did. When he appeared at Frances Coles' inquest, unannounced and uninvited, he argued *twice* with coroner Baxter, after demanding to be on the jury just as they were about to be taken to view her body in the mortuary. Coroner Baxter had refused him, and that's what caused the scene.

During the time he spent in prison, in Bristol, and working for the relief committee, no letters arrived at his home, and no murders were committed. When he then complained about his supposed wrongful conviction, he claimed he was going to travel to America, but nobody by the name of Albert Bachert is recorded as having travelled from anywhere, to any destination after that time. He is not recorded as having changed his name by deed poll, he did not go back to prison or join the Army and doesn't seem to have been admitted to an asylum, infirmary or workhouse. He made no further appearances either in court or in the newspaper, which would seem somewhat unlike him. It is wrong to believe that a serial killer will not stop killing unless they are caught, and countless similar offenders today have been shown to have done exactly that. Indeed, had he not been imprisoned for something else, died, or moved away, the killer may even have stayed living in the same district. He may have lived up to, and through, the Second World War, and for the rest of his life may have taken regular trips back to the crime scenes to relive his offences. He will have forever kept the souvenirs he had taken from his victims. It is shown today that when such an offender abruptly stops killing, it is often 'because he came close to being identified, was interviewed by police, or was arrested for some other type of offence.' Had Albert been the killer, he had indeed been very close to being apprehended on a number of occasions; particularly in Swallow Gardens, the apparent final offence, near his home, where PC Thompson had heard someone leaving the scene as he himself had approached it. The man Thompson had heard fleeing from the opposite end of Swallow Gardens as he discovered the murder was running in the direction of Mansell Street, which is the way Albert would have gone. Since then, Albert had also been spoken to by police regarding a separate offence and jailed, and any number of things could have happened inside prison to intimidate him. Three men, for example, were hanged as he served his sentence, though none apparently at the prison where he was being held.

Whatever happened to him between June 1893, and his reappearance on Sidney Street in 1901, there would appear to be absolutely no record of it. He appears to have stayed similarly silent for the rest of his days, and seems to have never been mentioned again. It might seem that with the exception of that brief, and obscure, mention in the 1901 census, after 1893, Albert Bachert had essentially disappeared.

The killer had, too.

Author Mick Priestley is regarded an as expert on serial killers and true crime and is the author of the award-winning book, Jack the Ripper: One Autumn in Whitechapel. *He has made numerous TV and radio appearances, appearing on CNN and CBS News in the States, and is a regular expert on the internet show* Murder With Friends, *on the Young Turks News Network.*

Chapter 3

Joseph Barnett – The Live-In Lover

By Keith Stride

Let's begin by asking the reader, what do you know about Mary Jane Kelly?

You might know that Mary Kelly is regarded by many to be the final victim of Jack the Ripper. Apparently, she was the youngest and prettiest of all the victims, and the only victim to have her own room at 13 Miller's Court. You may also know how her horrifically mutilated body was found lying on the bed in that tiny room on the morning of 9 November 1888. The only Jack the Ripper victim to have been murdered indoors.

But what do you know about her life prior to her murder? Seasoned Ripperologists may tell you that she was born in Limerick around 1863 and, after her family moved to Wales, she married at the tender age of 16 to a man named Davies, only to be widowed a few years later when her husband was killed in a mining explosion. She was 5ft 7in tall and stout. She had blonde hair (or ginger), blue eyes, a fair complexion and was said to have been possessed of considerable personal attractiveness. After her husband's death, she moved to Cardiff to live with a cousin who worked as a prostitute. It's here that Kelly herself fell into prostitution and from there she is believed to have made her way to London to become a prostitute in a high-class West End brothel. During this time, she had the company of a well-to-do gentleman who took her to Paris, which she was not too fond of, but where she may have acquired her alternative name of 'Marie Jeanette' and lived the life 'of a lady'. It is likely she came to the East End of London around 1883 or 1884, first lodging in Breezers Hill in St George-in-the-East and, by 1886, in Thrawl Street, Spitalfields.

Thus, we have the life of Mary Jane Kelly up until 1886. But there's a problem. So far, and despite decades of painstaking searches of the records, no researcher, armchair detective, enthusiast or historian has been able to find her, or her cousin or any of her family. It's like she never existed. Then you realize, almost everything we know comes from just one man: her former lover, Joseph Barnett.

Joseph Barnett was born on 25 May 1858 at 4 Hairbrain Court, Whitechapel, the fourth child (and third son) of John and Catherine Barnett. Joseph's parents had fled their native Ireland to settle in Britain and John was a dock labourer. By 1861 the family had moved to nearby Cartwright Street and were still living there in 1864 when John Barnett (senior), by now a Billingsgate fish porter, died of pleurisy in July. His widow was the informant on his death certificate. However this is the last time that Mrs Barnett appears on any official records and what became of her is unclear. It is speculated that she may have abandoned the family. Eldest son Denis would therefore have taken the responsibility as head of the family, although he married Mary Ann Garrett in 1869 and settled in Bermondsey. By the time of the 1871 census, four remaining Barnett children were living at 24 1/2 Great Pearl Street, Spitalfields (a notorious slum district). Denis, Daniel, Joseph and John all received their Billingsgate fish porter licences on 1 July 1878 and from this time (though dates are uncertain) Joseph is listed on his licence as living at 4 Osborn Street, St Thomas Chambers (a lodging house in Heneage Street) and North East Passage, Wellclose Square. He is also described as 5ft 7in in height with a fair complexion.

Barnett met Mary Jane Kelly on Commercial Street on Good Friday, 8 April 1887. That first night they had a drink together and agreed to meet again the following day. This was when they decided to remain together and Barnett took lodgings for both of them in George Street. From there they moved to lodgings in Little Paternoster Row, Dorset Street, but were evicted for non-payment of rent and drunkenness.

This seems awfully quick for them to move in together and it's unknown what Kelly was doing for money at the time, but if her past career was accurate then I can't see how that would have changed by moving to the East End. So, I have little doubt Barnett had probably paid for his first encounter with the woman and repeated the process the next day. Perhaps he took a shine to her and promised to take her away from her horrible life. In his own way, he probably felt he was saving her from the streets. Kelly probably thought herself extremely lucky that she had found a man with a steady income, willing to pay for her to live. Whether she really cared for him is anyone's guess.

Whatever the circumstances may have been, by March 1888 the couple were living at 13 Miller's Court, Dorset Street, a small partly furnished room owned by landlord John McCarthy, for which four shillings and sixpence was the weekly rent. Here they would stay for the next eight months. During this time Kelly doesn't seem to have got to know many people and it would seem very little was known of her. She kept to herself and the only time she came out of her shell was whilst drinking.

As far as we know everything seemed as normal as it could be for the time and area. However, things were about to turn sour. Somewhere between July and August 1888, Joseph Barnett lost his fish porter's licence. It's not known why this happened and there has been much speculation as to the reasons, namely, theft, drunkenness or simply being laid off. Either way, the money stopped coming in.

Here, unsurprisingly, we see the relationship deteriorate. Life became difficult for the pair from this point, with arguments growing more frequent and violent. At some point Kelly decided it was time to go back to prostitution. I would suggest that as soon as Barnett lost his job, she would have been back out to the streets. How else would they have survived? Where was the money coming from?

According to some witness reports, Barnett would never allow Kelly to go back to a life of prostitution, so it doesn't take a Sherlock Holmes to figure out this was probably the main cause of the arguments. Jealousy, anger and resentment must have tortured Barnett. The feeling of being inadequate, and the very real prospect that your pretty girlfriend is now in the arms of countless other men, must have affected him. But it seems there wasn't much he could do about it.

Kelly was different from the other victims of Jack the Ripper, as she was the only prostitute with her own accommodation and a place to which she could potentially bring clients back. After all it would be a lot more comfortable than performing sexual services out on the cold streets. From what we know about Mary Kelly, the evidence supports the fact that she did bring men back to the room. She also let prostitutes use her room as well, leading to more arguments. Kelly must have been using her room for her liaisons as there is no evidence to show that she traded solely in the back alleys and side streets with other prostitutes.

There are also reasons to believe that Barnett wasn't there all the time.

Where did Joseph Barnett go the nights Mary Jane Kelly was working?

Having looked at the available sources, I've reached the conclusion that when Kelly went out to prostitute herself, Barnett went and stayed elsewhere, maybe the pub, a friend's house or any one of the many lodging houses in the area. Wherever he went, he doesn't seem to have been present during these hours. He probably couldn't bear to see Kelly with other men and would have felt useless and inadequate, especially with no job and no money. He certainly wouldn't be in the room at the same time Kelly was servicing a client and I doubt he would have been keen to play happy families when she returned home after a night's work. This leads us to the reason why Barnett may not have been staying in the room that often. After July 1888, the couple were now, understandably, prone to brutal arguments, resulting in violence. We know Kelly had thrown something at Barnett and the object had crashed through one of the windows of their room. We know at that point he moved out, but it's extremely unlikely that Barnett would have stayed in the same small room and, more importantly, the same bed, during all the other previous arguments and fights. He, like most men in his position, would most likely have stormed off to drink his sorrows or just sleep elsewhere until it all cooled down. He also stated that Kelly was in the habit of bringing other women back to stay the night, out of sympathy for them. This means Barnett couldn't have been staying there at the time. There simply wouldn't be the room for three or four people.

Barnett making himself scarce while Kelly was working would also explain the conflicting testimony between his version of events and others that knew Kelly. Barnett claimed that Mary Kelly was sober in his company and he had only seen her drunk a few times. A report from the newspapers on 10 November, when Barnett was interviewed following Kelly's murder, said:

Reporter – 'Was she generally speaking of sober habits?'

Barnett – 'As long as she was with me and had my hard-earned wages she was sober.'

Reporter – 'Did she get drunk occasionally?'

Barnett – 'In my eyesight once or twice.'

Note his words, 'In my eyesight, once or twice', and 'As long as she was with me.'

The landlord, John McCarthy, who knew Kelly and was in a position to see her all of the time, stated that she was frequently drunk. We also hear from other sources that Kelly could be loud and angry when drinking, suggesting she had built a reputation for this. So how come Barnett had only seen her drunk with his own eyes once or twice? I feel we can safely conclude Barnett wasn't there all the time, certainly not on the nights she was out drinking, which seem to be the nights when she was also working. Earning money and drinking appeared to go hand in hand. We don't know where he could have gone but we know he could certainly move about. If we look at reports after the murder, he was recorded as living at 24 New Street, Bishopsgate and had been there for a while. Then he moved to his sister's home at 21 Portpool Lane and, according to *The Scotsman* on 19 November, he was back living with someone in Dorset Street. We also know he knew people in George Street and Brick Lane. It seems Barnett had contacts and had no issues finding places to stay. It's what I would expect from a man who has lived in the area his whole life.

Now they say absence makes the heart grow fonder but perhaps these little breaks from each other were beginning to appeal to Kelly. Perhaps she now found herself drifting away from Barnett's control and constant supervision. Feasibly he was now viewed upon as a clingy and controlling boyfriend from whom she needed to be distanced. She confided with a friend that she was sick of Barnett and had rekindled a romance with another man called Fleming. The fact she was bringing other working women back to stay in her small room could also have been a clever way of getting rid of Barnett. It makes perfect sense too. The girls were earning money; they may have even paid Kelly a small fee for the privilege of having a roof over their head. Barnett, having no money, contributed nothing to the household income and was no longer needed. He was in many ways, an awkward burden. I can imagine at some point during all of this, Barnett was being told to pay his way or get out.

For the purposes of this article and to build up a suspect profile, it is worth reminding the reader that Joseph Barnett losing his job and Mary Kelly returning to the streets also coincides with the start of what many consider to be the first murder committed by the man known as Jack the Ripper. On 7 August 1888, 39-year-old Martha Tabram would be found brutally murdered in George Yard Buildings, less than a four-minute walk from 13 Miller's Court. She was found on her back, her dress pushed up to the centre of her body and her legs spread apart. It was as if she was positioned for the act of sex, but instead had received thirty-nine stab wounds to the neck, chest and lower abdomen. Over the next seven weeks, four more prostitutes would be murdered in and around Spitalfields and Whitechapel. These were Mary Ann Nichols, Annie Chapman, Elizabeth Stride and Catherine Eddowes. (Eddowes was different as she was the only victim murdered in the Aldgate Area in the City of London).

By 30 October 1888, the odd relationship between Mary Kelly and Joseph Barnett had reached its peak. A fierce argument had erupted in their room which resulted in a window being smashed and Barnett leaving 13 Miller's Court for good. On this occasion we know he went to stay at Buller's Lodging House at 24 New Street, Bishopsgate, a place he may have been familiar with during his many arguments with Kelly. Although Barnett claimed he left willingly, I find his story simply unbelievable. This is due largely to the fact that for the next nine days he continually called round to see Kelly, bringing with him money, food or gifts for her. Are these really the actions of someone who has broken off a relationship or are they the actions of a man desperately hoping to make up with the angry girlfriend?

On the night of 8 November 1888, Barnett would visit Kelly for apparently the last time. According to his statements: 'I last saw her alive between half-past seven and a quarter-to eight on Thursday night last, when I called upon her.'

Maria Harvey had been staying with Kelly a couple of nights during the week and claimed to have been in 13 Miller's Court at the time Barnett visited. Before leaving the pair alone in the room she said, 'Well, Mary Jane, I shall not see you this evening again.' She also claimed to have left her with two dirty men's shirts, a little boy's shirt, a black overcoat, a black crepe bonnet with black satin strings, a pawn ticket for a grey shawl, upon which two shillings had been lent, and a little girl's white petticoat.

Nobody knows what Kelly and Barnett talked about in the room but the most likely scenario is Barnett had turned up once again with no money and asked Kelly to take him back or at least let him stay the night. Kelly had understandably asked for money and when he refused she had kicked him out again, or at least made it clear she didn't want him back.

According to Barnett, he left the room but would be well aware that Maria Harvey wouldn't be staying in Kelly's room that night. He returned to Buller's Lodging House on New Street. He would play a game of whist with some of the residents there before going to bed at 12.30am.

Eleven hours later, Thomas Bowyer was sent to 13 Miller's Court on the instructions of the landlord John McCarthy, who had realized that Kelly owed a huge amount of rent arrears. Bowyer knocked on the door of her room, but receiving no reply decided to go round to the windows and, noticing the broken pane of glass, put his hand inside to pull aside the curtain so he could peer into the gloom of the room. Bowyer saw the body of Mary Kelly lying on the bed in the most appalling condition, for she had literally been ripped and hacked to pieces. The existing photograph doesn't really convey the sheer horror that would have been etched on the faces of all who saw it. (A more detailed description of the crime scene is written in this book, in the chapter Person(s) Unknown.) When the police arrived it was found that the door was locked. John McCarthy had to prise it open using a pickaxe, to allow the police and the doctor in to examine the corpse.

What does the crime scene tell us?

An investigation of the room produced some points of interest. In the fireplace were the smouldering remains of a large fire, containing the remnants of burnt women's clothing, which included a skirt and a hat. Kelly's clothes were folded over a chair. Elsewhere in the room, the police found a clay pipe belonging to Joseph Barnett. Note that the killer seems to have ignored Kelly's clothes and only burnt the clothing left by Maria Harvey. Does this suggest a spiteful and jealous act? Some suggest the clothing was burnt to provide light for the killer to work with but this doesn't hold up when properly looked at. The clothing would have burnt up fairly quickly and thus fail to provide sustained fuel to light up the room for a great deal of time. And if that was the intention of the killer, he seems to have ignored Kelly's clothes, which would have given him a few more minutes of light.

According to the *St. James Gazette* on 10 November 1888: 'The bed sheets had been turned down, and this was probably done by the murderer after he had cut his victim's throat.'

This suggests the bed sheets were up over her body before the attack. There were also stab marks in the sheet, where her head would be and anyone looking at the crime scene photograph can clearly see what appear to be defence wounds on Kelly's arms. It seems the woman was asleep in bed at the time and was attacked as she slept. The clothes folded neatly on the chair would also support this conclusion. According to the doctors' reports, we know the killer doesn't have sex with his victims, so he was not sleeping next to her at the time and it's extremely doubtful Kelly would let a strange man sleep in her room during the Jack the Ripper manhunt.

How did the killer get in?

The door of 13 Miller's Court had a spring catch lock which could be opened from the outside with a key. Inside the room, the catch lock could be drawn back and kept in its open position. It means you could close the door and not lock yourself out, or if you wanted to, you could release the catch and then close the door which would then lock. But there's a problem.

During the investigation, Joseph Barnett claimed the key had been missing for some time and the only way to gain access was to put your hand through the broken window (broken by Kelly during an argument) and slip the catch back. However, this means the key must have gone missing around the same time as the argument that resulted in the broken window and Barnett leaving the room. I have already pointed out how I believe he was kicked out against his will and a sensible conclusion is he took the key with him as an act of spite. You can also imagine how he would have returned in the days after the argument and commented on how she managed to gain access to the room since the key was missing, and Kelly would probably have told him about the broken window technique. So, if she was asleep in bed during the attack, the killer must have either known about the window technique or had a key to gain access. Those that claimed to have seen her on the night of her death mention nothing about this unique door-opening technique and from at least one eyewitness it seems Kelly left the door unlocked when bringing men back to the room. So, you have to ask yourself, during the height of the Jack the Ripper scare would Kelly willingly:-

- Leave the door unlocked while sleeping?
- Allow strange men to know the technique for gaining access to her room?
- Fall asleep with a strange man in the room?

None of these suggestions seem plausible and by all accounts only one man knew how to open the door without a key and would have been in a perfect position to have had a key – Joseph Barnett.

Does Barnett act suspiciously?

At the inquest and in several newspapers, namely *The Scotsman* of 13 November 1888, Barnett attempts to link Kelly's murder with that of the other Jack the Ripper victims. He said: 'She used to ask me to read about the murders, and I used to bring them all home and read them. If I did not bring one, she would get it herself and ask me whether the murderer was caught. I used to tell her everything as what was in the papers.'

Note that Barnett says, 'I used to bring them all home and read them.' Is he saying he brought all the papers with any mention of the murders home? Surely that would be rather a strange thing to do, unless your interest in the murders went above the average resident of the East End. Either way he willingly points out that he was in the habit of collecting the newspaper accounts of the murders. One has to wonder whether Kelly really asked him to do this, or was he doing this by himself?

Some explain this habit of collecting the newspapers is a sign that Mary Kelly couldn't read and so she needed Barnett to get the papers and read them for her. But this contradicts the opinions of Maria Harvey, who knew Kelly well and had slept in the same room as the deceased on several occasions. She described Kelly's education as 'much more superior to that of the average person in her position of life'. John McCarthy also mentions that Kelly received letters from family. This would suggest she could read, and the fact other members of her family had also received the correct education to read and write would support this.

So why would Barnett bring up these newspaper articles if it wasn't true? The first impression that comes to my mind is deflection. He's pointing the public and the police in the direction he wants them to go. By mentioning how Kelly read all about the Ripper murders, he is basically saying this was a Jack the Ripper murder. He wants everyone to look anywhere else but his way. During the inquest he even senses his moment to push the deflection further when the coroner practically gives him his wriggle-out room by asking: 'Have you heard her speak of being afraid of any one?' Barnett replies, 'Yes, several times.' He then instantly jumps back to the Ripper by saying, 'I bought newspapers, and I read to her everything about the murders.'

But this idea that Kelly was somehow scared of someone seems to have been forgotten when he was interviewed by a reporter for *The Scotsman* on 13 November:-

Reporter – 'Did she go in fear of any particular individual?'

Barnett – 'No Sir; only with me now and again, and that was always shortly over – one moment rowing, and for days and weeks always friendly.'

And the idea that Kelly was afraid of someone was certainly not the opinion of Maria Harvey. When the coroner asked if Kelly had spoken to her about being afraid of any man, Harvey said she had not.

Something doesn't sit right with what Joseph Barnett is telling everyone. He even claims Kelly did not receive any mail from family, which conflicts with what the landlord says. Could it be that Barnett doesn't want any family members turning up on the scene to give the police a different version of how he really was with Kelly? Whatever the reasons, he was acting suspiciously and his own account about why he left 13 Miller's Court was also suspect.

Coroner – 'Why did you leave her?'

Barnett – 'Because she had a woman of bad character there, whom she took in out of compassion, and I objected to it. That was the only reason.'

Reporter – 'Why did you leave her?'

Barnett – 'Because she took in an immoral woman out of compassion. My being out of work had nothing to do with it.'

Note that each time he answers the question he has to add on an extra reassurance that he is telling the truth. Psychologically it's almost like he is trying to convince himself. We should now be looking very closely at this man.

Does he have an alibi?

According to some witnesses the murder must have happened around 4am when two women heard a cry of 'Murder!' coming from the courtyard. However, this isn't as clear cut as you might think.

The day after the murder *The Star* newspaper reported the following:

> 'The desire to be interesting has had its effect on the people who live in the Dorset-street-court and lodging-houses, and for whoever cares to listen there are a hundred highly circumstantial stories when carefully sifted, prove to be

> totally devoid of truth. One woman who lives in the court stated that at about two o'clock she heard a cry of "Murder." This story soon became popular, until at last half a dozen women were retelling it as their own personal experience. Each story contradicted the others with respect to the time at which the cry was heard. A *Star* reporter who inquired into the matter extracted from one of the women the confession that the story was, as far as she was concerned, a fabrication; and he came to the conclusion that it was to be disregarded.'

On the night of the murder, Barnett was in the New Street lodgings playing cards until 12.45am. After this time, he has no alibi. So, even if the witnesses were correct, he is still in the frame. The initial examination of Mary Kelly's body was made at 2pm the day she was discovered. It was noted that rigor mortis had set in, but increased during the progress of the examination. This placed her condition in the brackets of 'moderate to advanced' rigor mortis. This is between eight and twenty-four hours after death.

Eight to twenty-four hours gives us a very big window. There are reported sightings of Kelly at 11.45pm the night before and 1am and 2am that morning, but the accuracy of the witness statements have been subject to debate over the years. Interestingly, if we take all the eyewitnesses' accounts as genuine then Barnett's alibi still doesn't hold up and if we dismiss all the witness statements as confused or made up then Barnett, by his own admission, was the last person to be with Kelly the night she died and with the rigor mortis report, his alibi still wouldn't hold up.

Was Barnett interviewed by the police and his alibi checked out?

Joseph Barnett was interviewed by Inspector Fred Abberline following the murder. He wasn't charged with her murder and some take this as proof that Barnett is innocent. It should be noted that the police were not even looking for him. He volunteered himself to the police for questioning. We have no idea how that went or what questions were being asked. We don't even know if his alibi was questioned. According to *Lloyd's Weekly Newspaper* on 11 November, Barnett had been interviewed for four hours. However according to *The Star* he had only been questioned for two hours. So there is real doubt about how effective any questioning was. But how intensive would the police have been anyway? From the first discovery of the body, the idea that Jack the Ripper had struck again was firmly planted in the public mind. As far as the police were concerned the Ripper was some lone assassin unconnected to his victims. They were still busy investigating the other murders, following up false eyewitness reports and hoax letters, not to mention being totally swamped with theories. Would they really have considered Barnett, the former lover of Kelly and the man who lived with her, as the Ripper? How many other grieving partners and friends had they talked to over the past couple of months who had nothing to do with the crimes? I wouldn't be surprised if the questioning was just a routine exercise with no real effort or suspicion attached.

We've also got the issue about eyewitnesses. If just one of those witnesses was mistaken then it could have possibly given him a much-needed alibi. Unfortunately, we will never know what was discussed during the Barnett interview.

What's his motive for being Jack the Ripper?

Here lies the tricky part. We can definitely find a motive for him killing Mary Jane Kelly. A fairly obvious story of jilted love, resentment and revenge, much like hundreds of crimes of passion we've seen over the last 130 years. Pointing the finger at Barnett for her murder is easy. Who else knew how to gain access to her room? Who knew she was alone that particular night? Who doesn't have an alibi? Who would burn only Maria Harvey's clothes, the one woman Barnett blamed for being made to leave the house? Whose pipe was found at the crime scene? And who else would know that when alone with the victim he would not be disturbed in the act of killing? Nobody but Barnett!

But could he really be Jack the Ripper? To answer this question, we have to once again see what the experts at the time thought. On 25 October 1888, Dr Thomas Bond was asked for his assistance with the Ripper investigation. Bond examined all the evidence presented in the Ripper case and then wrote his response on 10 November. Mary Kelly had been killed the morning before, and Bond had spent much of that day performing the post-mortem examination. His report is considered one of the first examples of criminal profiling. Dr Bond stated:

> 'All five murders were no doubt committed by the same hand… . The mutilations in each case excepting the Berner's Street one were all of the same character… . In each case the mutilation was inflicted by a person who had no scientific nor anatomical knowledge… . The murderer must have been a man of physical strength… . He must in my opinion be a man subject to periodical attacks of Homicidal and erotic mania. The character of the mutilations indicates that the man may be in a condition sexually, that may be called satyriasis. It is of course possible that the Homicidal impulse may have developed from a revengeful or brooding condition of the mind...also he is most likely to be a man without regular occupation, but with some small income.'

If we can conclude that Joseph Barnett was the only one most likely to be in the position to kill Mary Jane Kelly and we agree with the doctors, we have to conclude Barnett is the most probable candidate for being Jack the Ripper. But how likely is it, that a man can be jilted by the woman he loves and end up on a crusade against prostitutes? Well, this is exactly what happened in the case of the most notorious serial killer of the modern age – the Yorkshire Ripper.

In 1969, Sonia Szurma was Peter Sutcliffe's regular Saturday night date and his serious girlfriend. In fact, she was the only girlfriend anyone had seen him with. He put her on a pedestal and spoke to work colleagues regularly about her.

However, she had been spotted by his brother Mick with an Italian man who was a local ice-cream salesman. Sutcliffe, feeling betrayed and utterly devastated, decided to confront her, but Sonia refused to answer any of his questions about the situation, or whether their relationship was over or not. They argued fiercely and Sutcliffe left her to lick his wounds. He felt angered and humiliated, his already sense of low self-esteem getting the better of him. It has been suggested that Sutcliffe was impotent.

That night, Sutcliffe decided to take his revenge by going with a prostitute. Perhaps it was his way of trying to deal with his sexual issues. Driving up Manningham Lane in Bradford, he went past the Royal Standard pub and, at a petrol station, he saw a prostitute waiting for customers. Having confirmed she was 'doing business', they agreed on a price of £5. They went back to her home and he unzipped her dress but it was clear Sutcliffe was not going to gain an erection. They decided to abandon the attempt and Sutcliffe told her to keep the payment but to give him his change. As they got back to the garage, the prostitute went into the garage and two minders came out and chased Sutcliffe off. As he was about to go, he saw the girl come out with another big-built bloke. They walked off together, having a laugh. According to Sutcliffe he felt stupid and drove home angrier than ever. He felt outraged, humiliated and embarrassed and developed a hatred for the prostitute and her kind.

Some weeks later, he saw the same prostitute in a pub in Lumb Lane. When he approached her about the money, she laughed at him and proceeded to go around telling everyone in the pub the details of their encounter. Before Sutcliffe knew what was happening most of the people in the pub were having a good laugh. Within weeks of this episode Sutcliffe was caught hiding in a garden just off Manningham Lane's red-light district armed with a hammer and knife. At the time he was charged with being equipped for a burglary. However, eleven years, thirteen victims and seven attempted murders later, we know exactly what he was planning to do at the time.

Peter Sutcliffe eventually married Sonia but would continue to seek out prostitutes to kill when she was working weekend nights and he was left alone with his thoughts. Likewise, with Mary Jane Kelly, would it not be logical to say she would be out at the weekends, when trade would be at its busiest, hoping to earn enough money to get her through the week? And if she was out on the weekend nights, would it be fair to say Joseph Barnett would be at his lowest point of self-esteem? Perhaps we've answered the age-old question of why were the canonical five victims of Jack the Ripper all murdered at the weekend.

We don't know what was going on in the tortured mind of Joseph Barnett or how Mary Kelly's rejection of him would affect his mental state. Perhaps he too found himself in similar circumstances. Perhaps he was impotent, just like Peter Sutcliffe. We know that for the rest of his life he never had any children of his own. Could this be a reason? Perhaps he blamed prostitutes and their kind for Mary Kelly being back on the streets or for how his life seemed to be spiralling out of control. Perhaps, in his despair, he too decided to go with a prostitute to take revenge on Kelly or even up the score, or even to prove himself a man, and perhaps he was unable to have sex. His anger exploded and he killed for the first time. Perhaps it was with Martha Tabram.

Here I remind the reader how Martha Tabram had been discovered on the stairwell on 7 August 1888, her dress pushed up to her waist and her legs spread, almost as though she was positioned for sex although no sexual intercourse had taken place.

Interestingly, while we are on the subject of the Yorkshire Ripper investigation, the police had plenty of photofits of a man with dark hair, gap in the teeth and a beard but were able to interview Peter Sutcliffe ten times and still not connect him to the person seen by witnesses. Joseph Barnett also closely resembles eyewitness descriptions of Jack the Ripper, right down to the exact age and height, (30 years old and 5ft 7in) and a fair moustache. One has to wonder if the police missed this obvious clue during their interview with Barnett.

There is also a robbery element to the murders. In the cases of both Annie Chapman and Catherine Eddowes, some of the contents from their pockets were found lying beside them on the ground. There are no reports of them being covered in blood. This suggests the killer went through their pockets before committing the mutilations. This placed the Ripper in the category of a man on the same social ladder as his victims and a man who desperately needed money. Perhaps to pay his way in a small room somewhere? None of the victims, despite being prostitutes, had any money on them when found. Was the Ripper taking their money? If so where was he going with it and who was he giving it to?

It should be noted that throughout the month of October there were no murders. Coincidently it was also the month which saw Barnett finally leave, or perhaps be kicked out of, 13 Miller's Court.

Matching the profile

Barnett also matches some of the criteria put forward by criminal profilers. In 1988, an FBI profile on Jack the Ripper was compiled by John E. Douglas of the National Center for the Analysis of Violent Crime. The findings are given here with the suggested relevance to Joseph Barnett:

White male, aged 28 to 36, living or working in the Whitechapel area.

- Barnett was 30 years old, white, and had lived within a mile of Whitechapel for his entire life.

In childhood, there was an absent or passive father figure.

- Joseph's father died when he was 6.

The killer probably had some sort of physical defect which was the source of a great deal of frustration or anger.

- According to one contemporary news report, Barnett repeated the last words spoken to him at the inquest. This may have been an indication of echolalia, a speech impediment.

The killer probably had a profession in which he could legally experience his destructive tendencies.

- Barnett was a fish porter, undoubtedly experienced in boning and gutting fish.

Jack the Ripper probably ceased his killing because he was either arrested for some other crime, or felt himself close to being discovered as the killer.

- Barnett was interviewed by the police between two and four hours after the Kelly murder (reports vary). If it was four hours then it would suggest they were not satisfied with him completely and may have come close to breaking him. We simply don't know. Some suggest the police were happy with his story or he wouldn't have been released. That's simply not true. The police in 1888, just like today, would have to find evidence to detain someone and if they couldn't charge that person then they would have to be released.

Again, I use the Yorkshire Ripper case as an example. When Sutcliffe was arrested with a prostitute in his car, he was interviewed for hours and the police were not happy with his story, but they couldn't break him. He finally confessed when a quick-thinking officer, deciding to go back and check the arrest site, found a concealed hammer and knife next to an oil tank. Up until then the interrogating team only had circumstantial evidence and would no doubt have had to let him go. It would have been the closest Sutcliffe had ever come to being captured and no doubt he would have been watched night and day. It's doubtful he would have risked going out to kill again. Just think how different the Yorkshire Ripper story may be today because of it. Joseph Barnett may have been in such a position but, lacking the crucial evidence, the police would have no choice but to let him go.

Did he know any of the victims?

Mary Jane Kelly allowed other prostitutes to use her room, which caused much tension with Barnett. Is it possible some of these women were the victims of Jack the Ripper? Look at what was reported in *The Daily Telegraph* on Saturday, 10 November, the day after the murder of Mary Kelly:

> 'Dorset-street is made up principally of common lodging-houses, which provide not less than 600 registered beds. In one of these establishments Annie Chapman, the Hanbury-street victim lived. Curiously enough, the warehouse at No. 26, now closed by large doors, was until a few weeks ago the nightly resort of poor homeless creatures, who went there for shelter. One of these women was Catherine Eddowes, the woman who was murdered in Mitre-square.'

We know Elizabeth Stride lived opposite Dorset Street and would no doubt have frequented the pubs in the immediate area – the same bars that Mary Kelly was reported to be drinking in. You could assume each prostitute would know one another from their own particular patches. You could also assume Barnett would know their faces as well. Eddowes was known to be working the Aldgate area the night she died and, coincidently, Aldgate was also a place Mary Jane Kelly worked. According to a newspaper reports, her landlord John McCarthy said: 'Since her murder I have discovered that she walked the streets in the neighbourhood of Aldgate. Her habits were irregular, and she often came home at night the worse for drink.'

Who were these women that Kelly was bringing back to 13 Miller's Court to shelter? Could it be possible some of the victims were among the ones staying under her roof? If they were, then there's a big possibility that Barnett knew who they were and of course, there's only one reason he didn't mention it at the inquest.

Can we place him anywhere else on any other murder dates?

The short answer is no. But there is circumstantial evidence which does make you think. On 30 September, Jack the Ripper killed twice in the same night. The first victim was Elizabeth Stride, killed shortly before 1am in Berner Street and for the first and only time in the case, the killer then decides to go to the Aldgate area in the City of London. The next victim, Catherine Eddowes, had only been let out of the 'drunk tank' at Bishopsgate Police Station around the time Stride's body was found. She would be discovered murdered at 1.45am in Mitre Square.

But if Joseph Barnett was Jack the Ripper, why would he be going in the Aldgate direction after the murder of Elizabeth Stride? There is one very good reason.

He might have been staying in Buller's Lodging House on New Street, Bishopsgate, while Kelly was working. Incredibly, New Street sits right beside Bishopsgate Police Station, where Catherine Eddowes had just been released. We know Barnett had stayed at this lodging house at least once. If Barnett was going towards New Street that night and Eddowes was coming from Bishopsgate, they would have almost certainly bumped into each other. Not convinced? Let's look at the timings.

If Joseph Barnett killed Elizabeth Stride around 12.50am he had a good twenty minutes to walk back to the lodging house on New Street. This would place him in the area around New Street at 1.10am, around the same time Eddowes was being released from Bishopsgate Police Station.

Eddowes would have had to pass New Street between 1.05am and 1.15am. If she met Barnett around the New Street area and decided to walk with him along to Houndsditch, without stopping to talk, both of them would have reached Church Passage within ten to twelve minutes. This makes the time about 1.27am. If they chatted it would be a few minutes later.

At around 1.30am, three men, Joseph Lawende, Joseph Hyam Levy and Harry Harris, saw a man and woman standing at the corner of Duke Street and Church Passage, leading to Mitre Square. The woman and the man are seen talking, she is relaxed in the man's company, and she has one hand on his chest, almost as though she knows him. Lawende would later confirm this was Eddowes.

At 1.45am PC Edward Watkins enters Mitre Square and finds the horrifically mutilated body of Catherine Eddowes. Some of the contents of her pockets are turned out. Any money she may have had is now gone.

The killer is now heading back to Spitalfields, stopping only to clean himself before going to his destination. This suggests that wherever the killer was going there were others present. If it was Dorset Street, then he only had to walk in a straight line for four minutes.

Meanwhile Catherine Eddowes is still lying in Mitre Square. According to PC Watkins, 'She was cut up like a pig in the market.' Or perhaps more accurately, gutted like a fish.

Barnett's life after the Kelly murder remains a mystery until 1906 when he was given a new porter's licence at Billingsgate. In 1919 he is recorded on the electoral register as living at 106 Red Lion Street, Shadwell with a Louisa Barnett who is listed as his wife. No evidence has surfaced to confirm if they were married. Joseph Barnett died aged 68 on 29 November 1926, with the cause of death being oedema of the lungs and bronchitis.

A retired journalist and resident of London's East End, Keith Stride is one of the original members of H:Division Crime Club. An interest in the Ripper murders started during the centenary year of 1988 and for the past thirty years Keith has produced many articles on the murders for crime magazines such as Top Detective, The Dagger *and* Murder Most Foul. *Keith is currently working on a book called* Witness 88, *which focuses on the stories told by the East End locals during the autumn of terror.*

Information provided from Jack the Ripper Wikipedia page.

Chapter 4

William Bury – The Dundee Connection

By Bill Beadle

It is now 130 years since the Victorian serial killer, whom we call Jack the Ripper, committed his atrocities in the East End of London. I was tempted to write that he stalked the streets of Whitechapel and Spitalfields but in fact 'stalked' would be the wrong word; 'slunk around' would be a more apt description because this nasty little creature pounced on his victims under cover of darkness to slake his abnormal desires on them.

The canonical Ripper murders began on 31 August 1888 and ended on 9 November. Since that nightmare autumn we have been deluged in theories about the Ripper's identity and motives, most of them puerile to the point of inanity. The crimes have bred generations of royal Rippers, sadistic aristocrats, deranged surgeons, masonic conspiracies and alternative serial killers. But amongst the names put forward are a handful whom I believe merit serious consideration: William Henry Bury, Hyam Hyams, David Cohen, Francis Tumblety, Charles Lechmere and Thomas Donoghue. Reasonable claims have also been advanced for George Hutchinson, Severin Klosowski and Aaron Kosminski, which I respect but find unconvincing.

Of the six whom I do believe could have been the killer, one name stands out, William Henry Bury. But before looking at him let us first see what sort of man Jack the Ripper would have been. This means examining Jack's profile, prepared by the FBI in the 1980s.

Offender profiling is defined as focusing on the type of individual likely to have committed the crimes. Profiles are based on a comprehensive survey of autopsy reports, scene of crime analysis, photographs, maps, witness statements and investigative feedback designed to create a psychological portrait of the perpetrator.

The Ripper was most likely to have been the following:

- A white, working class male, aged between 28 and 36, living in the locale of the crimes and, if employed, performing a menial job. He would have a good knowledge of the area.
- He would have originated from a dysfunctional home where the father was weak or absent, and the mother was a sexually promiscuous, heavy drinker. The killer was probably abused, sexually or physically, by a domineering female during childhood.
- He would have committed acts of arson and/or cruelty to animals during childhood.
- He might have had a minor defect such as a scar or speech impediment, making him feel inferior.
- Commencing in childhood, he would have indulged in deviant fantasies about dominating and mutilating women, stemming from his fear and hatred of them. As he grew older his fears would have been exacerbated by worries about the sexual power possessed by women, further fuelling his need to dominate, control and mutilate them. Additionally, he may well have had a morbid curiosity about female sex organs. If so, then the removal of the victims' organs was an attempt to neuter or de-sex them, so that they no longer posed a threat to him. He may even have eaten the organs.
- He was probably single, but if he did have a partner she would have been older than him and the relationship would have been shortlived.
- His appearance would have been neat and orderly.
- His habits would have been nocturnal.
- He would have been a loner who drank in the local pubs and relied on prostitutes for his sexual outlets.
- His poor self-image would have resulted in paranoia, creating the need to carry knives around for self-protection.
- He would have engaged in bouts of erratic behaviour and may have been interviewed by the police about the murders.
- He was likely to have returned to the crime scenes or visited the victims' graves as symbols of his control over them.
- He was not a doctor or any other professional person.

In addition to the FBI profile, another top serial killer expert, Robert Keppel, who led the hunt for Ted Bundy, makes the point that if this type of killer does have a wife then he is likely to regularly batter her. This, as we shall see is spot on, as are other aspects of the profile where we can check it against Bury. There are vast tracts of his life, especially his formative years, which we know nothing about. However, we know enough to be able to pinpoint Bury as a violent, paranoid, misogynistic loner; exactly the sort of man the Ripper was.

William Henry Bury was born in Stourbridge, Worcestershire, on 25 May 1859. He was the fourth and final child of William Henry Senior and Mary Jane Bury née Henley. The surname is also spelt 'Berry' in some documents.

Baby William's birth plunged Mary Jane into a depression from which she would never recover. Adding to the family's woes, the eldest child, 7-year-old Elizabeth Ann, died from a series of epileptic fits on 7 September. According to Dr Richard Lechtenberg in *Epilepsy and the Family*, siblings of epileptics will develop an inordinate fear of contracting it themselves. We will return to this later.

Worse, much worse, was to follow. On 10 April 1860, Bury's father was killed in a carting accident which saw a heavy wagon wheel pass along the whole length of his body, tearing it asunder. Logically, it would also have shredded his genitalia and disfigured his features. The parallel with the Ripper crimes is obvious – the images that we see in the police Ripper photographs were first created on a hill in Worcestershire.

Mary Jane broke down completely and was committed to Powick Lunatic Asylum from which she never emerged, dying on 30 March 1864.

We only have brief glimpses of Bury en route to manhood. In 1861, he was living with an uncle in Dudley and, in 1871, at a Bluecoat school at Old Swinford near Stourbridge. But there is a very clear pointer to an unhappy childhood in that Bury severed all connection with his family and refused to speak to them. Clearly, his traumatic entry into life had developed into a baleful upbringing.

The William Bury who greets us in adulthood is 5ft 3 ½in tall with a dark complexion, broad shoulders and a barrel chest. But he has a fair moustache. He left one job owing money, was sacked for theft from another, and was prone to violent outbursts, but dressed very respectfully.

We have a very good portrait of his personality in a report appearing in the *Midland Evening News* of 12 February 1889:

> 'His addiction to falsehoods is said to have been a continual habit... . He had a most plausible manner and was capable of inventing the most extravagant stories which he told with an air of the most innocent sincerity. He was…a hopeless and confirmed ne'er do well, a fellow whom it was quite useless to try and help. In drink he was wholly incapable of controlling himself and when sober had not the least compunction in deceiving his best friends.'

A classic serial killer in the making. Instant psychopath – just add alcohol.

In the study of serial killers, research shows that two thirds of serial homicides have drink and drugs related problems. FBI experts also noted financial difficulties and family problems are present in almost fifty per cent of murders investigated. Another precipitating factor is employment difficulties. As we shall see, all these coefficients settled around Bury's shoulders like a pall when he arrived in London from the Midlands in the autumn of 1887.

Bury ended up in Bow in the East End. Here he worked for a man named James Martin, delivering sawdust to businesses in East London. Bury also resided at Martin's premises, at 80 Quickett Street. Martin is euphemistically described as a general dealer but much of his merchandise was of the human flesh variety – 80 Quickett Street was to all intents and purposes a brothel.

One lady who worked there was 31-year-old Ellen Elliott. Technically, Ellen was in service at Quickett Street but she was also a working prostitute there. In 1883 she had given birth to a daughter, also named Ellen, whilst residing in Bethnal Green. Sadly, the little girl died in Poplar Workhouse Infirmary on 15 December 1885. Ellen senior commenced working at Quickett Street in spring of 1886, although she actually slept at another Bow address, 3 Swanton Road.

The odd thing is that Ellen had money; six railway shares, each with a nominal face value of £100. Presumably she was keeping her nest egg intact to attract a husband. But given her work circumstances he was always likely to be the wrong sort of spouse, and if ever there was a wrong man to hitch your wagon to, it was William Henry Bury.

Initially Ellen and he did not get on, but when he discovered her nest egg he began to court her. At least once during their courtship he beat Ellen up. Tragically she still accepted his proposal of marriage with the couple deciding to live at Swanton Road.

The week before the wedding found Bury beset by financial worries. Martin had sacked him for theft and was demanding recompense of £17.65. Bury was drinking heavily and was about to marry someone who, deep down, he despised. A few minutes' walk away was 19 Maidman Street. Here on 29 March 1888, a seamstress named Ada Wilson was attacked by a man who demanded money and stabbed her twice in the throat. She hovered between life and death for two weeks before recovering against expectation.

Five days later Ellen and Bury tied the knot. Echoing the profile above, he was three years her junior and the relationship would not last long. In fact, Ellen had difficulty lasting a week. On Saturday, 7 April their Swanton Road landlady, Elizabeth Haynes, attracted by a commotion from Bury's room, burst in to find him attempting to cut her throat. Since the wedding, he had also twice assaulted Ellen in public, clear indications of the erratic behaviour serial killers are prone to.

Ellen placated him by resolving his financial difficulties, selling one of her shares for £39.37. Martin was reimbursed, and Bury bought a pony and cart to set himself up in business as a sawdust salesman. But whatever money he made seemed to have gone on drink and prostitutes, because in May, Ellen discovered she had contracted 'the bad disorder' from him.

The course of treatment for syphilis was then around ten weeks, so Bury's treatment would have ended by the beginning of August 1888. It was at this time that a 39-year-old prostitute named Martha Tabram was hacked to death in George Yard Buildings, Whitechapel. Whether she was a Ripper victim continues to divide historians, but one of her injuries was an incised wound, three inches long and one inch deep, in her lower abdomen, which was the Ripper's signature mutilation on subsequent victims. Martha was subject to a form of epilepsy called 'rum fits' which are linked to alcohol. She had certainly been drinking that night and it is plausible that she went into a rum fit whilst servicing Bury who, with his own terror of epilepsy and fuelled by drink and paranoia, stabbed her to death in a virtual frenzy. The case against Bury being the Ripper does not hinge on Tabram being his victim but it would explain her savage end.

Four days later, Saturday 11 August, the Burys moved into their final Bow lodgings at 3 Spanby Road but left immediately for a week in Wolverhampton. This has all the hallmarks of getting out of town whilst things quietened down. One factor, which mitigates against other Ripper suspects, is that it is generally impossible to track their movements through those horrendous weeks in which 'Jack' danced the East End in terror on the point of his knife. Bury is the exception. The police later investigated him for these crimes. We do not, by a long way, know everything they found out because, along with a vast number of other Ripper files, Bury's is now missing.

But we do have a valuable insight into them through crime journalist Norman Hastings' contacts at Scotland Yard. Whilst certainly not unanimous, we know that some officers at the time believed Bury to be the Ripper. In 1929, Hastings wrote in *Thomson's Weekly News*:

> 'The knife the Ripper used was probably just such a one as that carried about by Bury, and on one occasion when he was definitely known to be staying in the East End. At the time of a Ripper crime he had absented himself from the house in the most suspicious manner.'

We do not know which murder the police were referring to here, but Hastings was more specific about Annie Chapman on 9 September when he wrote: 'Bury had went away from his home and his manner on his return the next afternoon suggested a madman.'

And when Mary Jane Kelly was murdered on 9 November 1888, Hastings wrote:

> 'The police established that he was missing from his lodgings on the night Mary Kelly was done to death and that he was in the habit of carrying that knife around with him. His description was very much like that of the man who had been speaking to Kelly on the night of the crime.'

The comments about the knife reiterate what the profile says of the Ripper carrying weapons due to a paranoid need for self-protection. In fact, as Ellen discovered, Bury even slept with one under his pillow. He was arguably more wedded to his knife than her.

That is not just circumstantial evidence – it is *damning* circumstantial evidence. A network of facts and probabilities similar to those which led to the recent conviction of serial murderer Levi Bellfield.

As 1888 wore on, Bury indulged more and more in heavy drinking, paying less and less attention to his fledgling business. He financed his lifestyle mainly through Ellen's money. In June he 'persuaded' her to cash in the rest of her shares, receiving £194.35 on them (about £12,500 in today's values). The sort of persuasion Bury applied is explained to us by his Spanby Road landlord, William Smith: 'He frequently assaulted his wife and on one occasion…I heard her screaming and had to interfere to prevent him further assaulting her.'

The latter attack may have been the beating which Bury inflicted on Ellen in October when she had to spend several days in bed as a result. It may be significant that October was the one month that the Ripper did not strike.

All pretence at running a business ceased early in December when Bury sold his horse and cart. In terms of walking distance, the Ripper's hunting ground was approximately thirty-five minutes from Spanby Road but the journey took much less time in a horse and cart. This was much more in line with the safety zone that serial killers establish between their abodes and murder sites. After Bury divested himself of his transport, Jack the Ripper never again darkened the streets of Whitechapel and Spitalfields.

In January Bury decided to leave London for good. Yet again, it is a common trait for serial murderers to leave a locale which has become, in their minds, too hot for them. Fear of apprehension is constant. After the double event murder of 30 September, the press had carried descriptions of the suspect with a moustache but no beard. In the aftermath Bury grew a beard.

In fleeing the East End, Bury indulged in his usual lies. Ellen was shown a letter purporting to come from a manufacturer in Dundee offering them both work. In fact, the letter was a forgery written by him. According to Ellen's sister, Margaret Corney, Bury could 'write in several hands'.

To William Smith, Bury said they were sailing to Brisbane, Australia, but on 19 January they set sail for Dundee. Once there, the Burys moved into what was to be their final dwelling, a basement apartment at 113 Princes Street consisting of two rooms. There, at some point between 5 February and 9 February 1889, Bury strangled Ellen with a ligature and mutilated her body.

What precisely led to this murder we do not know, but when the police went to Princes Street on 10 February they discovered two garish messages written in white chalk at the rear of the apartment.

On the rear door were the words:

'Jack the Ripper is at the back of this door'

On the rear stairwell outside the door:

'Jack Ripper is in this seller'

By February the Burys were almost broke but Ellen had some nice pieces of jewellery, her little pride and joy. There is little doubt that Bury was threatening to take these from her and sell them. It seems likely Ellen had some inkling of who he was and had threatened him with exposure if he tried to take her jewels.

The most plausible explanation for the chalked messages is that Ellen, who was not very well educated, wrote them to frighten him. However, it is doubtful she ever got as far as telling him before he was clawing at her neck with the rope ligature with which he ended her life. The autopsy describes the way in which she was killed: 'There was a mark of constriction around the neck passing in front between the hyoid bone and the larynx.'

There was speculation in the press in December 1888 that the Ripper first strangled his victims, and it was confirmed by two of the twentieth century's leading pathologists, professors Francis Camps and James Cameron. Strangulating his victims first meant that the Ripper would not come in to contact with spurting blood, a lesson which may have grown out of the Tabram murder. Ligature marks would have been obliterated by the throat wounds. In Ellen's case there was no need to ensure she was dead by cutting her throat as they were in their apartment, not a back alley.

But the very fact that he had slain her in their apartment set Bury a quandary. After he had mutilated her body, what would he do with it? He crammed Ellen's remains into a trunk, breaking one of her legs in the process, apparently intending to ship it back to London. Then another idea came to mind. His luck had always held in the East End. Why not here too?

Pausing only to slip one of his knives into his pocket (not the mutilation weapon) and the spoils of murder – Ellen's Jewellery – he set through the snow-covered streets for Dundee Police Station. He told them Ellen had committed suicide, but what the police discovered at

Princes Street would convince them – in Dundee at least – that the man they were dealing with was none other than the feared London Ripper.

It is Ellen's bodily mutilations which confirm the Ripper's signature. There was an incised wound extending downwards for four-and-a-half inches from the umbilicus and ending one-and-a-half inches above the pubis. Through this protruded part of the omentum and about twelve inches of intestine. Seen this before? Yes, in Whitechapel, Spitalfields and Aldgate, and in particular with Annie Chapman and Catherine Eddowes.

Looking at Mary Ann Nichols' murder, she had a number of incisions running across the abdomen. So did Ellen – one cut running downwards for seven-and-a-half-inches, another running parallel to it five inches long, and a number of further incisions also commencing at the umbilicus and running downwards to the pubis.

Turning specifically to Catherine Eddowes' injuries, some were like for like with Ellen's – incised wounds over the bridge of the nose, the perineum breached in both instances and the injuries extending right the way down to the thighs. Most of the injuries had been made within, at most, ten minutes after death although two were inflicted at a later time. According to the pathologist's report there were:

> 'Two other cuts on the abdomen, one, two inches from the inner lid of the right anterior superior iliac spine and a corresponding wound on the other side, both about half-an-inch in length.'

So Bury had returned to the corpse and eviscerated it again. Only serial killers do this.

Why did Bury perpetrate these mutilations? These were not attempts at dismemberment, any more than those inflicted on the London victims.

Ever hear the story of the scorpion and the frog? A scorpion enlists a frog to take him on his back across a stream, even though the frog is astute enough to protest that the scorpion 'will surely sting me and I will die.' The scorpion points out that if he stings the frog, he will die too. The trusting frog thus takes on his passenger, is stung by him, and the two creatures drown together. But before the frog drowns he asks, 'Why did you sting me, Mr Scorpion, even though it costs us both our lives?' The scorpion replies, 'Because I'm a scorpion and I couldn't help it, it's in my nature.' William Bury mutilated Ellen because he was Jack the Ripper and he had to.

There was one final link with the East End. Found strictly amongst Bury's possessions were two cheap brass rings. Bury wore his own, more expensive rings. But these two cheap rings do conform to the rings pulled off Annie Chapman's fingers. Serial killers keep such items to relive their kills. Found with them were other little knick-knacks. Were these items taken from other victims?

If the Dundee police believed they would be warmly congratulated by their London counterparts they were to be disappointed. Publicly, Scotland Yard dismissed Bury as the Ripper. Publicly. But hidden away in their dismissal was an intention that investigations into him would continue. We know that they did and what they discovered was a very interesting case against Bury, so much so that two detectives were sent to Dundee on the eve of Bury's execution, which took place on 25 April 1889.

The man who hanged William Bury was his namesake, James Berry, who similarly became convinced that Bury was Jack. According to Berry, when he entered the death cell, Bury greeted him with a sneering, 'I suppose you think you were clever to hang me,' with an emphasis on the 'me', as though he was not just a common killer. Bury went on to say, 'But because you are here to hang me you are not to get anything out of me.'

Almost exactly a century later, Ted Bundy said the same thing: 'If you bring the full weight of the state [execution] on them… you're a goner.' In other words, no confession.

James Berry repeated William Bury's last words to the Scotland Yard detectives who told him, 'We know all about his movements in the past and we are quite satisfied that you have hanged Jack the Ripper.' And so he had.

Bill Beadle is the author of Jack the Ripper: Anatomy of a Myth *and* Jack the Ripper: Unmasked. *He is also the honorary chairman of the Whitechapel Society in London. Bill has been a life-long contributor to the field of Ripperology and has been a regular attendee and guest speaker at the Jack the Ripper Conference in East London.*

Chapter 5

Montague John Druitt – Homicidal Suicide

By David Andersen

There is no smoking-gun evidence against any of the named, or known, suspects in the case of Jack the Ripper. And whatever evidence there is, it is only circumstantial and gleaned from what remains of the official Scotland Yard files, the memoirs and marginalia of police and other contemporary diarists, and rumour. The only official document, so far discovered, to actually name any suspects at all is the *Macnaghten Memoranda*.

During the 1950s, the late Daniel Farson presented a television series called *Farson's Guide to the British*. Several of the programmes dealt with the Whitechapel murders. Whilst researching for his programmes, Farson happened to mention to a friend, Lady Rose MacLaren, that he was busy preparing a programme on the subject of Jack the Ripper. It so happened that Rose MacLaren was the daughter-in-law of Lady Aberconway – the daughter of Sir Melville Macnaghten. Christabel Aberconway still had some of her late father's private papers. Among these papers made available for Farson was a draft copy of a confidential report which Melville Macnaghten had prepared for the Home Secretary in 1894.

It would appear that *The Sun* newspaper had published a series of stories on the Whitechapel murders in which they had named a certain Thomas Cutbush as the killer. Cutbush was the nephew of a police superintendent, who later committed suicide. Indeed, Cutbush himself also suffered a mental breakdown around 1888. At first, he appeared to be in the habit of pinching ladies' bottoms but had subsequently progressed to the more painful and dangerous pursuit of stabbing ladies' bottoms with a sharp pair of scissors. As a result of this he was now in Broadmoor where he died in 1903.

The Sun articles, naming Cutbush as the Whitechapel murderer, had caused a small sensation, and in anticipation of being questioned upon the subject, the Home Secretary had asked Macnaghten to prepare a brief on the matter. There are at least two versions of Macnaghten's report. The final, and official version, and Macnaghten's draft version, though the gist is the same in each. In the draft version, which Farson now held, Macnaghten names three men, any of whom, in Macnaghten's opinion would have been much more likely to have been the Whitechapel killer than Thomas Cutbush. They are:

> 'Montague John Druitt – a doctor of about 41 years of age and of good family, who disappeared at the time of the Miller's Court murder, and whose body was found floating in the River Thames on 31st December, ie; 7 weeks after that said murder. The body was said to have been in the water for a month or more. On it was found a season ticket between Blackheath and London. From private information, I have little doubt that his own family suspected this man of being the Whitechapel murderer; it was alleged that he was sexually insane.
>
> 'Kosminski – a Polish Jew and resident in Whitechapel. This man became insane owing to many years indulgence in solitary vices. He had a great hatred of women, especially of the prostitute class, and had strong homicidal tendencies: he was removed to a lunatic asylum in about 1889. There were many circumstances connected with this man which made him a strong "suspect".
>
> 'Michael Ostrog – a Russian doctor and a convict, who was frequently detained in a lunatic asylum as a homicidal maniac. This man's antecedents were of the worst possible type, and his whereabouts at the time of the murders could never be ascertained.'

In the same document Macnaghten also writes:

> 'Personally, and after much careful and deliberate consideration, I am inclined to exonerate the last two, but I have always held strong opinions regarding option number

> one and the more I think the matter over, the stronger do these opinions become. The truth however will never be known, and did indeed at one time lie at the bottom of the Thames, if my conjectures be correct.'

Both Kosminski and Ostrog are positively described as homicidal maniacs with criminal backgrounds, whereas suspicion seems to fall upon Druitt as the result of allegations voiced by his own family. For Macnaghten to be so convinced that Druitt was the killer he must have known more. We can be sure, therefore, that he is suppressing some known details, in contrast with the information he gives on the other two suspects. Even if that is not the case, there is still some suggestion that Macnaghten altered some of the details in the case of Druitt by adding ten years to his actual age, and by describing him as a doctor when in fact Druitt, a fully qualified barrister, had spent most of his working life as a schoolmaster. It could, however, be argued that the term 'Doctor' was often used as a form of address to schoolmasters. But despite these errors the Macnaghten papers have been acknowledged as the starting point for all subsequent research into the Whitechapel murders.

The importance of these highly confidential papers lies in the fact that they were the first papers known to actually name Druitt as the killer. But these are by no means the only contemporary papers alluding to Druitt as the main suspect. Major Arthur Griffiths had been a professional soldier before joining the prison service. He was also a crime historian, and a close personal friend of Melville Macnaghten. Four years after Macnaghten penned his now famous memo, Griffiths wrote:

> 'The police, after the last murder, had brought their investigations to the point of strongly suspecting several persons, all of them known to be homicidal lunatics, and against three of these they held very plausible and reasonable grounds of suspicion. Concerning two of them the case was weak, although it was based on certain colourable facts. One was a Polish Jew, a known lunatic, who was at large in the district of Whitechapel at the time of the murders, and who, having afterwards developed homicidal tendencies, was confined to an asylum. This man was said to resemble the murderer by the one person who got a glimpse of

> him – the police constable in Mitre Court. The second possible criminal was a Russian doctor, also insane, who had been a convict in both England and Siberia. This man was in the habit of carrying about knives and surgical instruments in his pockets; his antecedents were of the very worst, and at the time of the Whitechapel murders he was in hiding, or at least, his whereabouts were never exactly known. The third person was of the same type, but the suspicion in his case was stronger, and there was every reason to believe that his own friends entertained grave doubts about him. He was also a doctor in the prime of life, was believed to be insane or on the borderland of insanity, and he disappeared after the last murder, that in Millers Court, on the 9th November 1888. On the last day of that year, seven weeks later, his body was found floating in the Thames, and was said to have been in the water for a month. The theory in this case is that after his last exploit, which was the most fiendish of all, his brain gave way, and he became furiously insane and committed suicide.'

There is no room for doubt that Griffiths is endorsing and elaborating upon Macnaghten's suspicions as there is no conflict between Griffiths' description of Macnaghten's suspects – Kosminski, Ostrog and Druitt – with the facts which have subsequently been discovered about them.

Journalist George Sims, whose pen name was 'Dagonet', was a close friend of both Macnaghten and James Monro, the man in overall control of the investigations. Sims covered the case contemporaneously and seems to have been well acquainted with all aspects of it and the way in which it was being investigated. Just three weeks after the slaying of Mary Kelly, Sims, writing in *The Sunday Referee* newspaper of the re-appointment of James Monro to the position of police commissioner, had this to say:

> 'It would be strange if the accession of Mr Monro to power were to be signalised by such a universally popular achievement as the arrest of Jack the Ripper. From such information which has reached me, I venture to prophesy that this will be the case.'

This article was published on 2 December 1888 just two days before Druitt's death, and it is clear that Sims' purpose is to let the reader know that Monro is on to someone. Writing in *The Sunday Referee* fifteen years later, Sims tells us that a shortlist of seven suspects existed. He wrote:

> 'This list was reduced by a further exhaustive enquiry to three, and we were about to fit these three persons movements in with the dates of the various murders when the only genuine Jack saved us the trouble, by being found dead in the Thames, into which he had flung himself, a raving lunatic... . But prior to this discovery the name of the man found drowned was bracketed with two others as a possible "Jack" and the police were in search of him alive when they found him dead. It is perfectly well known at Scotland Yard who "Jack" was, and the reasons for the police conclusions were given in a report to the Home Office, which was considered by the authorities to be final and conclusive.'

In April 1903 Sims wrote in *The Sunday Referee*:

> 'No one who saw the victim of Millers Court as she was found ever doubted that the deed was that of a man in the last stage of a terrible form of insanity. No complete description was ever given to the press. The details were too foully fiendishly awful. A little more than a month later the body of the man suspected by the chiefs at the yard, and by his own friends, who were in communication with the yard, was found in the Thames. The body had been in the water about a month.'

The list of suspects, to which Sims refers in his December 1888 article, could not have been the *Macnaghten Memoranda* since Macnaghten had not yet been appointed to his office. It was to be a further three-and-a-half years before Macnaghten was to write his memo. Yet somehow Sims knew of the list of suspects. In his later article, Sims mentions a report made to the Home Office which was considered 'final and conclusive'. Later, in 1903, Sims reveals that he knew the real name of the suspect and that this man's friends had communicated with the police. It would also seem that Druitt's name was not only known to the police but had already circulated into the public domain.

In the 1922 book *My Life and a Few Yarns*, career naval officer H.L. Fleet made an interesting observation, as discovered by Paul Begg, which strongly suggests that rumours about Druitt may have been already in circulation as early as late 1888. He wrote:

> 'On January 1st, 1895, my promotion to Captain was gazetted; another spell of half-pay! At Blackheath we found a lot of old friends, and one of my old C-in-C's Sir Walter Hunt Grubbe, as Admiral at the college. The Heath itself had a bad reputation after dark. When we lived there formerly it was considered dangerous for the terrible series of crimes committed by "Jack the Ripper" were then being perpetrated, and many people believed that he lived in Blackheath. His victims were invariably women of the unfortunate class, and it was evident that he was a homicidal maniac with a grudge against such people. He was never caught, although it was sometimes stated that he had been and was confined in Broadmoor.'

The rumour that Jack the Ripper had lived in Blackheath could not have originated with the Macnaghten memo as the memo, an unpublished and highly confidential document, makes no mention of Blackheath. Furthermore, Captain Fleet appears to be describing – in January 1895 – a rumour which was known in the area when he had lived there at the time of the killings in late 1888. If this is the case then Captain Fleet's rumour predates the Macnaghten memo by six years. This makes it even more likely that the rumour may have originated locally in Blackheath, and quite possibly from George Valentine's school, where Druitt worked and resided until his death.

However, Druitt's name does not seem to have been known to MP and author Leonard Matters, although he had clearly heard the rumour of the 'drowned doctor'. In his book *The Mystery of Jack the Ripper* he came tantalizingly close to what might have been the truth...and then dismissed it. In chapter sixteen, he discussed the rumour that the body of Jack the Ripper had been fished out of the River Thames shortly after the last murder. He wrote:

> 'I have searched the columns of *The Times*, *The Daily Telegraph*, *The Daily News* and *The Star*, and have failed to find any reference, between 9th of November 1888 and March 1889 to this sensational find in the Thames. Surely if the facts could have been substantiated such a discovery would have been a sensation — to say nothing of a great relief to the awe-stricken East End of London.
>
> 'The finding of a body in the Thames would not, of itself, excite any interest. Bodies are taken from the river almost every day, but not the body of a murderer of the character of Jack the Ripper, for whom the entire police force were still eagerly looking. The suicide of Jack the Ripper is a possibility that cannot be lightly scouted, especially by those who accept the theory of the murders being committed by a lunatic, but to give it its full credence it is first necessary to believe that this lunatic disguised his violent mania for many months... . The theory that he was a lunatic, to be incarcerated if examined by a doctor, unaware of anything definite against him to prove his lunacy, will not bear consideration... . Many theorists were reluctant to declare that the murderer was quite sane, and they sought a compromise by suggesting that, while he was not mad, he was the victim of delusions and impulses.'

What Matters is telling us here is that there was a story about the body of Jack the Ripper being taken from the River Thames, and that the suspect was insane with apparent periods of lucidity. Matters then dismisses this possibility in favour of his mythical Doctor Stanley. If Matters had, however, extended his search among the periodicals of the day he might well have stumbled across the body in question. For, as we shall see later, a body was indeed pulled from the River Thames during the relevant period. Given Matters' own assertion that such a find would have been 'sensational', I strongly suspect that if he had discovered this fact to be true then his fictitious Doctor Stanley would never have appeared in print. As it was the world had to wait for almost another forty years before learning the name of a much more likely, and real, suspect.

Druitt, as the son of an eminent surgeon, is also identified in the following story which appeared in *The Bristol Times and Mirror* on 11 February 1891:

> 'I give a curious story for what it is worth. There is a West of England member who in private declares he has solved the mystery of "Jack the Ripper".
>
> 'His theory – and he repeats it with so much emphasis that it might also be called his doctrine – is that Jack the Ripper committed suicide on the night of his last murder. I cannot give details, for fear of a libel action, but the story is so circumstantial that a good many people believe it. He states that a man with blood-stained clothes committed suicide on the night of the last murder and that he was the son of a surgeon who suffered from homicidal mania. I do not know what the police think of the story, but I believe that before long a clean breast will be made, and that the accusation will be sifted thoroughly.'

The same story, slightly edited, appeared in other papers of the same date, notably *The Pall Mall Gazette* published in London.

The identity of the West of England Member (of Parliament) slipped out a little over a year later when the *Western Mail* revealed him to be Henry Farquharson the MP for West Dorset from 1885 until his death in 1895.

Farquharson lived only nine miles from the Druitt family home in Wimborne. He was the son of the Lord of the Manor of Tarrant Gunville, and principal landowner, and would have known the family well, not just as neighbours but also as part of the high Tory gentry of West Dorset. It is quite possible that Farquharson might have heard the story directly from a source in the Druitt family or through the Dorset grapevine. He might have heard it from Macnaghten himself or Farquharson might even have been the source of Macnaghten's own 'private information'. We are told that Macnaghten's initial suspicions appear to have been based upon information from either a friend and/or family of Druitt himself and confirmed from some kind of evidence 'of a factual nature', which came into his possession some time later. But what was this private information? And how did it leak into the public domain so soon after Druitt's death?

To find the answers to these questions we must use reasoned speculation based on what we do know about Druitt, and in particular the peculiar circumstances surrounding his sudden dismissal from the Blackheath school where he worked as an assistant master, and his sudden death less than a week later. We do know that Druitt was dismissed, for an unspecified 'serious offence', from his position on Friday, 30 November 1888, which was the day after he had won an appeal case in the law courts. The following day he purchased a return railway ticket and travelled to Hammersmith Station. Thirty-one days later his body was found floating in the River Thames at nearby Chiswick. The reasons for Druitt's dismissal from the school have never been explained. Some theorists have concluded, without evidence or justification, that it must have been for a homosexual offence, but it might have just as easily been due to a conflict between his legal work and his school duties. Or, if we accept the word of George Sims' article of 2 December, it is possible that Druitt became aware that the police were on to him.

The next we hear of Druitt is the report of his death and inquest. In 1970, I discovered the report in an archive copy of the local paper for 1888. This is from the *Acton Chiswick and Turnham Green Gazette:*

> 'FOUND DROWNED Shortly after mid-day on Monday (31st December) a waterman named Winslade [*sic*] found the body of a man, well dressed, floating in the River Thames off Thorneycrofts. He at once informed a Constable, and without delay the body was conveyed on the ambulance to the mortuary. On Wednesday afternoon, Dr Diplock, Coroner, held the inquest at the Lamb Tap, when the following evidence was adduced: William H. Druitt said that he lived at Bournemouth and that he was a solicitor. The deceased was his brother, who was 31 last birthday. He was a barrister-at-law and an assistant master at a school in Blackheath. He had stayed with witness at Bournemouth for a night towards the end of October. Witness heard from a friend on the 11th of December that deceased had not been heard of at his chambers for more than a week. Witness then went to London to make enquiries, and at Blackheath he found that deceased had got into serious trouble at the school and had been dismissed. That was on

> the 30th December. Witness had property of the deceased searched where he resided and found a paper addressed to him (produced). The Coroner read the letter, which was to this effect: "Since Friday I felt I was going to be like mother, and the best thing for me was to die." Witness continuing, said deceased had never made any attempt on his life before. His mother became insane in July last. He had no other relative. Henry Winslade was the next witness. He said he lived at number 4 Shore Street, Paxton Road, and that he was a waterman. At about one o'clock on Monday he was on the river in a boat when he saw a body floating. The tide was at half-flood running up. He brought the body ashore, and gave information to the police. PC George Moulsom 216T said he searched the body which was fully dressed excepting the hat and collar. He found four large stones in each pocket in the top coat; 2 pounds 10s in gold, 7 shillings in silver, 2 pence in bronze, two cheques on the London Provincial bank (one for fifty pounds and the other for 16 pounds), a first class season pass from Blackheath to London (South Western Railway), a second half return Hammersmith to Charing Cross (Dated 1st December), a silver watch, gold chain with a spade guinea attached, a pair of kid gloves and a white handkerchief. There were no papers or letters of any kind. There were no marks of injury to the body, but it was rather decomposed. A verdict of suicide whilst in an unsound mind was returned. Druitt's body was then transported to Wimborne in Dorset where, on the afternoon of the day following the inquest Montague Druitt was buried in Wimborne Cemetery. Relatives and a few friends attended the funeral.'

While this newspaper report only gives the gist of Druitt's 'suicide note' it does raise a number of other problems. Druitt's brother, William, himself a solicitor and coroner, who gave evidence at the inquest clearly committed perjury when he stated that there were no other relatives. The police constable who searched the badly decomposed body stated quite categorically that 'no papers or letters of any kind' were found on the body. We must ask therefore where the 'suicide note' apparently left for brother William was found. We are also told that a letter was left for Mr Valentine at the school, but if this is the case it clearly did not allude to suicide since Valentine later stated that he believed Druitt had gone abroad. Furthermore, if Druitt had intended suicide when he abruptly left the school it must be asked why did he purchase a return ticket to Charing Cross? And how did he end up in Chiswick? Thus far it has been assumed that Druitt left these papers at the school on the basis that they were found at the place 'where he had resided.' We are told that Montague was last seen alive on Monday, 3 December, two days after he had made his journey to Hammersmith. But we are not told where, or by whom he had been seen. Brother William had gone to London and had Montague's 'things searched where he [had] resided.' But we are not told where this residence was.

The date of Druitt's death is given as 4 December. It is clear then, since he had not used his return ticket that he must have stayed in the area where his body was found some three weeks later. But where? What connections did Druitt have with Chiswick? He must have stayed somewhere in the area for his last few days of life. Could this temporary refuge have been the place where he last resided and where he left his papers? Was there an attempt, by Druitt's family or friends, to conceal the fact that Druitt may have been the Ripper? The inquest into his death does not appear to have been as thorough as one might have expected considering his brother's perjured evidence, the ambiguity as to where Druitt had stayed while in Chiswick and the conflicting evidence of the policeman who claimed no papers were found on Druitt's body. The coroner, Dr Diplock, had trained as a doctor at St George's Hospital at the same time that Druitt's uncle was the chief medical officer of that hospital. Could that fact have influenced the coroner's inquiry? During his life Montague Druitt had been a keen and avid sportsman. He had played cricket for his Oxford University team. Two of his contemporaries at Oxford were the Tuke brothers who, in 1888, were running a private mental asylum in Chiswick, just 200 yards from where Druitt's body was found in the River Thames. It has been suggested that Druitt may have been a casual, almost informal, patient of the Tukes. They may have been the friends who, according to Macnaghten, feared for his sanity. They may have been the ones who found the 'since Friday' note and contacted William Druitt to tell him of his brother Montague's sudden disappearance. If this were the case then it is obvious that, by the end of December, William, and the brothers Tuke, must have known that Montague was dead and that it was just a question of time before his body would be discovered. George Sims certainly alludes to this possibility. He wrote:

> 'The homicidal maniac who shocked the world as Jack the Ripper had been once – I am not sure that it was not twice – in a lunatic asylum. At the time his dead body was found in the Thames, his friends, who were terrified at his disappearance from their midst, were endeavouring to have him found and placed under restraint again.'

There is, however, a much more concrete connection between the Tukes' asylum at Chiswick and the Druitt family. On 31 May 1890, just eighteen months after Montague's death, his mother Ann was placed under the care of Dr Tuke by her eldest son, William. She died there seven months later. It would seem odd, if not callous, to place her in a location just a few hundred yards from where her other son's body had been found. Even more telling is the fact that Ann's medical notes, compiled by Dr Tuke, make no mention of Montague's suicide, which was practically on the doorstep of the asylum, yet notes other suicides in her family as being relevant to her own mental condition. It is almost as if Montague had been erased from the family history.

Macnaghten tells us he believed Druitt's own family thought he was the Whitechapel murderer. Why should they hold such a belief without good reason? More importantly, when did Druitt's family formulate such a belief? If the family had held such a theory before Montague's disappearance, would they not have had him certified for his own protection? This could even have been the purpose for his visit to Chiswick. From what Sims has leaked to us it would seem that brother William might have confided his suspicions of Montague privately and through 'the proper authorities'. It is also quite possible that Montague Druitt himself made a confession. This would certainly constitute evidence of a factual nature, such as Macnaghten claims came into his possession some years later. If this is the case it may be asked to whom such a confession would have been made.

It is entirely possible that a confession was made, possibly to a close relative. Let us consider the following press report which appeared in the *Western Mail*, 19 January 1899:

WHITECHAPEL MURDERS DID "JACK THE RIPPER" MAKE A CONFESSION?

'We have received (says the *Daily Mail*) from a clergyman of the Church of England, now a North Country vicar, an interesting communication with reference to the great criminal mystery of our times – that enshrouding the perpetration of the series of crimes which have come to be known as the "Jack the Ripper" murders. The identity of the murderer is as unsolved as it was while the blood of the victims was yet wet upon the pavements. Certainly Major Arthur Griffiths, in his new work on *Mysteries of Police and Crime* suggests that the police believe the assassin to have been a doctor, bordering on insanity, whose body was found floating in the Thames soon after the last crime of the series; but as the major also mentions this man was one of three known homicidal lunatics against whom the police "held very plausible and reasonable grounds of suspicion" that conjectural explanation does not appear to count for much by itself. Our correspondent the vicar now writes: "I received information in professional confidence, with directions to publish the facts after ten years, and then with such alterations as might defeat identification. The murderer was a man of good position and otherwise unblemished character, who suffered from epileptic mania, and is long since deceased. I must ask you not to give my name, as it might lead to identification meaning the identification of the perpetrator of the crimes." We thought at first the vicar was at fault in believing that ten years had passed yet since the last murder of the series, for there were other somewhat similar crimes in 1889. But, on referring again to Major Griffiths' book, we find he states that the last "Jack the Ripper" murder was that in Miller's Court on November 9, 1888 a confirmation of the vicar's sources of information. The vicar enclosed a narrative, which he called *The Whitechapel Murders – Solution of a London Mystery*. This he described as "substantial truth under fictitious form. Proof for obvious reasons impossible – under seal of

> confession," he added in reply to an inquiry from us. Failing to see how any good purpose could be served by publishing substantial truth in fictitious form, we sent a representative North to see the vicar, to endeavour to ascertain which parts of the narrative were actual facts. But the vicar was not to be persuaded, and all that our reporter could learn was that the rev. gentleman appears to know with certainty the identity of the most terrible figure in the criminal annals of our times, and that the vicar does not intend to let anyone else into the secret. The murderer died, the vicar states, very shortly after committing the last murder. The vicar obtained his information from a brother clergyman, to whom a confession was made by whom the vicar would not give even the most guarded hint. The only other item which a lengthy chat with the vicar could elicit was that the murderer was a man who at one time was engaged in rescue work among the depraved women of the East End – eventually his victims; and that the assassin was at one time a surgeon.'

The vicar is telling us that he was given this information by a fellow clergyman. This may be one of the 'facts' that he had to change in order to disguise the identity of the 'confessor'. It is quite possible that it was this vicar, who seemed anxious that his name should not be revealed lest it led to the identity of his colleague, to whom the confession had been made. Could there be any truth in this story? Let us speculate here on what we are being told.

- The 'confessor' (the killer) was a man of good standing with an unblemished character.
- The man suffered from epilepsy.
- The man is dead.
- The man died shortly after the last murder.
- The vicar obtained his information from a fellow clergyman to whom a confession had been made.
- The man was at one time engaged in rescue work among the depraved women of the East End.
- The assassin was at one time a surgeon.

The East End in 1888

A view of Whitechapel High Street.

Above left: Public unrest following the Ripper murders.

Above right: Commercial Street around the time of Jack the Ripper's reign.

Looking down to Christ Church Spitalfields from Fournier Street.

The East End of London was rife with crime.

The poverty and overcrowding in Victorian London meant many people struggled to survive.

Whitechapel Murders

Above left: A popular image of Jack the Ripper.

Above right: Police conducted house-to-house searches in the East End.

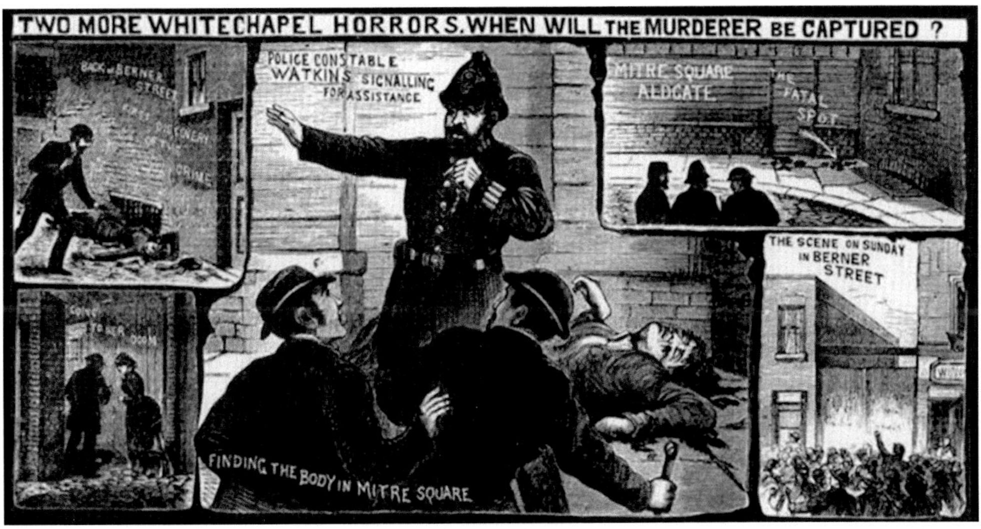

Newspaper report on the night of the double event.

BLIND-MAN'S BUFF.

(As played by the Police.)

"TURN ROUND THREE TIMES, AND CATCH WHOM YOU MAY!"

Above left: A satirical cartoon mocking the police for being taunted by the Ripper.

Above right: A reconstruction of one of Jack the Ripper's crimes.

The double event – the discovery of Elizabeth Stride and Catherine Eddowes on the same night less than forty-five minutes apart.

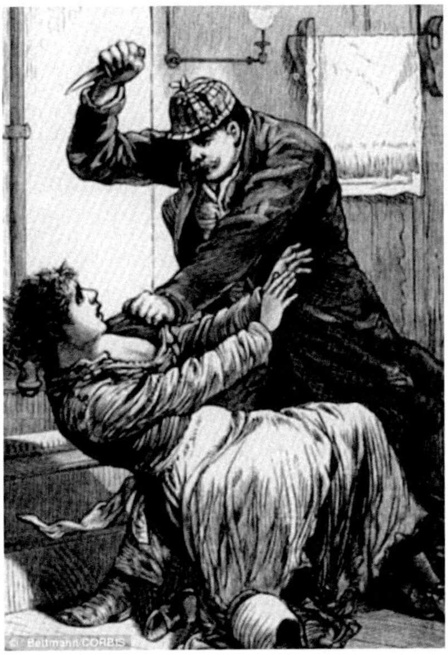

Right: One of the Whiechapel murders.

Below: Map illustrating where the Whitechapel murders took place.

The victims — in the order they happened.

Emma Smith.

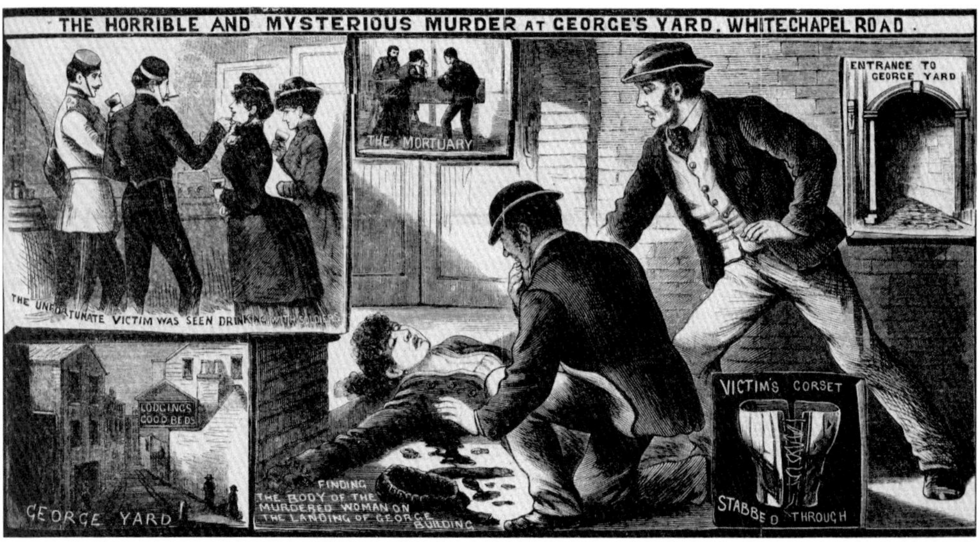

The murder of Martha Tabram.

Mary Ann Nichols last seen leaving her lodging house.

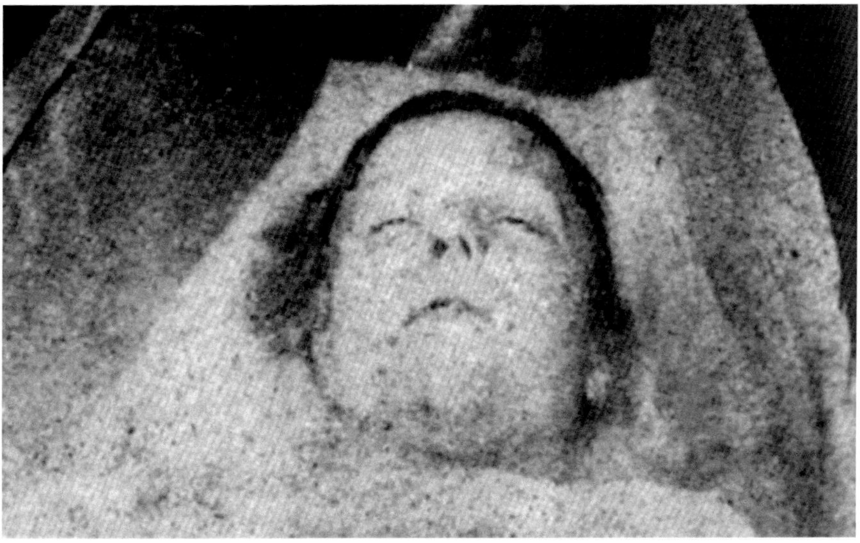

Mortuary photograph of Mary Ann Nichols.

Annie Chapman.

THE SCENE OF THE MURDER.

Pall Mall Gazette, 8 September 1888

Above left: Mortuary photograph of Annie Chapman.

Above right: The back yard of 29 Hanbury Street, where Annie Chapman's body was discovered.

Above: Blood stains at Hanbury Street from Annie Chapman's murder.

Below left: Crime scene photo of the back yard of 29 Hanbury Street.

Below right: Number 29 Hanbury Street.

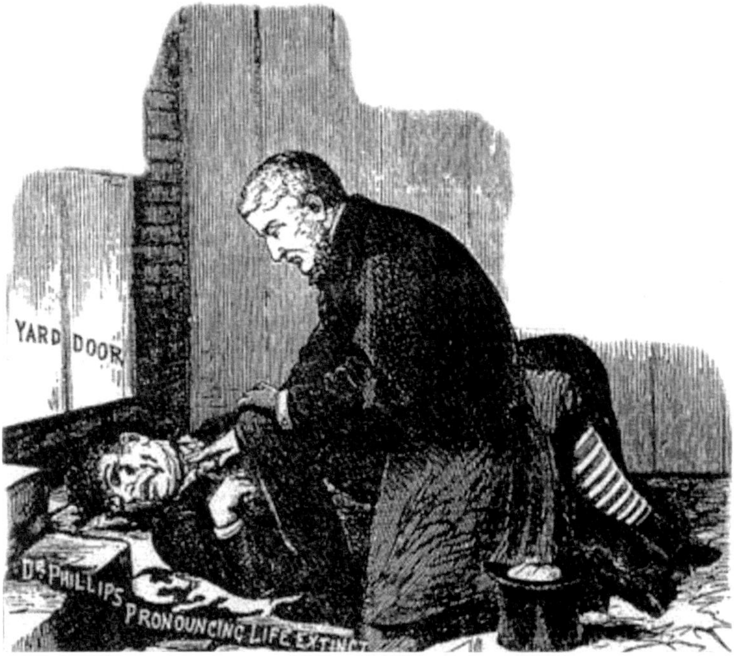

Dr Phillips examines the body of Annie Chapman.

Discovering the body of Elizabeth Stride.

Above: Berner Street, off which Elizabeth Stride was murdered.

Right: Mortuary photograph of Elizabeth Stride.

Above left: Catherine Eddowes.

Above right: Artist depiction of Mary Jane Kelly entering her lodgings.

The awful discovery of Mary Jane Kelly.

Rose Mylett.

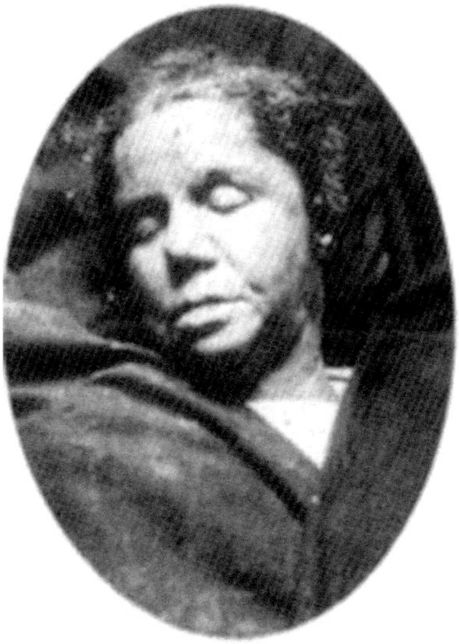

Above left: Mortuary photograph of Alice McKenzie.

Above right: The discovery of the 'Pinchin Street torso'.

Frances Coles.

Mortuary photograph of
Frances Coles.

Police

Above left: Chief Inspector Donald Swanson.

Above right: Inspector Fred Abberline.

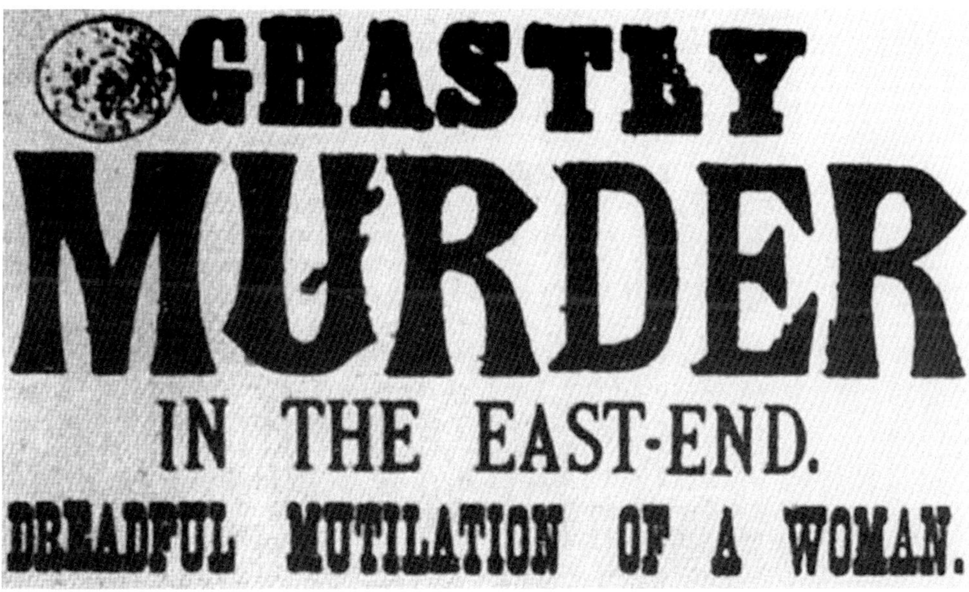

GHASTLY MURDER IN THE EAST-END.

DREADFUL MUTILATION OF A WOMAN.

Public notice of the murders.

Above Left: Sir Charles Warren.

Above right: Sir Melville Macnaghten.

Sir Robert Anderson.

Suspects

Right: Artist's impression of Robert Anderson's Jewish suspect often thought to be Aaron Kosminski.

Below: A suspicious Whitechapel character often used to depict Kosminski.

Left: An artist's impression of Jack the Ripper.

Below: Charles Lechmere (also known as Cross) in later life.

Charles Lechmere alerts a police officer following the murder of Mary Ann Nichols.

The Whitechapel mortuary where Robert Mann worked.

Francis Tumblety.

George Hutchinson sees Mary Kelly in the company of a man.

Joseph Barnett.

Montague Druitt.

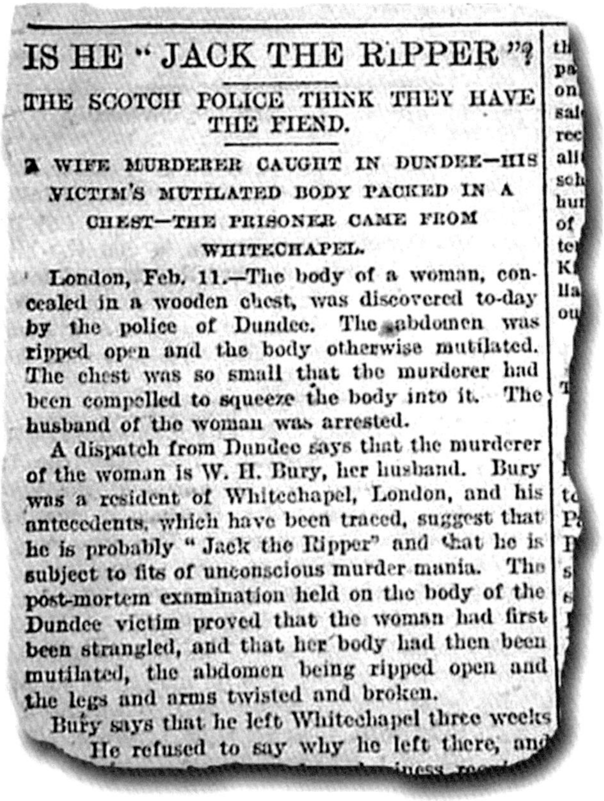

IS HE "JACK THE RIPPER"?

THE SCOTCH POLICE THINK THEY HAVE THE FIEND.

A WIFE MURDERER CAUGHT IN DUNDEE—HIS VICTIM'S MUTILATED BODY PACKED IN A CHEST—THE PRISONER CAME FROM WHITECHAPEL.

London, Feb. 11.—The body of a woman, concealed in a wooden chest, was discovered to-day by the police of Dundee. The abdomen was ripped open and the body otherwise mutilated. The chest was so small that the murderer had been compelled to squeeze the body into it. The husband of the woman was arrested.

A dispatch from Dundee says that the murderer of the woman is W. H. Bury, her husband. Bury was a resident of Whitechapel, London, and his antecedents, which have been traced, suggest that he is probably "Jack the Ripper" and that he is subject to fits of unconscious murder mania. The post-mortem examination held on the body of the Dundee victim proved that the woman had first been strangled, and that her body had then been mutilated, the abdomen being ripped open and the legs and arms twisted and broken.

Bury says that he left Whitechapel three weeks ... He refused to say why he left there, and

News of William Bury's arrest reaches the press.

Sir Robert Anderson's Jewish suspect identified at the seaside home. Was this Kosminski?

Above: Another artist's impression of Jack the Ripper.

Right: The only known illustration of Albert Bachert disarming an attacker in Whitechapel.

William Bury.

A modern photofit of what Jack the Ripper may have looked like.

Six of the seven facts listed fit Montague Druitt who was the son of a surgeon. That the killer was believed to have been a surgeon may account for this discrepancy (if it does refer to Druitt). It also presents some difficulty when considering the identity of the original vicar to whom the alleged confession was made.

Most telling, however, is the revelation that the killer had been engaged in rescue work among the prostitutes in the East End of London. Given Druitt's established association, as financial contributor, to The People's Palace in the Mile End Road and his possible links with the Oxford settlements and to Toynbee Hall, in the heart of Whitechapel, it would provide perfect cover for a killer acting as a lone vigilante in plain sight. The theory that the killer may have had associations with Toynbee Hall is strengthened when one considers Dr Canter's 'circle theory'. The concept of this theory is based upon the notion that all people, and thus offenders, operate in a limited spatial mindset creating imagined boundaries based upon pre-existing knowledge. If a circle is drawn around the area of the killings, the habitat of the killer may be located towards the centre. Toynbee Hall is in dead centre when the theory is applied to the Whitechapel murders.

Montague's cousin, Charles Druitt, was a vicar in Parkstone, Dorset, not far from Wimborne and would have been unlikely to describe Montague as a surgeon. But, since we also know that the vicar who gave the story to the newspaper had been tasked with distorting some facts in an attempt to disguise the identity, describing the confessor as a surgeon would achieve that objective. We should remember that the suggestion that the killer must have been a surgeon was quite consistent with the common belief at that time. Yet another possibility exists. The original vicar, to whom the confession was made, could have been former barrister John Lonsdale, sometime roommate of Charles in Wimborne and close friend of Harry Wilson of The Osiers, a male chummery a few hundred yards from the Tuke asylum at Chiswick. Wilson was also a close friend of HRH Prince Eddy (Prince Albert).

John Lonsdale, born in 1856, would have known Montague Druitt well. He had lived at Eliot Cottages in Blackheath just a few yards from George Valentine's School where Druitt was based. He had chambers alongside Druitt at King's Bench Walk in the Inner Temple. In 1887 Lonsdale had given up practising law and was ordained as an

Anglican priest, becoming the immediate successor to Charles Druitt as curate of Wimborne. More interesting is the fact that in 1887 Charles Druitt and John Lonsdale had shared a house for a time in East Borough, Wimborne. The Priest's House Museum in Wimborne holds another clue, in the form of a journal which strongly suggests that the Druitt family was concealing a family secret. Montague's uncle, James Druitt, his father's brother, had, sometime in the late 1800s commenced writing a memoir. The memoir was dictated to his daughter Barbara. For some unknown reason the memoir breaks off in November 1888, between the last murder and Montague's death. It recommences again in 1894, with the following words: 'Avoiding all mention of the defects which one hopes to conceal from one's neighbours.' We can only speculate what these defects might have been but clearly Uncle James was keeping it secret. Could James Druitt have received information, possibly from his nephew Charles, or from Charles' friend John Lonsdale to whom either, or both, Montague may have confessed? Both were ordained priests. Furthermore Barbara Druitt, Uncle James' daughter, to whom the journal was dictated, married, at the age of 36, the Rev Harold Holmes Blair who, like his father, was a vicar in Northumberland.

None of the above is evidence that Druitt was the Whitechapel murderer. But it is ample evidence that Druitt was the chief suspect at the time, and quite possibly even very shortly before his death, at which point the murders attributed to Jack the Ripper ceased. Some investigators have insisted that Druitt could not possibly have committed these killings and carried on his normal everyday existence including turning out to play cricket at the same time. I disagree. Such coolness and detachment from the crime is a prime characteristic of the psychopathic sexual serial killer.

Peter Sutcliffe, the so-called Yorkshire Ripper, lived an outwardly normal existence with his wife and friends. None of them ever suspected that he was a serial killer. Yet, in a period of five years he brutally murdered more than a dozen women. Peter Kurten, the mass killer of Dusseldorf, led an overtly blameless life until it was discovered that he had murdered at least nine women, each time in a frenzy of sexual sadism. The youngest of his victims was only 9 years old. Dennis Nilsen murdered more than a dozen young men. Some of his victims were disposed of by burning. Others were dismembered and boiled before the remains were flushed into the public sewers. Nilsen's crimes came to light when the drain outside his house became clogged up with rotting human flesh. During the day, Nilsen would go off to his job as a civil servant in a social security office. At weekends he socialized in the local pubs and gay bars of West London. Although essentially a loner he did form relationships. But when not in a relationship he killed, as he himself has intimated, for company. His most recent victim would often be left sitting upright in an armchair as if waiting to welcome him home from a hard day at the office. Until the bodies started to smell he would treat them as living companions. Yet no one could have guessed that this outwardly normal-looking, inoffensive clerk was a serial sexual murderer.

All three of these men killed more often than Jack the Ripper.

The fact that Montague Druitt played cricket and displayed signs of normal behaviour in between murders does not exclude him from the capabilities required of such a killer. Neither do Druitt's cricketing fixtures provide him with an alibi. We know that on the day following the murder of Mary Ann 'Polly' Nichols, Druitt turned out to play cricket at Canford in Dorset. We know too that he was playing cricket at Blackheath just six hours after Annie Chapman was murdered.

Here are Druitt's cricketing fixtures for the relevant period:

Saturday, 21 July ....Blackheath
Friday, 3/4 August ....Bournemouth
Friday, 10 August......................Bournemouth
Saturday, 1 September.............Canford, Dorset
Saturday, 8 September.............Blackheath

Polly Nichols' body was discovered before 4am on 31 August. Montague plays cricket the following day in Wimborne. If we assume that the match did not start before 9am, Montague would have had thirty hours to make the two-hour train journey to Wimborne.

Annie Chapman was killed before 6am on 8 September. Montague played cricket in Blackheath later that day, the match commencing at 11.30am. This would give him at least five-and-a-half hours to make the thirty-minute train journey from the East End to Blackheath. Trains from London to Blackheath were frequent. They ran from Charing Cross every ten minutes during the morning and evening rush hours, and every twenty minutes during the rest of the day. The same was true of Cannon

Street Station. Both stations are just a short walk from the murder area. No cricket was played on either 30 September – the day Elizabeth Stride and Catherine Eddowes were murdered – or on 9 November, the day of Mary Kelly's murder. Furthermore, given Montague Druitt's known association with The People's Palace in nearby Mile End Road, and the very strong likelihood of an association with the Oxford settlement in and around the environs of Toynbee Hall in Commercial Street, it is easily within the realms of probability that he may have made use of these resources if requiring a bolthole.

The railway season ticket found upon Druitt's body confirms that he travelled regularly between Blackheath and Charing Cross. In those days, the underground ran from very early in the morning until late at night for the convenience of market traders. Montague could easily have travelled from Blackheath to New Cross and then on the underground to Whitechapel. The journey is only five stops and such a service had been in operation since 1884. Montague Druitt does not have an alibi. His exact whereabouts, at the precise times of the Whitechapel murders, remain unknown. As the son and nephew of eminent surgeons he may well have possessed some rudimentary surgical knowledge. It may even be quite plausible to suggest that Druitt was one of the many vigilantes who patrolled the dark streets and alleyways of the area, looking for the killer. He was a strong and agile athlete and would have passed unnoticed among the many Oxbridge students who volunteered to keep watch in the Whitechapel area. And as such he would have had the perfect cover – in plain sight. He was also insane.

Such is an outline of the Druitt theory which has met every challenge since it was first aired by Tom Cullen and Daniel Farson. There is nothing left of the evidence which we know once existed. We are told that it has all been destroyed. Even Melville Macnaghten claimed that 'the truth will never be known', but added that it did 'at one time lie at the bottom of the Thames.'

I believe that it still does.

Author of the acclaimed Blood Harvest – My Hunt for Jack the Ripper, *David Andersen is a crime historian, researcher and local radio broadcaster specializing in mystery and unsolved crimes. He has lectured at the annual Jack the Ripper Conference and written new research articles and books on the subject of the Whitechapel murders.*

Chapter 6

David Cohen – Mistaken Identity

By Martin Fido

It's best if I explain just how I came to identify David Cohen. Too many people have tried to explain it as a scramble to find something – anything – to put as a substitute when it became clear that Aaron Kosminski could not have been Jack the Ripper.

It all began in 1985 as I was researching my *Murder Guide to London*. For this I read all the memoirs of the various knackers of the yard who had described their detective days. And so, for the first time, I read the Ripper musings of Ben Leeson, Robert Anderson and Melville Macnaghten. I had the greatest hopes of Leeson. I was aware of the widespread esteem for Inspector Fred Abberline's knowledge of the case, and believed that the ordinary police on the ground under his supervision were most likely to hold the key to the mystery. Leeson summed up the majority position ultimately to be gleaned from them: there was an inclination to suspect a 'a certain' unnamed doctor. Other than a vague suggestion that he was always in some way in the vicinity of the crimes, it wasn't clear why. And Leeson's memoirs were clearly unreliable. His claim to have been the third police officer arriving at the scene of Frances Coles' murder is not supported by inquest testimony. His writing showed a tendency for mild self-inflation. He had not usually been treated as important by previous Ripper writers. Donald McCormick accepted his story and invented dialogue for him, but McCormick himself was the least reliable of early Ripper writers.

From such writers, I was aware that the *Macnaghten Memoranda* – the version transcribed by his daughter, Lady Aberconway and quoted by Tom Cullen and Dan Farson, and the Scotland Yard version reproduced by Donald Rumbelow – now held pride of place as evidence accepted by serious Ripperologists with an understanding of historical research.

There was a problem. Macnaghten described the suspect Montague Druitt's age and occupation wrongly, but otherwise seemed reliable. His memoirs were less detailed, didn't name his suspect as Druitt, and made mysterious mention of evidence speculated to lie at the bottom of the Thames.

Anderson was almost universally dismissed by commentators. His claim that the Ripper had been identified as a poor Polish Jew from the heart of the district was rejected; he was scoffed at for saying the man had been incarcerated in an asylum before he was identified, and so was unfit to plead. A cheap excuse to cover the fact that he had no real evidence, said the commentators. The most extreme declared that Anderson was utterly dishonest, attempting to cover his force's disastrous failure in the Ripper investigation with an undisprovable pack of self-serving lies. Only Richard Whittington-Egan, doyen of true crime writers, withheld judgement, noting that Anderson's claim was highly plausible, but, unfortunately, unsupported by any concrete evidence.

What I noticed immediately was that Anderson's poor Polish Jew matched Macnaghten's second named suspect, Kosminski. There seemed little doubt that the two were talking about the same man: a local immigrant who had been (in Anderson's words) 'caged in an asylum'. Macnaghten told us his surname, added that he hated women, and dated his entry to the asylum at or about April 1889. It seemed strange that no one had ever seen that the two must be one, but then in a decade of reading books about the Ripper as they came out I had missed it myself. If the mind is focused on something else – trying to establish that M.J. Druitt or Sir William Gull or Alexander Pedachenko was the Ripper, or putting together a really readable and factual survey of the case, or looking for the errors that have crept into popular opinion, then the memoirs of two officers in what was widely seen as a deeply flawed investigation were hardly matter for detailed examination. But put together in the same perspective, they gave us clues to a very serious suspect, believed by one senior officer to have been positively identified, and by the other to have many strong reasons for suspicion standing against him.

How reliable, then, were my two police witnesses? This called for further research. It transpired that his colleagues almost universally spoke well of Macnaghten. He was enthusiastic, energetic, encouraging to others, and in the words of Frederick Wensley, the most distinguished of the four Metropolitan chief constables who rose from the ranks in the late nineteenth and early twentieth centuries, 'a very great gentleman'. Only the *Police Review*, a magazine representing the position of rank and file coppers, complained that he received credit for the work of others. But the *Review* opposed the appointment of the highest ranks from the gentleman classes, passing over experienced men who had been promoted from the beat.

Macnaghten was certainly not a liar, then, and not an obvious boaster: two failings supposedly abhorred by the traditional English gentleman. But he was demonstrably inaccurate. His account of his preferred suspect, Montague John Druitt, was riddled with error.

What about Anderson? A Protestant Irish lawyer with a record of aggressive Orange Unionism: was he the liar and boaster of popular report? Well, the first peculiarity to note was that he was, in his own mind, a dedicated Christian. He wrote two memoirs, one of them centering on his experiences as a police detective and twenty-seven books of theology, some of them still valued by minority evangelical groups today. He belonged to numerous religious missionaries and other societies, including the repulsive Protestant Truth Society which, well into the 1960s, kept a shop in Fleet Street selling scurrilous anti-Catholic pamphlets and the infamous *Awful Disclosures of Maria Monk*, an obscene fictitious exposé of nuns' lives. An eccentrically narrow-minded religious and political bigot then, probably capable of believing and passing on damaging untruths about Catholics and Irish nationalists. But would Anderson deliberately lie to boost the reputation of a force from which he had retired?

It seemed in the highest degree improbable. Brought up in a Quaker family and educated at a Methodist school, I knew something about the 'hypocrisy' of dissenting evangelicalism and fundamentalism. My school's motto, '*Esse quam videri*' ('To be rather than to seem'), was flagrantly mocked when we respected the Sabbath and on Sundays were forbidden to play tennis on the three grass courts on the hill at the front of the school, visible from the town. But we could play as much as we liked on the hard court at the back, hidden by the large science building. Like anyone who could read, I was familiar with the countless sexual scandals involving prominent evangelical Christians, from Henry Ward Beecher to Jimmy Swaggart and Jim Bakker. I don't personally see them as grotesquely wicked and hypocritical. As Doris Lessing's creating angel reported to God in her novel *Shikasta*, the creators seem to have made the sex drive too strong. Yielding to temptation may be easily forgiven in an admired figure such as Martin Luther King. Why should we be severely judgmental about other men who lie to preserve their reputations and whose sins need not involve elements of cruelty, insensitivity or manipulation?

But these sorts of lies are astonishingly different from the type of which Anderson was accused. I'm not aware of any vocal nonconformist Christian apologist who has been convicted of extreme barefaced lying intended to boost his secular professional reputation after his retirement. Anderson regarded detective work as inherently detrimental to a good Christian life, since it engendered suspicion rather than trust. Neither he, nor any other deeply committed Christian would be at all likely to go in for self-glorifying fantasy in published writing, even though Anderson's autobiographical work tends to emphasize his successes, endorse his own judgments complacently, and remain unaware of weaknesses including his failure to spot the value of new instruments such as the telephone and techniques such as fingerprinting. Since Anderson and Macnaghten both had access to all the Ripper files (including investigating officers' notebooks), they were the witnesses in the strongest position to know the most likely Ripper suspects. And of the two, Anderson was the more important. He worked directly on the case: Macnaghten joined the force just after the ongoing investigation was reined in. He himself regretted never having 'had a go' at saucy Jacky. And parts of his memoranda relating to Druitt were demonstrably wrong. Nothing Anderson said about the Ripper could be shown to be untrue.

By this time, I had completed the *Murder Guide*: we were into 1986, and foreseeing the Ripper centenary approaching I was ready to propose a book. I drafted the outline of the sort of book most of us now never want to see again: a blow-by-blow account of the canonical murders (as I named them at that time, almost everyone in those days accepting the *Macnaghten Memoranda* as the final evidence); a case-by-case dismissal of previous suspects, and a final chapter laying out my own theory. The only really new material was a careful examination of the police involved in the case (which established that Sir Charles Warren was not the military buffoon portrayed by previous writers, and Major Smith was an unreliable blowhard, as well as detailing what I had found out about Anderson) and a presentation of the evidence that the police had begun by suspecting that the Ripper was probably a local Jew, but had come to soft-pedal publicizing this belief as it aroused anti-Semitic disturbances. The specimen chapter I offered was the final one, and the last sentence read: 'So when we can examine the asylum records we should find a patient called Kosminski, who will be the most plausible suspect ever named.'

Weidenfeld and Nicolson released a bombshell in accepting it. 'You're obviously right,' they said. 'So go and find him, and get the manuscript in by next year. We want to be first in the market for the centenary.' I had little money, a year to trace my man, and the 100-year closure of asylum records which meant that I would not be able to go to the vital source before publication.

I went to work on infirmary records. A pauper lunatic would have gone through the workhouse infirmary before being transferred to an asylum. That was where I found no Kosminski, but one Nathan Kaminski, treated for syphilis early in 1888 and resident at almost the exact centre of the murder sites, in Black Lion Yard. This fitted well with the route taken by the murderer who dumped his part of Catherine Eddowes' apron in Goulston Street. Kaminski was a bootmaker: a possible user of a leather apron, and I had already established the probability that John Pizer was not Leather Apron, and that the police continued to suspect the unknown man with this nickname. Kaminski was one of three possible forms of the name in Lady Aberconway's transcript of Macnaghten's notes that Dan Farson had cited. But since Macnaghten's Ripper file had been purloined, Dan was unable to remember why he had offered variants, and not having seen the original document then I did not know that this was because the paper was damaged at the point where the name was written.

I contacted Richard Whittington-Egan, who was hugely enthusiastic. He had never dismissed Anderson's opinion out of hand. He accepted immediately the obvious identity of Anderson's suspect and Kosminski. He was also very impressed by Black Lion Yard as the heart of the Ripper's territory. But I was stymied by Kaminski's complete disappearance from all subsequent records. Not even his death was listed over the next 100 years. I was examining all the possible records that might help: death registers, census lists, voter registrations, lists of pauper lunatics supported by parishes, and other East End workhouse infirmaries. In these I missed a Kosminsky being sent to Mile End Old Town Infirmary in 1890. His name was so badly written that, like Charles Nevin, then of *The Daily Telegraph*, who actually knew it was there somewhere, I completely failed to identify it. It fell to the brilliant researcher Keith Skinner to trace that early hospitalization of Aaron.

Much of my work took place in the City of London Records Office in Northampton Street. The staff got used to me and told me that, as a serious researcher, I would probably be given permission to see asylum records. And so I started my huge trawl through all the records of all the London asylums between 1888 and 1890, noting the names of all Jewish patients. (My notebooks have since been posted on the internet in How Brown's Ripper forum). No Kosminski. In April 1889 a Whitechapel Jew named Hyam Hyams was admitted to Colney Hatch Asylum. (A photograph would show that he was almost a dead ringer for Macnaghten's third suspect, Ostrog.) But he was committed by his wife which ruled him out as Kaminski under an assumed name.

I telephoned every Kaminski in the London telephone directory. I checked Montreal voters' lists after finding one emigration. I got nowhere, but felt convinced that this man was really the figure who had been maddened by his syphilis into seeking revenge on prostitutes – (something the *Murder Guide* work had shown me was an occasional motivation). You will note that my evidence was still very thin.

I went back to the asylum records, and there, the first entry I noted in the Colney Hatch Day Book showed me a man who really seemed capable of being the Ripper. David Cohen, a Whitechapel Jew of exactly the same age as Kaminski, was the first of his race and parish to be arrested after the murder of Mary Jane Kelly. His incarceration in early December would explain the cessation of the murders: almost the only real clue we had. He was the most violent Jewish patient in the two years I had covered: dangerous to others and potentially suicidal. He was brought to the infirmary by the police, where he immediately threw himself on the floor, and subsequently tried to tear down bars and screens. He was sent on to Colney Hatch Asylum under restraint two weeks later. He spoke almost nothing but Yiddish (described as German). He had no known relatives. He took ill at the end of December, and his condition fluctuated throughout 1889, until in October he died of exhaustion of mania and inflamed lungs.

He was said to be a tailor. This would not have given him a leather apron, but I knew that a royal commission on immigrants had established that unskilled Jewish immigrants were immediately sent by their communities to bootmaking or tailoring sweatshops, to learn as they went along, so that they did not become a charge on their parishes. A 'Leather Apron' who wanted to be rid of his incriminating garment and change his identity would have been able to find instant alternative employment as a tailor.

The name Kosminski, I assumed, was some recollection of his having been known under the name Kaminski. How this became heard as Cohen I could only speculate – perhaps a little wildly. Might this demented Yiddish speaker have mumbled inaudibly? It was only after I had published that I was contacted by people called Cohen who told me their immigrant ancestors had been given the easy name Cohen by immigration authorities who couldn't remember, spell or pronounce their Russian or Polish surnames. In those days I could never remember that Danny Kaye's original name was Kaminsky. It had always been just something long and Polish and unfamiliar to me.

And so, I submitted my manuscript for *The Crimes, Detection and Death of Jack the Ripper*. Imperfectly satisfactory. Another very complicated explanation, starting from something that appeared wonderfully straightforward at first, but including frustration I was coming to expect in Ripper research: trails that ran stone-cold for no reason. Kosminski went into an asylum in April 1889? He certainly did not. It seemed he never went in at all: there was no Kosminski! Nathan Kaminski fitted everything? Well, as long as he existed he did. But where did he go after his treatment for syphilis? Where did he die? He must have done that at some point.

But as everyone who's published a Ripper book looking for the killer's identity knows, publishers insist on their pound of flesh. You must say you've found him. And so Stewart Evans and Paul Gainey, probably Melvin Harris, possibly Keith Skinner and Martin Howells, possibly Shirley Harrison, possibly many others, and I, have all been pressed to make positive declarations that we might like, with hindsight, to have made more restrainedly. My manuscript was submitted. But all was not over.

The illustrations editor failed to come up with satisfactory new material, and the publishers asked if I could add another thirty pages. I was delighted. This gave me a chance to find out more about my suspect David Cohen. So, having found his details in the Colney Hatch Day Book, I now had time to send for the Admissions and Discharge

Book to look for further details. There were some interesting additions. At one point he had been separated from other patients and dressed in 'strong garments'.

But in the Admissions Book I found Kosminski. The Day Book stopped in 1890. The Admissions and Discharge Book ran to 1892. Aaron Kosminski had been admitted in February 1891, and then sent on to Leavesden Asylum for Imbeciles in 1894. There he finally died in 1919. I had to signal Weidenfeld and Nicolson immediately. I would certainly have to rewrite the last chapter, and might have to rewrite most of the book. (And I had to pay the printing costs of re-setting.) The task before me was to see whether Kosminski really was the Ripper and whether David Cohen had anything at all to do with the case.

The accumulating evidence made it quite clear that Kosminski was not. He was a hairdresser, so if he was the Ripper the suspicion of Leather Apron had been completely misplaced. He believed that voices in his head told him what everyone was thinking. He believed that he should never take a bath, and stoutly resisted attempts to make him do so. He was harmless: not dangerous to himself or anyone else, although he had once picked up a knife and threatened his sister. In Leavesden he once used a chair in an attempt to fight off attendants who were going to bathe him. And for a full fourteen months after the murders stopped he had gone harmlessly about his business, picking up food from the streets. In 1987 we believed that the sudden end of a sequence of serial killings must indicate that the perpetrator had died, moved to another locality to continue killing, or been incarcerated for some reason. Today we know from DNA evidence that Gary Ridgeway, the Green River Killer, and Dennis Rader, the BTK (Blind, Torture, Kill) murderer, both stopped killing and led law-abiding lives for years before they were chemically identified. But both men were capable of rational thought. Neither suffered hallucinations or obeyed voices in their heads. And both realized that they were prime suspects and likely to be arrested and convicted if they made one small mistake in any future killing. Aaron Kosminski was not like them. It is probable that the City Police were watching him closely and suspiciously. It is unlikely that he was aware of this and still more unlikely that he would have known how to take rational defensive action had he needed it. Mistrusting food that he hadn't found for himself and physically resisting attempts to bathe him were not the actions of a man capable of lying low and looking innocent.

Kosminski looked mad but harmless, and that, we may be sure is what he was. I added him to my book but discounted him immediately.

This still left an inconclusive and complicated story. Adam Wood pointed out that Nathan Kaminski seemed just one name too many in a story of Aaron Kosminski and Aaron Davis Cohen (the name the police gave David at the magistrates' court). At that stage Kaminski appeared partly because his was the first Kosminski-like name I had found in the records; partly because Richard Whittington-Egan had been so encouraging and enthusiastic about a Black Lion Yard suspect; but mainly because I still needed some explanation for how the name Kosminski got into the *Macnaghten Memoranda*.

And such an explanation turned up almost immediately when the grandson of Chief Inspector Donald Swanson came forward with his grandfather's notes, written in the margin and the back cover of his copy of Anderson's memoirs *The Lighter Side of My Official Life*. *The Daily Telegraph* received them from Mr Swanson. They consulted Donald Rumbelow, who told them to consult me, and soon Donald and I found ourselves mulling over these mystifying notes. They said Kosminski was Anderson's suspect. He was taken by the Met 'with difficulty' to 'the Seaside Home' to be identified, but the Jewish witness refused to swear to his identification of a fellow Jew. Kosminski was then released to his brother's home in Whitechapel, until he was taken, with his hands tied behind his back, to the infirmary, and later sent on from there to the asylum where he died shortly afterwards. Donald confidently explained to me the watch maintained by the City Police in Metropolitan Whitechapel. This was a case with so much prestige attached to solving it that either force would willingly have poached secretly on the other's territory. He could not understand the reference to the Seaside Home – a police convalescent home in Brighton used by both forces. Though convalescing officers had been sent to various ad hoc boarding houses in Brighton since 1887, and a single house was preferred after 1891 until a permanent home was opened in 1893, this last was the one usually described, and this would make the identification extremely late in the day. Why was the suspect taken there anyway? What sick policeman might have been thought of as a reliable witness to the perpetrator's identity? And why was there any difficulty in taking anyone anywhere in this critical case? 'All I can say,' said Donald, 'is Kosminski existed, and he was not the Ripper.' But that was just what my book had said. It didn't explain these mysterious notes.

It wasn't until two days later when I was going to meet Charles Nevin that the explanation occurred to me. First, the various statements about the suspect clearly confirmed that Kosminski and Cohen had been confused with each other. Swanson said that the suspect was called Kosminski and he lodged at his brother's home in Whitechapel. This was absolutely true of Aaron Kosminski. But Swanson also said that Kosminski was taken to the infirmary with his hands tied behind his back, and died soon after his transfer to the asylum. This was quite untrue of Kosminski, who was committed by his family and not under arrest. Cohen, on the other hand was explicitly reported as being under restraint when he was taken to the asylum, and as his first act on arriving at the infirmary was to throw himself on the floor and roll around, he may well have lacked the use of his hands.

But more important still, Swanson said Kosminski soon died in the asylum. He wrote that in or around 1910 when Anderson's memoirs appeared. And Kosminski had another nine years to live before he would die in another asylum. It is unthinkable that the Metropolitan Police would have casually assumed that their man had died when they heard he was no longer in Colney Hatch. They would definitely want to watch him closely in case he was to be discharged as cured. There can be no doubt that someone that Swanson and Anderson thought of as a suspect – and in Anderson's case as the definite Ripper – died in an asylum. Without anticipating this piece of evidence, I had already researched every Jewish patient in every asylum in London between 1888 and 1890. And only one had died of anything but old age. The one I had already identified as Anderson's suspect and the possible/probable Jack the Ripper. David Cohen.

So how did the confusion come about? The hint was there again in Swanson's reference to the City Police keeping obbo in Whitechapel – Metropolitan territory. And the *Macnaghten Memoranda* said that the Met had used a City PC as the witness who saw the Ripper outside Mitre Square. As Donald had said, the two forces were poaching on each other's grounds. We know that the Home Office and the Met both complained that the City gave them no real information about what they were doing and discovering in their investigation. We may suspect that the Met played their cards equally close to their chest when liaising with the City. So, neither knew the other was following a 23-year-old Polish Jew from Whitechapel who was incarcerated in Colney Hatch. And by the time they found out, the Met's Jew was dead, and they assumed he was the same man the City had been watching. Now the Met had never been certain about their man's name. They called him Aaron Davis Cohen at the magistrates' court, and David Cohen at the infirmary. Goodness knows where they got either name from, or learned of his occupation as a tailor. He was an incoherent maniac with no known relatives, and unlike Aaron Kosminski, he is not described by any named witness who knew him. The name Cohen may even, as my correspondents pointed out, have been simply applied to him as a Jew whose name was for some reason uncertain.

But the City Police, as Donald had pointed out to me, knew their man's name quite definitely. He was called Kosminski. They were aware of his brother, who was perfectly sane. And so, the Met (or those of them in the know) who knew their man was dead and had stopped watching him, accepted the name given them by the City. And Anderson's suspect is still tagged as Aaron Kosminski by people who don't know my underlying research which unearthed Aaron.

What do people think today? American police, used to boundary problems between sheriffs, city police and state police find it immediately convincing. John Douglas, former head of the FBI Criminal Investigation Analysis Department, together with his colleague Roy Hazelwood, compiled a psychological profile of the Ripper. Shown the evidence against Druitt, Prince Albert Victor, James Maybrick, Walter Sickert and Aaron Kosminski, they unhesitatingly declared for Kosminski 'or someone very like him'. Subsequently John's co-author Mark Olshaker came across my work and drew it to John's attention. This changed his mind completely. It resolved the problems left in his mind by Kosminski, and he declared firmly: 'Jack the Ripper was David Cohen, or someone very like him.'

In England, Cohen received a regretful rejection by Richard Whittington-Egan. 'I like it,' he wrote to me. 'I want to believe it. But I can't.' Donald Rumbelow robustly declared, 'There must be a simpler explanation.' But he has never been able to propose one, and the case he and Stewart Evans make for Thomas Sadler as the Ripper and the Seaman's Home as the Seaside Home is markedly more complicated and less convincing.

Most other commentators have been trying to sweep away Cohen so as to make room for new proposals of their own. Melvin Harris used the political attacks of Anderson's Liberal enemies to cast doubt on his integrity, making great use of his dubious role in the Parnell letters scandal and Winston Churchill's attempt to extract the Liberal government from blame years later by casting it all on Anderson. Harris also attempted to use a memory failure of Anderson's old age, nearly twenty years after he had first recorded his belief that the Ripper's identity was known, to suggest that he was unreliable. Others have used Anderson's responsible investigation of claims in the 1890s that the Ripper had been belatedly discovered to suggest that he cannot have believed him identified in 1888. Stewart Evans and Paul Gainey follow a sleight-of-hand devised by Melvin Harris, which pretends that I made up the Kaminski-Cohen trail after finding and dismissing Kosminski, and says there is no evidence to support it. They are silent about Swanson's evidence that those who suspected Kosminski believed he had died shortly after admission to the asylum, and the fact that the only Jewish patient to die at that time and place was David Cohen – coincidentally a Whitechapel resident of exactly Kosminski's age.

I will not consider the ravings of Bruce Robinson here.

The most cogent question I have ever faced came (unsurprisingly) from Paul Begg. 'What would you have done, Martin,' he asked, 'if you had found Kosminski first and seen that he was not the Ripper?' What would I have done? I was contracted to write a book proving that he was, for publishers who believed I had already established it. What would they have done with a manuscript contradicting this? It would have been outrageous to go looking for an alternative to fill in. It was pure chance that I had already replaced Kosminski in my mind with Cohen, and had found Kaminski as an uncertain pointer to a source for the name. I don't know what I should have done.

But I do know that the *Swanson Marginalia* establish, beyond a shadow of doubt, that he and pretty certainly Anderson (with hearsay confirmation from Inspector Abberline who said he 'knew all about' the theory) believed that the Ripper had died in an asylum. And only David Cohen fits this description. And none of my challengers has ever addressed the problem.

I assert without fear of contradiction that David Cohen is the most plausible suspect ever named as Jack the Ripper. But I acknowledge Charles Nevin's caveat: 'Martin, you're not in a field that is particularly noted for plausibility!'

A literary historian specializing in the nineteenth century social novel and a junior research fellow of Balliol College, Oxford, Martin Fido is regarded as one of the most influential writers on the subject of Jack the Ripper and the Whitechapel murders. Originally finding fame as a freelance writer and broadcaster, his Murder Guide to London *series led to a specialization in true crime, with his first book on Jack the Ripper appearing in 1987. Martin's book* The Crimes, Detection and Death of Jack the Ripper *uncovered for the first time a top suspect who today is regarded as one of the leading contenders to be Jack the Ripper.*

Chapter 7

George Hutchinson – A Person of Interest

By Bob Hinton

The drama was over, the last scene had been played and the cast were assembled on stage to take their final curtain.

In the front row were the leading lights of the show, Her Majesty Queen Victoria, Prince Albert Victor, Inspector Abberline and Sir Charles Warren all waiting to give their final bow.

Behind them came the supporting cast, Druitt, Tumblety, Pizer and a thousand others and right at the very back were the stage fillers, the urchin, the chestnut seller, the newspaper boy – these were destined never to see the front row, never to bask in the limelight of fame.

But wait what's that? Someone from the motley crew in the back is forcing his way to the front, pushing aside the leading man he stands in the spotlight, arms akimbo like a really good *Blackadder the Third* and in a voice that could only belong to a graduate of the Dick Van Dyke school of how to speak like a cockney utters the immortal lines:

'Here guvnor I saw something I did – I want to make a statement!'

Ladies and Gentlemen, I give you George Hutchinson – a person of interest.

George Hutchinson couldn't really be described as a minor character in our drama. His sole appearance was when he went to Commercial Street Police Station at 6pm on the evening of 12 November and asked to make a statement about Mary Jane Kelly. Until that moment no one had ever heard of him. This is what he said:

> 'About 2am 9th [the morning of the murder] I was coming by Thrawl Street Commercial Street and just before I got

to Flower and Dean Street I met the murdered woman Kelly and she said to me, "Hutchinson will you lend me sixpence?" I said, "I can't I have spent all my money going down to Romford." She said, "Good morning I must go and find some money." She went away towards Thrawl Street. A man coming in the opposite direction to Kelly tapped her on the shoulder and said something to her they both burst out laughing. I heard her say "all right" to him and the man said "you will be all right for what I have told you." He then placed his right hand around her shoulder. He also had a kind of small parcel in his left hand with a kind of strap round it. I stood against the lamp of the Ten Bell [deleted and Queens Head inserted above it] Public House and watched him. They both came past me and the man hung down his head with his hat over his eyes. I stooped down and looked him in the face. He looked at me very [end of first page of statement, signature at bottom of page George Hutchinson] stern. They both went into Dorset Street I followed them. They both stood at the corner of the court for about 3 minutes. He said something to her. She said, "All right my dear come along you will be comfortable." He then placed his arm on her shoulder and gave her a kiss. She said she had lost her handkerchief he then pulled his handkerchief a red one out and gave it to her. They both then went up the court together. I then went to the court to see if I could see them but could not. I stood there for about three quarters of an hour to see if they came out they did not so I went away.

'Description age about 31 or 35, height 5ft 6 complexion pale, dark eyes and eye lashed dark [deleted] slight moustache curled up each end and hair dark very surly looking, dress long dark coat collar and cuffs trimmed astrakhan and a dark jacket under. Light waistcoat dark trousers dark felt hat turned down in the middle button boots and gaiters with white buttons, wore a very thick gold chain, white linen collar black tie with horse-shoe pin. Respectable appearance [end of second page and statement signed at bottom "Geo Hutchinson"] walked very sharp, Jewish appearance. Can be identified.'

Now I am quite sure that most of you are familiar with the statement but I have taken the liberty in reproducing it so that you can refer to it as we go along.

What I propose today, ladies and gentlemen, is that we all adopt the persona of an investigator par excellence, a veritable Sherlock Holmes, a Poirot of the first order, a Lord Peter Wimsey if you must; in other words, we are going to CSI the heck out of this bad boy.

The first thing you must do is remember the creed of the investigator, the sacred A B C.

Accept nothing.

Believe no one.

Check everything.

When a piece of evidence drops in your lap, before you get all caught up with the content check the feasibility of it. For example, let's say I make a statement to you here and now. I say, 'This morning, on leaving my house I noticed a green 7 series BMW parked outside registration number P999PRU.'

Now before you dash out checking the whereabouts of said car, the first thing to do is check if I was actually at home this morning. If I wasn't that should switch on a warning light.

In other words, check to see if the statement is plausible.

Looking at Hutchinson's statement there should already be some warning lights flashing. Put yourself in his position. He is walking up Commercial Road going north. He meets Mary Kelly going south; they exchange a few words and then carry on, him going north and her going south. He then says a man travelling in the same direction as him – north – stops Kelly going south and says something to her.

How is that possible? Unless he has eyes in the back of his head or is walking backwards how can he see what is happening behind him?

Warning light one.

This statement is all about what he saw, so the next thing we have to do is to find out whether or not it was possible for him to actually see these things.

The event took place in the early hours of the morning, so what were the conditions like at that time?

The streets were lit by gas. Gas mantles had been invented by 1888 but they were reserved for the posher areas of the city. In Whitechapel it was a simple gas flame, rather like a large Bunsen burner. The amount of light that was given out depended on the quality of the gas and the cleanliness of the glass surrounding the flame.

The lamps were not meant to illuminate the road or the pavement but simply to act as markers, the idea being that you made your way from one glow to the other. Since pedestrians could be sure to walk by each lamppost, they became the favourite spot for prostitutes to ply their wares. Lilli Marlene wasn't underneath the lamppost by accident. The lamps were placed at varying distances apart; there was usually one on a corner and then one about every thirty to eighty yards. Now what condition were these lamps in?

We are lucky to have an inspection report on the state of the lamps in Whitechapel very close to the relevant time. On 26 November 1888 the Lamps Committee minuted:

> 'The Chairman suggested the importance of an inspection of the lighting of the whole District; and after consideration it was resolved that arrangements be made to ascertain the condition of the lighting of the District by actual inspection of the several streets of the District.'

After the first inspection on 3 December 1888, they reported back:

> 'That a communication be addressed to the Commercial Gas Company complaining of the dirty state of the lamps generally throughout the District and of the defective condition of the burners and broken glass in lanterns.'

As you can see they weren't too good. So, if we cannot rely on the lamps how about some moonlight?

The moon was in its first quarter that night, a very small sliver. But what about the weather? Was it a bright starlit night? Unfortunately not. The weather report for the night of 8/9 November states: 'Overcast with rain all night. Cold with minimum temperature 3° Centigrade, fourth day of new moon.'

As you can see that night was very dark, the weather was awful and the street lighting next to useless, so the chances of Hutchinson actually seeing anything are very remote. This is also overlooking the fact that there would be other people out that night who would have blocked his view.

More warning lights.

The statement takes a strange turn as Hutchinson now admits that he is closely watching Mary Kelly, for what reason we do not know. He positions himself outside the Queens Head pub and waits for the couple to walk by. When they draw abreast he stoops down to get a good view of the man's face. First of all, that would be a waste of time. The light on the Queens Head was high on the wall; the man wore a wide-brimmed hat, therefore his face would be in shadow. It just wouldn't work.

He makes a big thing of the man having a small parcel in his left hand and his right arm around Mary Kelly's shoulder. If they are walking north then Kelly is nearest the buildings and the man is nearest the road. For Hutchinson to stoop down and look at the man's face he would have had to walk right in front of Kelly, bringing the couple to a dead stop. He also asks us to believe that in this brief glance at the man, his peripheral vision is good enough to see not only the man's eyelashes but also his boots. Yet all the man did in face of this rather aggressive act was look at him sternly!

Hutchinson follows the couple into Dorset Street where, for some obscure reason, they hang about in the freezing rain to have a quick chat about red handkerchiefs. Hutchinson must have been practically looking over their shoulders to have heard that. He also decides to hang about for some time in the miserable weather for no discernible reason and then toddles off.

Warning lights going off like fireworks at this point.

Hutchinson's famous statement fails the logical test on all counts:

- Hutchinson walking north could not have seen what was happening behind him.
- The lack of illumination and other people would have made it impossible for him to have seen more than a very few feet ahead.
- He would not be able to hear what was said at that distance.
- He would not have been able to stoop down as he claimed.
- It is impossible to see so much in such a short glance.
- He would not have been close enough in Dorset Street to hear their conversation.
- He would not have been able to tell what colour the handkerchief was.

The other point is that it is just totally implausible.

The weather was close to freezing and it was raining – a miserable night. No one with such a warm overcoat would leave it open to the elements, displaying not only his jacket but his waistcoat as well.

No one with such obvious wealth would leave it so openly on display in such a dangerous area.

The red handkerchief and small parcel part of the statements echo earlier statements made by previous witnesses about earlier murders.

Why would anyone wearing such an overcoat carry a small parcel? He would just put it in his pocket.

The whole description is far too theatrical.

On top of all this there are two very important questions that need to be answered.

Question one. Where was he going?

Hutchinson states he was travelling north on Commercial Street. He had walked past his lodgings, which were shut to him. According to him he had no money for more lodgings, yet he was going somewhere for a reason that was so important it was worth walking the streets in the freezing rain. However, as soon as he meets Kelly all this goes out the window; he abandons his original journey and goes to Miller's Court instead. This makes no sense at all – unless his original destination was Miller's Court. Then it all makes perfect sense.

Question two. Why did he take so long to come forward?

This all happened on the morning of Friday, 9 November. Many other people gave statements to the police on that day but not Hutchinson. He didn't tell anyone on Friday or Saturday or Sunday and waited until Monday evening before coming forward. Why?

There are only two reasons people do things – one is they want to do them and the other is they have been forced to do them. According to Hutchinson these events took place on the morning of 9 November, yet the first anyone knows about it is when he walks into the police station on Monday evening. What happened to force him to make the statement at that time? The only thing that had any relevance was the inquest on Mary Kelly, and at that inquest a witness, Sarah Lewis, stated that she had seen a man waiting outside Miller's Court on the morning of the murder. Hutchinson was now in a cleft stick, either he could just ignore it and hope he didn't run into Mrs Lewis in the streets or he could go to the police and give his own version of why he was there. That is the choice he made.

I do hope that by looking at the statement in greater detail I have given you something to think about. One final point – the statement was found to be totally unreliable only a few short weeks later, and Sir Robert Anderson and Melville Macnaghten both dismissed it as being unreliable.

Remember what Anderson says in his memoirs, *The Lighter Side of My Official Life*: 'I will merely add that the only person who ever had a good view of the murderer… .'

And again, in the *Macnaghten Memoranda*: 'No one ever saw the Whitechapel murderer (unless possibly it was the City PC).'

Now in the past when those statements have been examined, it has been from the point of trying to identify who the witness was. Was it Lawende or Schwartz, was it a City or Metropolitan PC? The most glaring thing about these statements to me is not the quality of the witnesses but the quantity. If Hutchinson's statement was true, the person he saw was obviously the killer. Hutchinson described the man down to his button boots, so why is it when two senior police officers talk about witnesses later on, they completely dismiss Hutchinson as a witness? For if Hutchinson was accepted as a credible witness then Anderson would have said 'two people saw the killer'. Macnaghten would have said 'only one man saw the Whitechapel murderer.' But they don't. Both of them talk about there either being one witness who ever saw the killer or none, and neither of them refers to Hutchinson.

Another interesting point, which up to now has not had an explanation, is something the reporter, George Sims, wrote on 2 December 1888, five days after Monro officially took over the post of commissioner. He wrote: 'It would be strange if the accession of Mr Monro to power were to be signalised by such a universally popular achievement as the arrest of Jack the Ripper. From such information which has reached me, I venture to prophesy that such will be the case.'

Where did Sims get the tip that an arrest was imminent?

The statement made by Hutchinson is deemed to be so important that Inspector Abberline is immediately summoned. He interviews Hutchinson and afterwards reports to his superiors: 'An important statement has been made by a man named George Hutchinson which I forward herewith. I have interrogated him this evening, and am of opinion his statement is true.'

For most people this settles the matter. After all if Abberline, a highly experienced detective, was satisfied, who are we to argue? I agree totally – *if* Abberline was satisfied – but I don't believe he was. This leads inexorably to the conclusion that Abberline filed a false report, which is exactly what I think he did.

Put yourself in Abberline's position – here at long last is something he knows without a shadow of a doubt is wrong. I'm not saying for one moment that he knew Hutchinson was the Ripper, of course not, I believe he was too good a detective for that, but he still knew something was amiss. Like Hutchinson he has two options. He can say to Hutchinson: 'This is a load of rubbish' to which all Hutchinson has to reply is: 'Prove it' and walk away. Or he can pretend to believe him; this will at least give him some breathing space to plan his next move. I believe he took the second option as the only safe course.

Naturally his main concern is to prevent any more killings. Again, if he suspects something, he can either lock Hutchinson up, which wouldn't work as he has no direct evidence to hold him, or he can take steps to isolate him. Again, he takes option two. It is a recorded fact that for two weeks after Hutchinson made his statement he was accompanied by two detectives. The official reason for these two police escorts was 'in case Hutchinson should recognise the man he saw.' This is a little bit flimsy to say the least. If this was the real reason, why did none of the other witnesses (Mrs Long, Israel Schwartz, Joseph Lawende, Mathew Packer etc) have such an escort? It is more believable that the two officers were there to prevent a suspect offending again.

However, Abberline now faces a grave problem. If he tells the truth and puts in his report that he doesn't believe Hutchinson, how long would it be before that was splashed all over the papers? Time after time, information that the police would have liked to have kept quiet appeared in the press almost as soon as the ink was dry on the official police reports. Look at what happened when they got to hear of 'Leather Apron'. Before they could act on it, the papers were letting everyone know they were looking for John Pizer, whereupon he promptly went and hid himself. The same thing happened with the statement of Israel Schwartz; the police naturally wanted to keep the description he provided secret, but the very next day he was being interviewed by reporters. Again, when a landlady reported that a mysterious lodger had left some bloodstained shirts in her house, the papers plastered it all over the front pages and scared him off before the police could trap him.

There is no doubt that certain police officers were supplementing their meagre incomes by selling information to the press. Perhaps if the Metropolitan Police had been a little more forthcoming with the press they could have worked together – as it was they were constantly at loggerheads. Whatever the reason, Abberline knew, without a shadow of a doubt, that if he put in his report he had any suspicions about Hutchinson at all, he could expect it to be in print the very next day.

I believe Abberline wrote out his report and took it directly to James Monro. Why Monro and not his predecessor Sir Charles Warren? It is true that Warren resigned from his post of commissioner on 8 November, the day before Mary Kelly's murder, however his resignation wasn't officially accepted until 10 November, and even then he continued in office until he was relieved by Monro on 27 November. Even so I believe Abberline would have been reluctant to go directly to Warren with his information. Warren had been the cause of Monro's original resignation and was not very popular among the detective branch. The detectives saw Monro as a professional policeman, one of them, and Warren was definitely not. Don't forget Monro knew and respected Abberline, he had personally ensured he was transferred to Scotland Yard, and I'm sure the feeling was mutual. Besides which, if Abberline had gone to Warren he might have seen this as a straw worth clutching to, and have forced Abberline's hand.

I believe that at the time it was common knowledge who was going to succeed Warren, and Abberline would see nothing wrong in going direct to Monro with the information. He would say something along the line of, 'Despite what I have written in my report I do not trust Hutchinson's statement. I believe the man is lying. I have placed two detectives with him in an effort to avoid any more attacks, and I need some time to investigate further.'

I certainly don't think Abberline would openly say, 'I've caught Jack the Ripper.' I think he was far too good a detective for that. Monro would of course, either by memo or spoken word, inform those other senior officers he would consider essential to be in the know. Whoever he would inform would be at the very top, as a general dissemination of this kind of information would lead to a leak. As the statement stands, it fails every test. However if you look at it a different way then it all makes sense. Hutchinson was infatuated with Mary Kelly: he returned from Romford that night with only one purpose in mind, he was going to visit her. So, he walked all the way from Romford in filthy weather and started walking towards Dorset Street. Halfway up Commercial Street the object of his desire is walking towards him. However, she only wants money and carries on down the road in search of business. Hutchinson stops and watches her meet her customer, not astrakhan man but a normal punter. He follows them back to Dorset Street and waits outside until the man leaves, then he enters Kelly's room and, in a fury, murders her. Now the whole scenario makes sense. But where did the description of astrakhan man come from?

When I first read the description of the man Hutchinson said he had seen, it struck me as being totally theatrical. It was if he was describing the perfect villain, a figure conjured up from someone's imagination. All that was missing was a poor, pregnant servant girl being turned out into the snow. Then it dawned on me, what Hutchinson was describing wasn't a real figure at all – it was a dummy. Look at the description: everything is perfect, the overcoat, followed by the jacket then the waistcoat, all with the correct jewellery, and of course don't forget the buttoned boots with white buttoned spats. I can almost see Hutchinson standing outside Stones Millinery and Mantle Emporium at 60 Market Place, Romford, gazing with intensity at a magnificent dummy in the window display. It might have an equally well-attired lady with him; perhaps with a board which says: 'What the Well-Dressed Gentleman and his Lady Companion are Wearing this Season.' How many hours did he stand staring at them, seeing not two dummies, but himself with Mary Kelly on his arm? No wonder he had to return to the East End, she would be longing to hear from him about how everything was going to turn out. Of course, this is pure speculation, apart from one tiny detail.

I spoke to the costume department at the Victoria and Albert Museum and a very pleasant American lady there confirmed what I had thought. You see the chances of Hutchinson seeing someone wearing spats at 2am are practically non-existent. Spats are worn between breakfast and luncheon. No one with that amount of obvious wealth would be wearing them to chat up prostitutes at that time, but of course Hutchinson wasn't very knowledgeable in the correct dress code for Victorian gentlemen.

It is interesting to note that when Hutchinson next tells his story, to the press the following day, certain details have changed. These aren't the details based on fact such as the description of the clothes (although he does add that the watch chain now carries a red stone seal, additions and subtractions from a story indicate accuracy) but the details that he would have had to invent for himself – the features. It is unlikely that the dummy (if that's indeed what he used) had any discernible features, so these are the points to watch very carefully, and sure enough these have totally changed.

FIRST STATEMENT	SECOND STATEMENT
Complexion pale	Complexion dark
Slight moustache	Heavy moustache
Dark eyelashes	Bushy eyebrows

It would appear that our eagle-eyed witness isn't so eagle-eyed after all. How can you possibly trust anyone who says he can describe the colour of a man's boot buttons, but changes completely the man's face? Far from dismissing these discrepancies as 'not significant' as one author has done, I believe these discrepancies are vital to disproving the validity of the entire statement.

I believe that we have now reached the stage where we can say without fear of contradiction that Hutchinson's statements are false.

So, if we can file the statement in the rubbish bin, what about the man who made it?

Who was George Hutchinson and where did he come from?

In my book, *From Hell*, I identified him as being born in Shadwell in December 1859. Later on, I came to doubt my choice and posted on the casebook site that although I was still sure he was the killer, I was not still sure I had the right one. I based this on the fact that I had compared his signature on his entry in the marriage records with his signature on the statement and could not find any similarities.

Further research was unfortunately curtailed by a series of personal circumstances which left me without access to my records; circumstances which prevailed until recently. Since then I have been digging even deeper and have uncovered a series of facts that will indeed make George Hutchinson a person of interest.

Firstly, I now have not one but three signatures of my Hutchinson to compare.

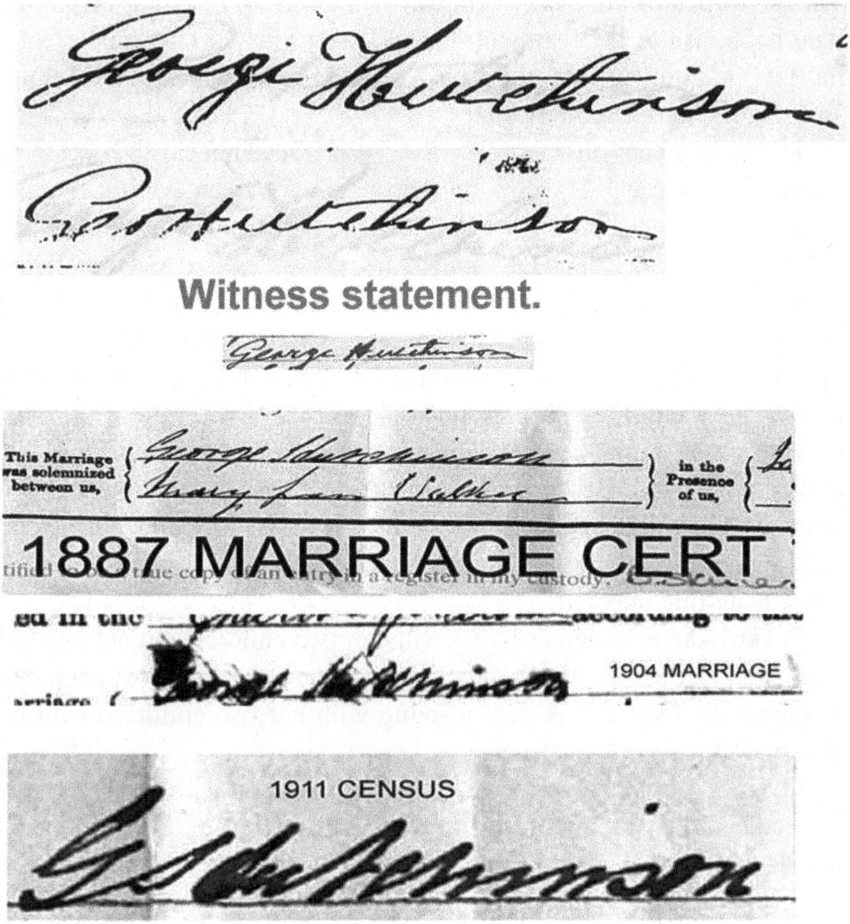

However, let us go back to the beginning. Our story starts in Yorkshire where two cousins, Joseph and John Hutchinson, took up with two sisters Hannah and Sarah Mallinson. Leaving Yorkshire, they all travelled to London where they married, with Joseph marrying Hannah. It must have been a shotgun wedding as they were married in July 1857 and their first child was born the same year.

Joseph carried on business as a licensed victualler and ran a pub called the Crooked Billet in King David Lane, Shadwell and it was here, on 10 December 1859, that George was born. Over the years they moved around the area but always with Joseph running pubs or coffee shops and always with his family working alongside him. This changed in 1876 when Hannah died of cancer of the womb. George was just 16.

The doctor who signed the death certificate was W. B. Laing Fergusson, who happened to be a surgeon to the Queen. In 1881 we find George has left the family circle and is now working as a barman in the John of Jerusalem pub in Clerkenwell.

The next event in George's life is in December 1887 when he marries a 41-year-old widow by the name of Walker, who is fourteen years his senior according to the marriage certificate. Mrs Walker had led an interesting life. Her maiden name was Mann and her father, Henry Mann, was a cab driver and coach proprietor. The first thing that we notice about her is that she gave the wrong age on her marriage certificate – she was not 41 as claimed but was, in fact, 50. She was born in Marylebone in 1837. Sometime between 1851 and 1859 she had taken up with a man named John Walker by whom she had a child, Henry. She had another child, George, and then they decided it was time they got married. They published the banns on 3 July, 10 July and 17 July but then apparently called the whole thing off as there is no record of them actually getting married.

In 1861 she is shown as living with her two children and her brothers and sisters, the assumption being that her parents are dead. No occupation is shown. In 1871 she is shown living with her two children, with her occupation given as dressmaker.

In 1881 she is shown living alone with her son and her occupation is needleworker. In Victorian times the occupation of dressmaker and needleworker were often euphemisms for prostitute and it does not take a long stretch of the imagination seeing this poor woman, who was completely on her own, taking to the streets to earn her living. In December 1887 she tells a little white lie about her age and marital status and marries Hutchinson. Somewhere along the line she adopted her mother's Christian name to go with her own. The certificate reads 'Mary Jane Walker'.

It is interesting to note that there are no witnesses from either her family or Hutchinson's at the ceremony. The witnesses are James and Susan Calvert. James is a cab driver and groom. After the wedding their lives are intertwined and so we can now look at them as a couple. There is no record of either of them in the 1891 census.

In 1892 George's father, Joseph Hutchinson, dies. His will, dated 1891, leaves his entire estate to his son, James Francis Hutchinson, whom he also appoints sole executor. This is rather strange as there is absolutely no mention of George Hutchinson, the oldest son. What is even stranger is that James Francis is not his son but his nephew. The next time we hear of George Hutchinson is in the 1901 census. His occupation is given as insurance collector and he is still living with his wife, Mary Jane Hutchinson. On 11 January 1904, Mary Jane dies of a blood disorder. Her age is incorrectly given as 60 when she is, in fact, 69.

Eight months later George marries again, this time to a Sarah Anne Hopton from Wales. The 1911 census shows them still married but without any children living in Surrey.

And so comes to and end, for now, the story of George Hutchinson.

Not a lot is known about Hutchinson from the records of the time. Some papers have his occupation as a groom and Hutchinson mentions Romford in his statement. One of his sisters was born in Romford and his wife's father certainly had connections to grooms, in fact he had one as a witness at his wedding. What happened to Hutchinson's family? Why did none of them attend his wedding? Why was he cut so completely out of his father's will, even down to his father proclaiming a nephew as the son that he was?

Was George Hutchinson Jack the Ripper?

It's impossible to say, but in the modern parlance he is certainly a person of interest.

Bob Hinton is a dedicated researcher and author of the Whitechapel murders, producing several acclaimed articles and dissertations in the field of Ripperology. His interest in the case began while serving in the Navy. After reading an article on victim Mary Jane Kelly, in a copy of Weekend Magazine*, Bob began his own investigation into the crimes. Realizing that most Ripper books started with a suspect and then built a case against them, Bob decided to do it in reverse and go through the suspects and eliminate them one by one. When he came to George Hutchinson, try as he might he couldn't discount him. This led to his book* From Hell – the Jack the Ripper Mystery *in 1998. Since then Bob has managed to discover new facts which only strengthen the case for George Hutchinson being Jack the Ripper.*

Chapter 8

Kosminski – Prime (Unknown) Suspect

By Steve Blomer

The idea that Jack the Ripper was caught but, for some reason, never identified has been a popular theory for many years. This has promoted countless conspiracy theories, books and debates on social media and internet forums across the world. Usually it's because the killer is someone of great importance and his identity would rock the foundations of the Empire. Thus, the evidence must be destroyed and the case stamped 'unsolved'.

But what if there is a much simpler and straightforward explanation for the Ripper not being identified?

An unnamed key witness at the time refused to testify. Let's examine this probability.

One of the most hotly debated topics in the study of Jack the Ripper is known as the *Swanson Marginalia*. These are pencil notes written by Chief Inspector Donald Sutherland Swanson, who was a highly regarded police officer of his time, and described as 'one of the best class of officers' by colleague John Sweeney.

During the Whitechapel murders, the officer in charge of the investigation, Sir Robert Anderson, took a leave of absence due to stress. This left Donald Swanson in charge of the investigation from 1 September 1888 until 6 October 1888. He took several statements from key suspects during police enquiries and had access to all the information gathered by the investigating officers. On Anderson's return, Swanson liaised between the assistant commissioner and the detectives on the ground, continuing to be a key figure in the hunt for Jack the Ripper. However, Swanson's importance in the Ripper case has only truly been acknowledged since the publication of the so-called *Swanson Marginalia* in 1987.

But what is the *Swanson Marginalia*?

Swanson remained friends with Anderson for years following the murders, and when his old boss published his memoirs, *The Lighter Side of My Official Life*, in 1910, Swanson managed to get a copy. In the book, Anderson had a definite suspect in mind as Jack the Ripper, but he refused to name him, only describing him as a poor Polish Jew from Whitechapel. Anderson wrote: 'The only person who had ever had a good view of the murderer unhesitatingly identified the suspect the instant he was confronted with him; but he refused to give evidence against him.'

At this point, in Swanson's personal copy of the book, in handwritten notes, Swanson added: 'Because the suspect was also a Jew and also because his evidence would convict the suspect and witness would be the means of murderer being hanged, which he did not wish to be left on his mind.'

In the margin of the book he also wrote: 'And after this identification which suspect knew, no other murder of this kind took place in London.'

On the other page of the book Swanson then wrote:

> 'Continuing from page 138, after the suspect had been identified at the Seaside Home where he had been sent by us with difficulty in order to subject him to identification, and he knew he was identified. On suspect's return to his brother's house in Whitechapel he was watched by police (City CID) by day & night. In a very short time the suspect with his hands tied behind his back, he was sent to Stepney Workhouse and then to Colney Hatch and died shortly afterwards – Kosminski was the suspect – DSS'

This was groundbreaking information. So, the big question is who was Kosminski?

The same name is used by Assistant Chief Constable Sir Melville Macnaghten when he wrote a memo in 1894, naming three likely suspects. He wrote:

> 'Kosminski – a Polish Jew & resident in Whitechapel. This man became insane owing to many years indulgence in solitary vices. He had a great hatred of women, especially

> of the prostitute class & had strong homicidal tendencies: he was removed to a lunatic asylum about March 1889. There were many circumstances connected with this man which made him a strong "suspect".'

That means two senior officers gave the same name as a person of interest, which is really three, given that Swanson is commenting on Anderson's assertions. Now there are those who claim there are too many mistakes in both these documents to allow them to be taken seriously and indeed there are many mistakes. The memorandum by Macnaghten gets details wrong about another suspect called Montague John Druitt and names a third suspect, Michael Ostrog, who can be shown not to have been available to commit the murders as he wasn't even in the UK. There are also different versions of the *Macnaghten Memoranda* and in one version, Kosminski was locked away in an asylum in March 1889 (the issue of versions of the memoranda is something I shall return to). It appears that Macnaghten may have used faulty information, and it would be easy to dismiss all three named persons on that basis alone. However, if one takes an holistic approach one can see other evidence which, to a degree, backs part of what Macnaghten says.

It seems that early in 1889, there were rumours that the killer had drowned in the Thames or had been locked up in an asylum. This suggests that Macnaghten did not just pluck the names out of thin air. Let's now return to the issue of the various versions of the memoranda. There are certainly two different versions in existence:

1. The 'Scotland Yard version' first published by author Donald Rumbelow in *The Complete Jack the Ripper*, some seven pages in length and in Macnaghten's own hand.
2. The 'Aberconway version', copied from an original draft by Macnaghten's daughter and discovered by Dan Farson in 1959.

In addition to these, a third version is said to have been seen in the early 1950s, referred to as the 'Donner version'. Its existence and authenticity is, however, much debated. There are several differences between the two known versions. With regards to Kosminski, this amounts to the Aberconway version stating that: 'This Man in appearance strongly resembled the individual seen by the City P.C. near Mitre Square.'

There are several points here: firstly if this is a copy of an original, then we do not have that original draft. While it is conceivable that the copying process could omit some details, it does not seem reasonable that an addition such as this could occur by accident. It seems that there may well have been additional drafts of the document that we have not seen. The copy at Scotland Yard would appear to be a draft and not the final document. If a final document was ever sent to Government, as appears to be the obvious aim of the memoranda, it is unknown. Secondly, saying that the man strongly resembled the man seen by an unknown City PC suggests that some form of identification took place. We shall return here later.

Let us now look at Sir Robert Anderson.

He first published his autobiography – as mentioned above – in Blackwood's *Edinburgh Magazine* in March 1910. In this he claimed that: 'The conclusion we came to was that he and his people were low-class Jews.'

He also said the suspect was identified but that the witness would not testify because he was a fellow Jew: 'When he [the witness] learned the suspect was a fellow-Jew he declined to swear to him.'

That would suggest the suspect may not have been of obvious Jewish appearance. Anderson also added that he was tempted to give the name of the killer, but that doing so would be of 'no public benefit' nor would it be beneficial to the reputation of his old department. The book also contained details of his other work, information gathering and spying. Understandably, this did not go down well in Westminster. There he was ridiculed by many, including none other than Winston Churchill. There was an attempt to write off much of his work as the ramblings of a man in old age, but this may well have been for purely political reasons. Modern researchers also use this to dismiss his version of events, pointing out that Anderson was not in charge of the investigation for the majority of the murders. It was also clearly seen by the Jewish community as being anti-Semitic. Leopold Greenberg, the co-owner of *The Jewish Chronicle*, wrote an article on 4 March 1910, which was heavily critical of Anderson. After some heated exchanges between Greenberg and Anderson, changes in the text were made in the book version, which was published later in the year.

'Low-class Jews' become 'certain low-class Jews'.

Anderson also changed the comment about the witness refusing to testify because he was a fellow Jew to just 'he refused to give evidence against him.' These changes suggest that Anderson could see part of the argument made by Greenberg, and was willing to accommodate some of those points of view. It certainly does not suggest the anti-Semitism his views are sometimes displayed as. What should be noted is that at no stage does Anderson give a name for his suspect.

John Littlechild, the head of Special Branch, referred to Anderson's Polish Jew theory when writing about another suspect called Francis Tumblety in a letter to journalist George Sims in 1913. Littlechild dismissed the theory by saying Anderson 'only thought he knew.'

Surely by definition that implies Anderson believed what he had put forward and it was not just vanity talking. It also suggests Littlechild was aware of the theory before the publication of Anderson's autobiography.

We now return to Donald Swanson and the annotations he made in Anderson's book relating to the apparent identification 'after the suspect had been identified at the Seaside Home where he had been sent by us with difficulty in order to subject him to identification, and he knew he was identified.'

Unfortunately for us, Swanson doesn't elaborate more on what or where the 'Seaside Home' is. The home has been greatly debated among researchers for years and the police convalescent home in Hove near Brighton is often put forward as the possible location, but it is far from certain. However, it seems odd that Kosminski is apparently taken to the witness, and suggests that the witness is waiting for him at the Seaside Home. It also suggests that this is done away from London to keep it low key and under the radar of the press. It is also conceivable that the witness does not want to be involved; indeed the suggestion is that it is a face-to-face event, maybe one person is led into a room where the other is waiting. The probability is that Kosminski is taken to the witness, rather than the other way round, because the non-cooperation of the witness is supported, to an extent, by the apparent reluctance of the witness to testify. Of course, that is to assume that the identification actually occurred. Who the witness was is another matter entirely.

Swanson only gives the name Kosminski and, just like in the *Macnaghten Memoranda*, there is no first name. This is frustrating as it leaves the door open for mass speculation among researchers. The assumption, for many, is that Kosminski equals Aaron Kosminski, a low-class Polish Jew from Whitechapel, who was first admitted to Mile End Old Town Workhouse on 12 July 1890. He spent three days there before being released into the care of his brother. However, by 4 February 1891, he was back again. This time he would be locked away for good. He was admitted to the Colney Hatch Asylum and by April 1894 he was moved to Leavesden Asylum, where he would eventually die in 1919. But if Swanson's Kosminski is indeed Aaron Kosminski, then there is a problem with the Swanson notes, although it is not insurmountable. He claims Kosminski died soon after he was admitted to the asylum, but this is blatantly incorrect, and thus diminishes the content. It is claimed that if the date of death is wrong then Swanson is also wrong, or must be referring to someone other than Aaron.

Now I said it is claimed the date of death is wrong, and I say claimed for a specific reason.

At the start of this work I asked a question, who was Kosminski? And only now am I about to look at that question. I'm well aware that Swanson's Kosminski may not be Aaron, and we shall look at this possibility in a moment, but let us for the sake of argument assume he is. How do we then account for Swanson saying he died shortly after entering the asylum?

We know Aaron was sent to Colney Hatch in February 1891, being committed by his family, not the police, and remained there until April 1894, when he was transferred to Leavesden. He remained there until his death in 1919. Thus, it cannot be ruled out that these transfers somehow got confused with his death. By 1895, Swanson was reported to have been of the opinion that the killer had died. This could have been borne out of the fact Kosminski was no longer in Colney Hatch Asylum, having been transferred the previous year. One can already hear the cries of 'Do you really think they would lose track of him if he were the Ripper?' but that depends on who the reports would have been made to. Any reports would not have been given directly to Swanson, therefore it may have been garbled in transmission. It also cannot be overlooked that if Aaron Kosminski truly was the suspect of several senior officers, and it seems he probably was, they may have wanted to keep that point quiet. In which case, the only notification they requested once he was safely locked up may have been if he said anything or if he tried to escape. There may have been an annual report sent, and when he moved that may just have stopped. Indeed, there is no real reason for the asylum at Colney Hatch to have known the suspicions of the police, it was after all the family who had him committed, not the police. The police may have taken the view that, lacking evidence for a prosecution, if he was locked up and no longer a danger to the public that was good enough for them.

Before moving on further with the question of who was Kosminski, there are a few other bits of information to consider.

There are also the statements of two detectives, Robert Sagar and Henry Cox, who, during the investigation, were keeping watch on an individual who was Jewish. Both said he was very likely linked to the crime in their opinion. Robert Sagar said the suspect was placed in an asylum by those close to him: 'Identification being impossible, he could not be charged, he was placed in a lunatic asylum, and the series of atrocities came to an end.'

Sagar made a second statement, which appeared in *Reynold's News* in 1946, some twenty-two years after his death: 'There was no doubt that this man was insane, and after a time his friends thought it advisable to have him removed to a private asylum. After he was removed, there were no more Ripper atrocities.'

This all fits with what Macnaghten says about the asylum, but it should be noted that Sagar says 'private' asylum while Aaron Kosminski went to the public one at Colney Hatch.

Macnaghten backs up Swanson regarding the suspect being closely watched by the City Police. Sagar said the suspect worked in Butcher's Row Aldgate, which may not point at Aaron Kosminski. Henry Cox was also a City detective and there was an article in *Thomson's Weekly News* printed in December 1906. It contained an in-depth description of the surveillance he was involved in. This includes following the suspect one evening and the suspect appeared to be aware of this. It would seem that this surveillance did not occur at the same time as Robert Sagar's, for although he does not give a location, he says they told the locals they were factory inspectors watching tailors and capmakers, which does not really seem to fit with Butcher's Row. One interesting comment in the article is this: 'He occupied several shops in the East End, but from time to time he became insane and was forced to spend a portion of his time in an asylum in Surrey.'

This again fits partly with both Sagar and Macnaghten and it may well be that Kosminski did go into a private asylum in March 1889, and stay there for a period. Although searches of asylum records have yet failed to show an Aaron Kosminski being admitted, the possibility remains that such may be found. This conforms to what Swanson says about the City Police watching the suspect. It should again be noted that it is highly possible the two reports are not talking about the same surveillance and it could be two separate individuals who are being watched. The surveillance conducted by Cox appears to be earlier, possibly in late 1888 or early 1889. One assumes there must have been an official report, the same for Sagar, which are both now sadly missing. Such a report could arguably be the source of part of the *Macnaghten Memoranda*. All of the above may be academic if the 'Kosminski' mentioned is not Aaron Kosminski.

Let us look at when and how the name Kosminski got linked to Aaron Kosminski.

The name Kosminski did not appear in the official police suspects file – now missing – but neither did those of Dr Francis Tumblety, Montague Druitt or William Bury to name but a few well-known suspects. This file may have included those interviewed by the police and then cleared, but with the file missing it is hard to say. The *Macnaghten Memoranda* did not surface until 1959 and the *Swanson Marginalia* was first published in 1987. Neither of these gave the name Aaron. This eventually came in the late 1980s from research by author Martin Fido, who was looking to find Sir Robert Anderson's Polish Jew suspect. The only Kosminski he found committed to an asylum in the timeframe was Aaron, whom he eventually dismissed. However, he found another Polish Jew by the name of David Cohen, locked up in December 1888, who was very violent and died soon after committal. Fido attempted to link him to an East End character named Nathan Kaminski and argued that David Cohen was not a real name but more a sort of John Doe name given by authorities to unidentified Jewish individuals. Subsequent research appears to have identified Cohen as Aaron Davies Cohen, and some argue that this was Anderson's Jew. But if this was the case, why were the police still following suspects later than this?

The answer of course is that they did not decide he was the killer until sometime later. It is a neat solution but far from convincing. Indeed Mr Fido has changed his mind and, while once dismissing Aaron out of hand, is apparently now prepared to consider the possibility that he may have killed Elizabeth Stride, based on his supposed home address. The truth remains that there were several individuals going by the name

Kosminski in the East End at the time, and many were anglicizing their names, as indeed Aaron's own family did when they changed to Abrahams. So he may have used both surnames in everyday life. He appeared in court in 1890 for being in control of an unmuzzled dog when the reply about giving an incorrect name caused some hilarity in the court.

There was a Kosminski living in Goulston Street, another living in Chicksand Street and a furrier called Martin Kosminski, none of whom appear to be related directly to Aaron. However, it does demonstrate that even the surname, if correct, does not necessarily mean Kosminski needs to be Aaron. And if the name given is not the correct name, we have more possible suspects who may fit Anderson's suspect and the two detectives' statements. Jacob Levy, Hyam Hyams and Solomon De Leeuw have all been named at various stages as possible Rippers. Now, from this it must seem to the average reader that when we say Kosminski, we are not really sure who we are talking about. However, when most people talk of Kosminski, it is clear they are talking about Aaron. There is no other Jew of that name who was incarcerated around that time, in the asylum records.

And so, let's have a little more background on Aaron.

Aron Mordke Kosminski.

Born in Kłodawa, Poland, in 1865, his parents were Abram Jozef Kosminski and Golda Lubnowska, and he was the youngest of seven. His eldest brother, Isaac, having changed his name to Abrahams, came to Britain in about 1871 and established himself as a tailor. Aaron may have followed the family tradition by becoming a tailor initially but then changed to being a hairdresser. It appears he came to London in 18881/82. We hear nothing more about him until December 1889 when he appears in court for having an unmuzzled dog. He gave the wrong address when stopped by the police and on his appearance in court, a brother, it is not clear which, accompanied him and there is some debate about his correct name. *Lloyd's Weekly Newspaper* of 15 December reported that his brother said the name was not Kosminski but Abrahams. It may well be that he had given the address of his brother, when he was not actually staying there. The paper wrote that the defendant said his name was indeed Kosminski but that he went by the name Abrahams. It also reported that the defendant said he could not pay the fine of ten shillings on a Saturday as it was the Jewish

Sabbath. I make this point that it is Aaron speaking, because there are arguments that his brother did all the talking, implying that Aaron was incapable of answering for himself.

A second report in the *City Press* on 18 December appears to back this up: 'I goes by the name Abrahams sometimes, because Kosminski is hard to spell" (laughter). The defendant called his brother, who corroborated that part of the evidence which relayed to the name.'

The next we hear of Aaron is on 12 July 1890, when he goes, or is most probably taken, to the Mile End Workhouse where he is detained for three days before being released into the care of his brother. This fits with Donald Swanson's account of the events of the identification at the 'Seaside Home'. In February 1891 Aaron is again taken to the workhouse where this time he is committed to the asylum. He is not taken by the police, or even by his immediate family, but apparently by Jacob Cohen who, it has been argued, was not only a family friend and business partner of his brother Woolf, but also possibly Woolf's brother-in-law, and the possible owner of the dog from the 1889 event in Cheapside. Why did Cohen take Aaron rather than his brother Woolf? Perhaps Aaron had moved from Woolf's home. However, he was then living at 16 Greenfield Street with his sister Matilda and her husband Morris, so why had they not taken him? Maybe it was because the immediate family could not bring themselves to take action and lock Aaron away for the rest of his life, even though maybe they knew he had to be detained for his safety, for theirs and everybody else's. Or just maybe they knew he had to be locked away from the arms of the police.

Much of our view of Aaron is coloured by the certification made by Dr Houchin. The doctor's report is of a deluded man:

- He is guided by an instinct, which controls him.
- He knows the movement of all mankind.
- He refuses food from others and only eats from the gutter.

Jacob Cohen adds that Aaron threatened his sister with a knife, but does he mean Aaron threatened one of his own sisters or does he mean Aaron threatened Jacob's sister? If he was Woolf's brother-in-law, this could be the reason for Jacob taking Aaron to the workhouse. He states that Aaron is dirty, practises self-abuse and has not worked in years. This description convinces many that Aaron could not be the killer in 1888, but this may be an incorrect reading of events. His certification says his illness started six months before, whereas at Colney Hatch it says six years.

Which is correct?

Maybe both are as we know that mental illness is often cyclical with periods of improvement, followed by relapses. It may well be that the six months applies to the latest attack. Some claim this fits well with the July appearance at the workhouse, but it may also fit equally well with immediately after it – if he had been identified this would make sense. The six years may well account for the first onset of illness. None of which tells us his condition in late 1888. His appearance at court strongly suggests that, at that stage, he appears well in public. He apparently lived with various members of his family, most often with Woolf who was closest in age to him, at addresses south of the Whitechapel Road, including 38 Berner Street, right next door to the site of Elizabeth Stride's murder. He also lived in Providence Street, a stone's throw away from that murder site, and Yarford and Greenfield streets and Sion Square, which was his address in July 1890. It is, unfortunately, true that we do not know exactly where he was at any given time, we can only assume he was living with family. He missed the census.

Let us now look at what, if any, evidence there is against him.

Firstly, it has to be admitted that apart from the comments of the senior police officers, Sir Robert Anderson, Donald Swanson and Sir Melville Macnaghten, there is nothing at all. Aaron Kosminski is a non-person. He almost does not exist. We know where members of his family lived, but there are no specific records on the man himself. Apart from the court appearance in 1889, the two instances at the workhouse, the scant surviving records from Colney Hatch and Leavesden, his death certificate and of course, a grave, we really have nothing else. A point worth making is that the family were not poor, they were a group of successful tailors. Woolf is reported to have had an expensive gold watch and the elder brother, Isaac, ran a hotel in Ramsgate for a few years, before returning to London to be the landlord of the Dolphin Pub, all of which requires a certain amount of capital. It appears that in 1889 Woolf, at least, fell on hard times; moving from Providence Street to the more downmarket Yarford Street and he removed his daughter from school at about the same time. What could have been the cause of that? Bad business? Or maybe, just maybe the family had an additional expense to pay. Possibly a brother in a private asylum. Pure speculation yes, but certainly plausible.

Let us return to the identification which, if genuine, is the most telling evidence against any suspect so far produced. Who could the witness have been? Many researchers go with Joseph Lawende, who claimed to see Ripper victim Catherine Eddowes with a man just before her death. But did he really see her or just another couple? It's impossible to say. Others go for Israel Schwartz who claimed to see Elizabeth Stride being physically attacked by a man close to where her body was later found. However, many question his account, particularly the fact that he was not called to give evidence at the inquest. And of course, let's not forget the Aberconway version of the *Macnaghten Memoranda*. This says that a man was seen by an unnamed police officer. This would suggest to be either PC Edward Watkins, who discovered the body of Catherine Eddowes, or PC Harvey, who was patrolling the area around Mitre Square where Eddowes' body was found. The problem is, neither man made any such claims, or if he did, it has remained unknown to all researchers. But there may be another possibility.

That evening in St James Place, close to the murder site, there was a fire station, and there was a nightwatchman there called James Blenkinsop. He gave an account to *The Star* on 1 October 1888 that he was approached at about 1.30am by a respectably dressed man, who asked if he had seen a couple going towards the square. The vast majority of researchers suggest that either this account is made up or that the timing is at least ten minutes out. However, asking if he had seen a couple go towards the square after the murder leaves out a very important question. Did he see anyone leave? There is a possibility that this individual was a plain clothes detective, and that the event occurred before the discovery of Eddowes' body. It is conceivable that this man could be the unknown police witness.

The one remaining question is, when did those senior officers come to the conclusion it was Kosminski?

The answer must be sometime in the 1890s, once the murders had stopped. It is easy to see how they could say, 'Well we did wonder about him. And now the murders have stopped when he is locked up.' One thing worth noting in relation to the possible private asylum in March of 1889 is that voluntary admissions were often for a set time, maybe three months. Such would, of course, allow Alice Mackenzie to be a

Jack the Ripper victim. Equally, one needs to exclude Frances Coles, as Kosminski could not have killed her.

Aaron is the only member of his family buried under the name Kosminski. He is not even buried in the same cemetery, which seems a little odd.

Was this the family caring about him, but ultimately wishing to distance themselves from him?

It remains a possibility.

A former employee of both King's College London and the Medical Research Council, where he worked for over thirty years in medical research, Steve Blomer took early retirement in 2015 and now divides his time between watching cricket, Egyptology and full-time research on Jack the Ripper and the Whitechapel murders. For the past year he has been working on a research project on the murder of Ripper victim Mary Ann Nichols in Buck's Row.

Chapter 9

Charles Lechmere – Hidden in Plain Sight

By Edward Stow

You will not find the name Charles Allen Lechmere in any mainstream book on Jack the Ripper, yet he is there all the same – hidden in plain sight.

He was, of course, listed in the contemporary record as Charles Cross and is the only witness involved in the official record of the case whose true identity remained unknown until just a few years ago. An anonymous local man, he spent virtually his entire life in the East End; the bulk of it in the area known as Tiger Bay – a district near the docks that was known for its squalor, criminality and as a major centre of prostitution. It was the most crowded part of London and an area that experienced the first waves of Jewish migration from Eastern Europe in the 1880s.

This was a far cry from the background into which Charles Allen had been born. His grandfather, Charles Fox Lechmere, was the younger son of the Lord of the Manor of Fownhope in Herefordshire and was variously listed as a 'gentleman' or 'farmer'. But being a scion of the landed gentry did not guarantee a rosy future in the early years of the nineteenth century. To keep estates together only the eldest son inherited, and if the advantages of birth were not seized upon, descent to the lower orders could be swift. That harsh reality played itself out.

Charles Fox's son – John Allen Lechmere – became a cobbler and married Maria but it did not work out well. Two children were born to the union – the second being Charles Allen Lechmere in 1849. But soon after his birth, for unknown reasons, the father abandoned his wife and children in the East End of London, to set up with a new family in Northamptonshire. Young Charles was left without a father figure until he was 8 years old, when Maria bigamously married a policeman who was eleven years her junior. This man – Thomas Cross – died eleven years later in 1869.

Maria was undoubtedly a remarkable lady. She engaged in a second bigamous marriage in 1872, this time to Joseph Fosdyke, who was ten years her senior. It might be noted that most of Jack the Ripper's victims became street prostitutes after their marriages broke down for one reason or another. This fate was not shared by Maria.

Charles Lechmere married an illiterate local girl called Elizabeth Bostock in 1870. They were to have eleven children although two died in infancy. The second eldest – called Mary Jane – for some reason was brought up by her grandmother Maria.

In 1868, Broad Street Goods Station (which was then adjacent to Liverpool Street Station) opened and Charles Lechmere started work there as a carman for Pickfords who had the contract for the delivery of goods. This was when he was about 18 or 19 so it wouldn't have been his first job. Broad Street was an important hub for the rail transportation of meat from the provinces to feed the growing population of the metropolis. A carman was the equivalent of a white van driver and Charles Lechmere would have carted goods to local businesses.

In June 1888, Charles Lechmere with his family (apart from Mary Jane) left the Tiger Bay area and moved to Doveton Street, which was just to the east of Whitechapel. This was the first time that he had moved any appreciable distance away from his mother.

Two months later, early in the morning of Tuesday, 7 August 1888, Martha Tabram was found murdered on the staircase of George Yard Buildings, which was just off Wentworth Street. Wentworth Street was on the most direct route from Doveton Street to Broad Street.

At about 3.45 in the morning of Friday, 31 August 1888, Robert Paul was walking down Buck's Row on his way to work when, in the gloom ahead, he saw a man standing in the road. The man approached and Paul took fright, attempting to avoid him, thinking he was about to be attacked. Instead the man directed Paul to a woman who was lying in the street where he had been standing when Paul had seen him. Her dress was pulled up to her hips and her hat lay by her side.

The man touched her arms and Paul felt her breast and thought he detected movement, which seemed to indicate that she was alive. Paul suggested propping her up – presumably thinking she was drunk or had passed out after being raped. The man refused to help so Paul contented himself with pulling her dress down to partially cover her legs.

Callously they decided to leave what was actually the freshly slain body of Mary Ann 'Polly' Nichols, and go on their way to work. They could have easily knocked up anyone from the many neighbouring houses or a caretaker or nightwatchman from a nearby business to help this woman – who if not dead was obviously in distress – but they chose not to.

They walked up to Baker's Row (now Vallance Road) and came across a policeman (PC Mizen) engaged in knocking-up duty. There are different versions of what now took place, which we will come back to later. In the meantime, another policeman – PC Neil – found Polly Nichols. In the sensationalized reports in that evening's newspapers, at the inquest which opened the next day, in all newspapers printed that Saturday and Sunday and in the initial internal police report, PC Neil was credited with finding the body. With one exception, because a Sunday evening newspaper, *Lloyd's Weekly Newspaper*, published an exclusive. They had managed to interview Robert Paul on the Friday evening but had sat on their scoop.

Lloyd's reported that Paul had seen 'a man standing where the woman was' and recounted that they left her there and then informed a policeman around the corner. This made it clear that PC Neil had not independently found the body.

The police reacted by issuing a statement that Sunday night reiterating that PC Neil had found the body and that the two PCs at either end of Buck's Row had seen no one 'leave to attract attention.' Neil said he summoned both PCs by his lantern to come to his assistance. In other words, they debunked the *Lloyd's* account. The next morning's (Monday, 3 September) newspapers contained the police statement which maintained PC Neil as the first finder. The inquest also reopened.

PC Mizen took the stand and recounted how he had been directed to the murder scene by a man who passed him and said he had been sent there by a policeman as a woman was lying in the street. A man was brought into court and PC Mizen identified him as being the same person.

PC Mizen's account did not contradict PC Neil's nor the official police statement from the night before, except in the detail that PC Neil thought he had summoned Mizen with his lamp, whereas Mizen thought PC Neil had sent a messenger to get him.

The next witness to take the stand was that man. He named himself as Charles Allen Cross and withheld his real name, which was Lechmere. It was an obligation to give one's true name and, in all instances, where an alias or alternative name was used and known about, the true name would also be given. This did not happen. Lechmere seems to have been trying to mask his identity for some reason. We know his wife was illiterate and they had only just moved into Doveton Street. We know that future generations of his family were ignorant of his involvement in the case. We know that in over 100 records in his life (including several in 1888) he called himself Lechmere and never Cross.

His first stepfather, who had been dead for nineteen years, was called Cross and this is clearly where he got the name from. However, family names are often used as subterfuge as they are memorable and the first that spring to mind. The highwayman Dick Turpin used his mother's maiden name and the Yorkshire Ripper used his cousin's surname for example.

One correspondent at the inquest, who wrote for *The Star*, recorded Lechmere's correct address. No other reporter even got an approximation. Did he mumble it? Did he neglect to declare it and *The Star* obtained it from the clerk during the recess? It is another oddity.

In contrast to the other witnesses, Lechmere was also described as appearing in his work clothes – bizarrely including his apron. Why didn't he take it off? Was he trying to look the part? The anonymous humble carman?

In the stand, Lechmere contradicted Mizen. He claimed he had said there was a woman either dead or drunk in the road and Lechmere denied telling Mizen the constable was wanted by a policeman.

No one explored this discrepancy further – not the police in their internal reports, nor the press who were usually eager to seize upon any apparent loose end. Lechmere must have come across as a bland, believable, inoffensive nobody. Why was this missed?

By the time Lechmere appeared, the police investigation was already well underway and on a different track with a seemingly promising suspect called Leather Apron. We have a long list of people who came under suspicion and who were eliminated or looked at but Lechmere (or Cross) does not appear, and the police clearly did not determine that his true name was Lechmere.

The coroner at the inquest reprimanded the police for failing to interview all but a handful of residents in Buck's Row, so clearly their investigation was less than thorough. The coroner's patience with the police was stretched by a number of other errors that came to light during the inquest, such as when Polly Nichols' body was undressed, or whether another PC had got his cape instead of going straight for Dr Llewellyn.

These factors conspired to allow the Mizen/Lechmere dispute to remain unnoticed. If Mizen – who had an unblemished record as a policeman and who lived his life, during and after his service with the police, as part of a Christian community – was telling the truth, then Lechmere lied to him by appearing to be a simple messenger, and bluffed his way past without giving his name or any details.

Had Robert Paul not blabbed to the press would Lechmere have come forward at all? As the police contradicted Paul's story late on the Sunday night, Lechmere can only have presented himself after this – after the publication of Paul's story which implicated him as standing alone near the body of a freshly slaughtered woman. Had Lechmere not come forward he would sensibly have been concerned that a search would go out for him, so he really had no choice.

There are other contributory factors which point to Lechmere's guilt.

When Paul left his house, he would have been walking some forty yards behind Lechmere all the way up to the time when he actually saw him in the road. Yet he neither saw nor heard him walking just a short distance in front of him on a quiet night.

Dr Llewellyn estimated the time of death to be less than thirty minutes before his arrival. As inaccurate as such timings are, this would have been roughly when Lechmere was there. Neither Lechmere nor Paul reported any blood despite being literally in touching distance of the body, nor did they get any on themselves, yet subsequent witnesses saw a pool of it. This suggests that the blood had yet to flow out of the wounds. These factors should tell us that Polly Nichols had only just been killed when Paul arrived on the scene.

Of all the Whitechapel murders where the victim had suffered abdominal wounds, this was the only instance where they were covered up. Polly Nichols' ghastly wounds were not left 'on display', which seems to have been an integral part of the Ripper's shock and awe ritual. This indicates that the culprit had been disturbed. Had Paul disturbed Lechmere?

If he had been disturbed, Lechmere chose to confront Paul rather than flee into the night. Lechmere would have been confronted by the 'flight or fight' conundrum. If he was the culprit then he must have been a psychopath, and psychopaths invariably choose 'fight' rather than 'flight'. This was confirmed by Superintendent Andy Griffiths of Sussex Murder Squad who re-investigated the case in conjunction with a TV documentary. Taking control of the situation by going up to confront Paul (and Paul thought he was about to be attacked) instead of running off into the arms of a possible policeman around the corner, would have been exactly the behaviour we should expect.

Lechmere also had the opportunity to kill. He said he left home at 3.30am yet seems to have taken fifteen minutes to cover the seven minutes to Buck's Row. Timings can never be relied upon absolutely but Lechmere's, as given, provide a significant window of opportunity.

Polly Nichols was the only victim found twice, and she was the only victim where the supposed first finder was seen standing by the body before summoning help.

So much for the murder of Polly Nichols. Can Lechmere be linked to any of the other Ripper murders?

On the night of the Nichols' murder, after leaving PC Mizen, Lechmere and Paul walked down Hanbury Street, right past No 29 where, eight days later, Annie Chapman was murdered. Paul left Lechmere and turned into Corbett's Court just 100 yards on from No 29.

Unlike Lechmere, Robert Paul did not present himself to the police as a witness after the Nichols' murder. Paul did eventually appear at the inquest, but not until 17 September – nine days after the Chapman murder. Paul gave another interview to *Lloyd's* at the conclusion of the inquest, complaining, 'he was fetched up in the middle of the night by the police, and was obliged to lose a day's work the next day.'

Walter Dew was a young PC in 1888, and he went on to have an illustrious career with the Metropolitan Police. In his memoirs, *I Caught Crippen*, he said Paul's 'behaviour was certainly suspicious.'

However, Dew's memory played tricks with him and he forgot that Paul had eventually been located: 'The police made repeated appeals for him to come forward, but he never did so,' he wrote.

Why did he remain silent? Was it guilty knowledge that caused him to ignore the appeals of the police?'

Clearly Paul came under suspicion and the police made a particular effort to find him. Was it because he had not come forward and then the next murder had happened yards from his work? It seems likely.

The Nichols and Chapman murders were in comparative quick succession. Did Lechmere deliberately locate his next crime near to Paul's work to throw suspicion in another direction and prompt a dragnet for the man who had originally implicated him?

The so-called 'double-event' murders took place in the early hours of Sunday, 30 September 1888. These were the only crimes in the Whitechapel murder files that took place the night before what would have been for most people their only day off work – Sunday.

Elizabeth Stride was found in Dutfield's Yard on Berner Street at about 1am – considerably earlier than other victims had been discovered. She had her throat cut but no abdominal injuries, leading many to suspect that her killer had been interrupted by the arrival of Louis Diemschutz with his horse and cart. Diemschutz was a regular at an anarchists' club next door that was frequented by Jewish radicals. Dutfield's Yard was pretty much on the direct route between Lechmere's mother's house (where one of his daughters was also living) on Mary Ann Street and Doveton Street.

Dutfield's Yard was also very close to James Street, which was Lechmere's address up to that June. Was he visiting his mother and daughter or looking up old acquaintances in a local pub that night? This was the only one of the generally accepted Jack the Ripper murders to take place south of the main east-west thoroughfares – Whitechapel Road and Commercial Road – which would have acted as psychological barriers to those on the northern side who were unfamiliar with both districts.

The police believed that the Whitechapel murderer (he had not yet been popularized as Jack the Ripper) had been interrupted and thwarted from completing his attack by the arrival of Diemschutz. Just forty-five minutes later, the brutally butchered body of Catherine Eddowes was found in Mitre Square – a mile to the west and just inside the City of London. Mitre Square was near a well-known haunt of prostitutes in the vicinity of St Botolph's Church in Aldgate and was yards from what would have been Charles Lechmere's old route to work at Pickfords when he used to live at James Street. Did that familiarity inform the killer's choice?

After this murder it seems the Ripper moved back east. Part of Catherine Eddowes' blood-soaked apron was found in Goulston Street at a site now occupied by Happy Days fish and chip restaurant. Above the apron was some freshly chalked graffiti that read: 'The Juwes are the men that will not be blamed for nothing.'

Was this the Ripper deflecting blame for the two murders that night onto the Jews? Psychopathic serial killers often project in that manner. Lechmere would have known that the Berner Street club was mostly used by Jewish people and, having been brought up in the district that experienced the first waves of Jewish migration in the 1880s, he would not have been alone in harbouring anti-Semitic attitudes. Whatever the case, Goulston Street was on Lechmere's direct route home from Mitre Square to Doveton Street.

Then we come to Mary Jane Kelly. Uniquely among the Whitechapel murders, she was found inside her lodgings and her body had been literally torn apart. Had she invited her killer into her room? Or did the killer break in while she was asleep? Had she been soliciting and taken the killer back there as a customer? Did she know the culprit? There are many theories, none of which can be answered at this remove. Mary Jane Kelly's true identity has not even been established. Was it her real name or was it assumed?

Prior to moving to Dorset Street with her last boyfriend, Joseph Barnett, Mary Jane Kelly had been living at 1 Breezers Hill right by the London Docks. Recent research has confirmed her as living among a group of people who appeared in the contemporary records, such as Mrs Boeuki (Buki), Mrs Felix (Phoenix), the Morgernsterns and Mrs Carthy. An interesting character called Stephen Maywood also lived at 1 Breezers Hill, which seems to have been a brothel up to 1888. They had all moved with Maywood to the same area of Limehouse by 1891 and continued to be associated with prostitution. Maywood had extensive criminal connections and may well have been the controlling pimp.

Maywood's children attended the nearby Betts Street School until the summer of 1888 – the same school as some of Charles Lechmere's children until they moved to Doveton Street, also in the summer of 1888. It might be noted that Lechmere's daughter, who lived with his mother, was called Mary Jane. Furthermore, Dorset Street was also on one of Lechmere's direct routes to work.

There were other murders on the official police Whitechapel murder file: Rose Mylett (found dead near the Poplar Pickfords depot); Alice Mackenzie (murdered just off Lechmere's Wentworth Street route to work and across from the Pickfords depot at White Swan Yard on Whitechapel High Street) and Frances Coles (who had visited the White Swan on the corner of White Swan Yard – as had Martha Tabram.)

However, the most interesting of these other murders is the so-called 'Pinchin Street torso', a female body – less its head and legs – which was found under a railway arch on Pinchin Street in Stepney on 10 September 1889.

Lechmere lived in Pinchin Street in 1861 when it was called Thomas Street. His mother had lived in Pinchin Street until the railway arch, under which the body was found, was constructed. In 1889 she was living just around the corner on Cable Street. Mrs Fosdyke (as she then was) was a horse flesh dealer for cats' meat. Did her premises contain the tools of her trade and the means to dismember a body?

There are certain similarities between the Pinchin Street case and the other Ripper murders. There were abdominal wounds, but also there was some graffiti left on a fence near the arch that read 'Lipski' and a bloody rag was found in the foundations of St Philip's Church (which now houses the London Hospital Museum), which would have been on the route back to Doveton Street from Pinchin Street.

The Pinchin Street torso links Lechmere to the other torso murders that took place in London concurrently with the Jack the Ripper murders. He had a mode of transport to dispose of the remains and the potential to dismember the bodies via his mother's horse flesh dealership. The victimology is similar and the cuts and wounds on the bodies of some of the torsos seem to have had a similarity with some of the Ripper victims.

In total, and along with other unsolved Ripper type murders and unexplained deaths (such as two bodies fished out of the Regent's Canal near where he ran a business in the 1890s to which he can be linked), Lechmere may have been responsible for over twenty murders from the early 1870s to the late 1890s. The so-called Jack the Ripper murders may 'just' have been a phase in the middle, occasioned perhaps by his moving out of his mother's immediate vicinity or the illness of his youngest daughter who was born in January 1888 and died in October 1890. Perhaps the death of his last stepfather in December 1889 removed one degree of resentment. Perhaps his immersion in local businesses from the early 1890s acted as a distraction. We can't know. Maybe he continued until he got too old...maybe he didn't do it at all!

What can we say of Lechmere?

His mother must have had a strong personality. She married three times, twice bigamously. She brought up one of Lechmere's children and ran her own business. The Ripper murders started within a few weeks of Lechmere moving away from the vicinity of his mother. Judging by his meticulous record keeping, he was very exact. He also ran several businesses while working as a carman. Yet he chose to withhold his true name from the inquest – and his involvement in the case became a secret from his family. He was from a prosperous family background but ended up living in the most overcrowded district in London, which was a notorious haunt of prostitutes, with no father figure in his formative years. Did this lead to resentment?

He was involved in the case but seems to have not been investigated. He was the only 'witness' spotted by a body prior to raising the alarm. That victim – Polly Nichols – was the only one to be 'discovered' twice and had been freshly murdered. Lechmere was late coming forward and only did so when a newspaper report mentioned his presence.

Other 'suspects' cannot have their case examined murder by murder. They are phantoms placed magically in the crime scenes with no context, invisibly flitting away as Lechmere supposedly innocently trudged up Buck's Row on his way to work, or passed by George Yard, Hanbury Street, Dorset Street or Castle Alley. Lechmere is that Holy Grail sought by amateur sleuths. The anonymous local man – the man involved in the case yet ignored by the police, by the press and by generations of Ripperologists. The man sought but not seen – hidden in plain sight.

Edward Stow graduated in History from Queen Mary College in the East End and lived for many years just a short walk away from Whitechapel. He was the adviser for the TV documentary Jack the Ripper – The Missing Evidence, *which featured the Lechmere case, and he was a consultant for the* East London Advertiser *for a series of articles marking the 125th anniversary of the crimes. He also gave a talk at the Whitechapel Ideas Store to mark the 125th anniversary. He wrote a best-selling Jack the Ripper guide book and regularly conducts walking tours of the East End for the Whitechapel Society (for whose journal he is a regular contributor) and for the Stairway to Heaven Memorial Trust (which is a charity that raised funds for a permanent memorial to the victims of the Bethnal Green Tube Disaster).*

Chapter 10

Jacob Levy – A Syphilitic Butcher

By Tracy I'anson

The name of our suspect is Jacob Levy. For many years, it had been hypothesized Jacob could have been related to the witness Joseph Hyam Levy. It took seven years of research before we could categorically confirm that Joseph and Jacob were without doubt related. They were, in fact, first cousins. Simple? Easy? No! There were hundreds, if not thousands of Levys living in and around the vicinity of Whitechapel. We had to decipher the scribbles of the census-takers, the misspellings and the re-christening of people; but we got there and we will show our research below to explain our results.

To prove our theory that Joseph and Jacob were cousins we had go back to the Great Synagogue of London's birth records of 1810 when Hyam Levy was born. It's recorded that the parents of Hyam were Isaac Levy and Sarah Levy. Isaac and Sarah were married pre-1812 and although a date of birth for Isaac is yet to be recorded, we know through census records that Sarah was born in Amsterdam, Holland in 1777. Further research found that Isaac and Sarah had another five children besides Hyam. Esther was born in 1812, Elias 1816, Moss 1818, Joseph 1822 and Elizabeth 1826.

The birth certificate of Hyam Levy also showed the address Petticoat Lane (later to be renamed Middlesex Street). The address was likely to be 36 Petticoat Lane, which would be in the family for at least another eighty years. He had also married Frances Napthali and was the father to three children, Isaac, Napthali and Sarah. Moving on to the 1851 census records we found that Hyam's mother Sarah was still living at 38 Middlesex Street, now aged 74 but still classed as a butcher. Living with her were her two sons, Elias and Moss. Hyam and Frances were still living at 36 Middlesex Street with their children Isaac, Napthali, Sarah, Joseph Hyam, Elias and Henry. Also living there was Leah Napthali, mother-in-law to Hyam. This is the first entry into the census for Joseph Hyam Levy who was born in 1842.

An interesting side note showed that also living with Sarah Levy at 38 Middlesex Street were husband and wife Morris and Maria Napthali – Morris was brother to Frances and son to Leah. In my and Neil I'anson's article, published in the 124th edition of the online magazine *Ripperologist*, we stated that in 1848, Hyam's brother Joseph Levy left home to marry a widower, Caroline Solomon, and set up home. We now know the year stated was an error. Caroline had two children from a previous marriage, Rebecca and Jane Solomon to her previous husband Joshua Solomon. He died from phthisis (tuberculosis of the lungs) on 22 March 1846. The address on his death certificate was 5 Love Court.

The birth certificate of Hannah Levy, Joseph and Caroline's eldest child, noted that she was born 14 September 1847 at 5 Love Court. This shows that Joseph and Caroline were living together before their marriage in 1848 and subsequently moved to 4 Little Middlesex Street as shown in the 1851 census. Living with them were Caroline's two daughters from her previous marriage, Rebecca and Jane and also Joseph and Caroline's children Hannah and Elizabeth.

By 1861 Sarah Levy had moved out of 38 Middlesex Street and was living as a boarder with Morris and Maria Napthali at 23 Hutchinson Avenue. She was no longer carrying on the trade of butcher and her occupation showed no trade. Hyam was still trading as a butcher from 36 Petticoat Lane, living there with Frances and their children Sarah, Elias, Elizabeth and Joseph Hyam. Joseph and Caroline were no longer living at 4 Little Middlesex Street as it was demolished to make way for Little Goulston Street and surrounding streets. They moved to 111 Middlesex Street. Joseph was still classed as a butcher. With them are their children Jane, Hannah, Elizabeth, Isaac, Abraham, Moss and 5-year-old Jacob.

This is the first census record of Jacob, born in 1856. The above narrative shows that Joseph Hyam Levy and Jacob Levy were without doubt first cousins. They were also in the same trade, butchery, lived very close to each other and Jacob Levy would eventually buy the house and business that Joseph Hyam Levy grew up in. The 1871 census recorded

Joseph Hyam Levy now resided at 1 Hutchinson Avenue with his wife Amelia Lewis. They had married at The Great Synagogue in 1866. Joseph's occupation was listed as butcher. Jacob Levy was now 15 years old and living at 111 Middlesex Street with his parents and siblings. Jacob was no longer recorded as a scholar but now a butcher following in what appeared to be a family business; his grandmother, grandfather, uncles, cousin, father and brother were all recorded as butchers over the generations.

This occupation would have provided Jacob with the required knife skills and the basic anatomical knowledge needed to kill and mutilate the Ripper victims.

On 25 November 1872, Hyam Levy, Joseph Hyam Levy's father, died at his home of 36 Middlesex Street after a painful illness lasting forty hours. His will left everything to Frances:

> '22 September 1873 Will of Hyam Levy – Effect under £100 The will of Hyam Levy late of 36 Middlesex Street, St Botolph, Aldgate in the City of London, Butcher who died 25 November 1872 at Middlesex Street was proved at the Principal Registry by Frances Levy of 36 Middlesex Street widow of the relict the sole executrix.'

May 28 1875 was a date that would have left a permanent scar on Jacob and his family, for it was when his elder brother Abraham committed suicide. This account is from the *Glasgow Herald*, Friday, 28 May 1875:

> 'Results of Unfortunate speculation. Yesterday, Mr Humphries, the coroner for the Eastern Division of Middlesex, received information of the death of Mr Abraham Levy, age 22 years, carrying on the business of butcher at Whitechapel, London. Deceased had bet heavily on the Derby and on the arrival of the news of the result he appeared very desponding. At a quarter past six the door of his bedroom was found to be locked and on it being burst open he was discovered suspended by a rope. A doctor was called in, but life had been extinct for some time. On account of the Jewish custom, an inquest will be held this day [Friday].'

The inquest added some additional details, as reported by *Lloyd's Weekly Newspaper* Friday, 28 May 1875:

Suicide on Derby Day

> 'On Friday, Mr Humphries held an inquest at the Coach and Horses, [129] Middlesex Street, Whitechapel, on the body of Abraham Levy, aged 22, who committed suicide on Derby night. The evidence proved that the deceased, the son of a butcher, lived at 111 Middlesex Street. On Wednesday evening, shortly after 6pm he left the shop and went up to his room for the purpose of dressing, but nothing being heard of him, suspicions were aroused, when one Joseph Levy, brother to the deceased, going up he found the door locked. After repeated knockings, and no answer being given, the door was burst open, when he discovered suspended by a rope line from the neck to a nail which he had fastened in the wall. The jury returned a verdict of "suicide whilst of unsound mind".'

We know that the Joseph mentioned in the report was Jacob, a name he used in the 1881 census, which means not only did he have to come to terms with his brother's suicide, he also found his body. Whilst Abraham's death was noted due to having a bad day at the races, we have found no evidence that he was a gambler, so we're not sure of the reason behind his suicide.

After Abraham's death, Jacob married Sarah Abrahams on 23 April 1879 and moved to 11 Fieldgate Street, after living in Middlesex Street for twenty years. He was still living there in the 1881 census and moved back to Middlesex Street around 1886. He actually moved in to 36 Middlesex Street, taking over the house and business from his aunt, Frances Levy, and was still living there at the time of the murders in 1888. Jacob had a past record for mental instability, petty theft and violence. In March 1886, he was arrested for theft from a neighbour, Mr Hyman Sampson of 35 Middlesex Street, for a piece of meat worth seven shillings. Jacob had £32 10s 9d in his pocket when he was arrested by PC Samuel Bacon, the equivalent of £2,153 in today's money. Back in 1886 this would have been the equivalent of ninety-eight days' wages for a skilled worker, so we can certainly rule out financial gain for the reason of the theft. Which begs the question why did he steal the meat?

For this criminal act Jacob was sentenced to one year hard labour on 5 April 1886 and sent to Holloway Prison. He was transferred to Chelmsford Prison on 19 April. A few weeks later, on 21 May, Jacob was certified insane after a suicide attempt and was admitted to Essex County Lunatic Asylum on 26 May 1886. His intake records from the asylum show that Jacob was married and had four children, although he didn't know the age of the youngest child. He recorded butcher under the heading of former occupation and his state of bodily health was described as 'Good'.

It was confirmed by medical staff that this was his first attack and that it had lasted about three weeks. Jacob was described as suicidal, due to 'fretting about business and family.' A document titled *Chief Delusions or Indication of Insanity* came in two parts: the first part was given by the medical officer and included his observations of the patient, and the second part was observations made by others. For his part, the medical officer noted Jacob showed evidence of 'rambling and incoherent talking, restlessness and insomnia.'

The second part was recorded by temporary warder Wade, whose comments on Jacob were that he had attempted suicide by strangling and that he was 'shouting, restless and talking at night. Violence. Incessantly talking of imaginary people.' The document was dated 26 May 1886 and signed by the medical officer E.H. Carter.

Another document from the intake file from Chelmsford has a handwritten explanation of Jacob's state of mind at that time:

> 'He is in a state of melancholia, cries without adequate cause – is very despondent from the fact that he attempted suicide by strangulation at Gaol and that a brother committed suicide and insanity is hereditary is in his family. I consider him suicidal and insane. He is in fair health and condition.'

This is dated 3 June 1886 and signed G.A.

Jacob was released two months earlier than his sentence date and, on 3 February 1887, was discharged from the asylum and moved back to 36 Middlesex Street. Hyman Sampson and his family were still living at 35 Middlesex Street although Hyman Sampson died just eight weeks after Jacob's release, on 2 April 1887, with his wife continuing the butchering business until she moved to new premises a few years later.

While it can be imagined that Jacob's subsequent arrest and trial would have lost him customers, Sarah was obviously keeping the business afloat as Jacob appeared in the 1888 business listings.

Towards the end of May 1888, Jacob's mother Caroline died aged 69 from cancer, bronchitis and haemorrhagic collapse. In 1890 Jacob returned to an asylum, this time Stone, City of London Lunatic Asylum in Kent.

The first paper from here is a letter titled the *Certificate of Medical Practitioner Form* and explains to us how and why Jacob had been sent to the asylum:

> 'In the matter of Jacob Levy of 36 Middlesex Street Aldgate E in the City of London, Butcher and alleged lunatic. I the undersigned Henry James Sequeira do hereby certify as follows:- I am the person registered under the Medical Act of 1858, and I am in the actual practice of the medical profession. On the 14th day of August 1890 at 36 Middlesex Street Aldgate E in the City of London, I personally examined the said Jacob Levy and concluded that he is a person of unsound mind and a proper person to be taken charge of and detained under care and treatment. I formed this conclusion on the following grounds viz:- Facts indicating insanity observed by myself at the time of examination viz Known patient several years, formerly shrewd businessman, now quite incapable of earning on same. Giving wrong change and money back for things bought. Says he feels a something within him, impelling him to take everything he sees. Feels that if he is not restrained he will do some violence to someone. Complains of hearing strange noises. Facts communicated by others viz:- Sarah Levy 36 Middlesex Street, wife, deposes – That he has nearly ruined her business, being quite incapable of taking care of money, making away with every penny he can put his hands on. Orders goods indiscriminately and is continually taking other people's goods, carrying them off. Wanders away from home for hours without any purpose. Does not sleep at night, raves he is continually fancying someone is going to do him bodily harm. The said Jacob

> Levy appeared to me to be in a fit condition of bodily health to be removed to an asylum, hospital or licensed house. I give this certificate having first read the section of the Act of Parliament printed below.
>
> Dated this fourteenth date August 1890.
>
> Signed H.J. Sequeira of 34 Jewry Street Aldgate London E.'

So, in summation, on 14 August 1890, Sarah requested Dr Henry Sequeira of 34 Jewry Street, brother to George William Sequeira who attended the scene of Catherine Eddowes' murder, to examine Jacob at his home – 36 Middlesex Street. On examining Jacob, Dr Sequeira declared that he was of unsound mind and needed to be placed in an insane asylum.

The next paper was titled *The Relieving Officer of the Poor Law Union in the City of London*:

> 'Whereas I the undersigned, and one of her majesty's Justices of the peace in and for the City of London on the 14th day of August received notice from you that Jacob Levy a person chargeable to the City of London Union is deemed to be a person of unsound mind.
>
> 'I therefore hereby order and require you to bring the said Jacob Levy before me, on the 15th day of August in the year of our Lord One Thousand Eight Hundred and Ninety at Eleven o'clock in the forenoon, at Guildhall Justice room in the said city or before such other Justice of the Peace for the said [City] as may then be there to be dealt with according to Law. Given under my Hand and Seal, at the Guildhall Justice Room in the said City, this 14th day of August in the year of our Lord, One Thousand Eight Hundred and Ninety.
>
> Signed James Whitehead.'

Included in the intake file for Stone is another paper dated 14 August 1890 and titled *Order for a Pauper Lunatic Wandering At Large*:

> 'I, George Robert Tyler, Esquire, being an Alderman and Justice of the Peace of the City of London having called to my

> assistance Henry James Sequeira of 34 Jewry Street Aldgate, a duly qualified medical practitioner and being satisfied that Jacob Levy of 36 Middlesex Street Aldgate is a pauper in receipt of relief and that the said Jacob Levy is a person of unsound mind and a proper person to be taken charge hereby direct you to receive the said Jacob Levy as a patient into your asylum. Subjoined is a statement of particulars respecting the said Jacob Levy and I hereby require you Walter Boscher a Relieving officer forthwith to convey the Lunatic aforementioned to the Institution herein named.
>
> Signed George Robert Tyler Esquire.'

Within the file is a record of financial transactions: the charges for the examination and diagnosis of Jacob and transport needed (which are quoted directly but don't add up):

> 'The Guardians of the City of London Union W. Boscher Relieving Officer re Jacob Levy (a Lunatic) Expense incurred on conveying the above named person from 36 Middlesex Street to Guildhall therein to Stone, City of London Lunatic Asylum. Stamps at Guildhall 5.6 Cab fare to Justice Room 2.0 – Railway fare (Special compt) 10.4 Cab fare at Dartford 3.6 Expenses for patient and attendant and R.O 7.6 Total expenses £1.8.10.'

Other reports in the file described Jacob as being married and that he was Hebrew. His occupation was recorded as butcher. One question that stands out from the others is when asked whether any relative had been afflicted with insanity Jacob answered yes, elder brother **cut his throat**. [my emphasis] Jacob only had two elder brothers, Isaac and Abraham. Isaac didn't die until 1901 so that left Abraham who we know committed suicide by hanging in 1875. Could this just be another coincidence or had Jacob developed a fixation with cutting throats?

On Jacob's intake records he was described as not being epileptic, suicidal or dangerous and his education was classified as 'Good'. He was described as covered with scratches, deeply stained with copper-coloured discolouration, most likely syphilitic, and that he also had a wound upon his right buttock and a wound upon his left index finger.

There were two marks of recent boils on his back. His height and weight were measured at 5ft 3in and 9st 3lb.

Jacob's medical notes from the asylum give us an insight into his health and everyday life in the asylum.

The first entry, dated 18 August 1890, described how he had recently taken to drink and how he used to be a, good father and husband but had become neglectful. The next entry dated 21 August, showed Jacob was suffering from mania and that he 'felt compelled to do acts contrary to the dictates of his conscience by a power which he cannot withstand.'

Physically, Jacob was free from disease of the lungs and heart and, with the exception of evidence of syphilitic disease, he was in good health. The report from 27 August described him as well-behaved since admission, he no longer suffered insomnia, was sleeping well and was eating food with a keen relish. It's noted that he worked on the farm daily. There's an added comment that there was a nonchalance in his manner, which was much unfitted to his condition and which suggested that he was conscious of a feeling of exaltation.

On 4 September, the entry is a lot shorter and states that there has been a slight improvement and that Jacob was feeling much better and was asking when he could go home. His weight was given as 10st. From 10 September to 16 October there was no change of importance but that changed on 26 October when it was noted that Jacob had felt out of sorts for the previous two to three days and that morning had had an attack of giddiness and faintness that lasted a few minutes.

He was described as being very depressed, crying for no reason and had lost his appetite. His heart was normal although his pupils were unequal, with the left much larger than the right.

The next entry was dated 8 November and described how Jacob had had an epileptic attack that day. The convulsions were confined almost entirely to the left side. His left pupil was much enlarged. The 4 December report showed that Jacob had had an eczematous eruption on his thighs but that it was yielding to medication. There had been no change mentally, he was always bright and lively, and there had been no despondency since the 8 November entry. His weight was recorded as 9st 3lb. The last entry from 1890 was on 30 December and showed the eczematous eruption was quite well and he was content with himself and things about him. The first entry of 1891 was dated 31 January and detailed how Jacob had been transferred to No 4 Ward and that he still worked on the farm. He was still in the same exalted state.

The entry on 6 March showed Jacob was still exalted and his pupils were markedly unequal. His weight was now 10st. On 5 May, it was described that he'd had a boil on his neck which was getting better. However, 15 July showed a marked difference in Jacob, explaining that he was much worse mentally and he was losing strength and weight. He now needed special feeding and it was observed his pupils were very unequal. His weight was 8st 7lb.

The next entry was just one week later on 22 July, which detailed how Jacob was now much weaker and very troublesome. He needed two or three attendants to dress and undress him and he required spoonfeeding. The last entry for his medical journal was on 29 July and described Jacob's final hours. At 8am on 29 July, Jacob suffered an epileptic attack and when he was seen at 8:30am his pulse and respiration were very rapid and feeble. His pulse was 120 beats per minute and respiratory rate was forty. There were no physical signs of pulmonary congestion when examined. He had bruises on his left arm and sternum and on the pelvis caused by falling. He resisted examination thoroughly.

At 5pm his respiratory rate was forty and moist sounds were noted from the back of both lungs. His pulse couldn't be counted at his wrist but was noted as 140 at brachial. At 7:52pm Jacob Levy died.

The final record for Jacob was an entry from the coroner. Jacob's name was at the top of the entry with the date of 30 July 1891. The report showed Jacob Levy, 35 years old, a butcher of 36 Middlesex Street Aldgate died at 7:52pm on 29 July 1891.

The cause of death was recorded as 'general paralysis of the insane' and that he had had the disease for 'some years'. There is an entry, which states clearly that a post mortem had been refused, and charge attendant Mr Hewlett and Mrs Levy (his wife) were there at the time of death. The report was signed by Ernest White.

In our opinion Jacob Levy is one of the best suspects. He was a local-born Jewish man who lived in the area all his life. He would have known the maze of alleyways throughout Whitechapel and the surrounding area. He also would have been a familiar face to the people in and around the area, able to blend in and talk to people without raising suspicions.

Did this knowledge of the area give Jacob an edge when evading capture by the police at the time of the murders?

We know that Jacob was an experienced professional butcher. Did this give him the requisite skills needed to kill and mutilate a body with the speed and accuracy within the timeframe and the lack of lighting the killer had?

Abraham Levy committed suicide by strangulation. Jacob was the person to discover the body hanging from the ceiling. Did this affect his mental state?

At the end of May, Jacob's mother Caroline died. Could this have been the stressor needed for the Jack the Ripper killings?

We know Jacob was the cousin of Joseph Hyam Levy and was the correct height of the suspect as seen by Joseph Hyam. Did Joseph recognize this man as his Jacob Levy?

He'd suffered trauma from his teen years with the suicide of his brother, and his mental health was in steady decline from his arrest for theft in 1886 onwards due to neurosyphilis. Did this affect his mental state to the point where murder and mutilation were the only things to satisfy his cravings and ease his mental trauma?

The Jack the Ripper files were officially closed within a year of Jacob's death.

Could Jacob's death be the closure the police were waiting for?

Tracy I'anson was born in Hartlepool in 1978. She attended St Cuthbert's Primary and English Martyrs Secondary School where her interest in history first began. After raising Nathan, her son, Tracy went to work in her local brewery as a tour guide but it was her fascination with true crime that led her to the mystery of Jack the Ripper. Alongside her father Neil, she explored the possibility that suspect Jacob Levy could be the world's most notorious serial killer. After years of painstaking research her findings will finally be revealed in the book, Jacob the Ripper, *published in 2019.*

Chapter 11

Robert Mann – The Mortuary Assistant

By Mei Trow

Because he was never caught, the Whitechapel murderer has assumed a supernatural quality. He is the ultimate bogeyman, creeping silently through the scum-smeared streets of Whitechapel, slashing unfortunates with his knife and vanishing into the darkness without a trace. Add to this our bewildering propensity to believe that serial killers come from the upper classes and we have the legend of the top-hatted, cloaked monster with peculiar eyes and a black Gladstone bag.

Experts who work on serial murder know that none of this is true or realistic. Dozens of people came forward to the police and/or the newspapers in the autumn of 1888 with their eyewitness descriptions of men they saw talking to a victim on the night she died. Although we make notoriously bad eyewitnesses, especially to humdrum events, and we have several contradictory accounts, it is likely that at least one of the men in question was actually Jack the Ripper. Like his near namesake, 'Spring-heeled Jack', who leapt from rooftops to terrorize women in the middle of the nineteenth century, an ordinary flesh and blood human being has been turned into an uncatchable demon.

We need to establish some ground rules in our endless hunt for the identity of Jack. Serial killers, as we call them today, or the 'habitual homicide' as our Victorian forebears called them, were an unknown 'species' in 1888. The poisoner, Mary Ann Cotton, has a strong case to be called Britain's first serial killer, responsible as she was for as many as twenty-one deaths from the early 1850s until her arrest in 1872. She is not remotely the same type of killer as Jack, however, a 'lustmorderer' who attacked random strangers in a 'blitz' assault, using his superior strength, surprise and a sharp knife. Research into other serial killers of our own time has shown that such people target their own social class, people with whom they can blend, people who will trust them on first – and often last – meeting. Builder John Wayne Gacy picked up apprentice builders, offering them jobs before assaulting, murdering and burying them in the crawl space under his home in Norwood Park, Chicago. College student Ted Bundy lured college co-eds into his yellow Beetle car before murdering them in various locations across the States between 1971 and 1978. On that basis, we can eliminate all the famous who have been cited as potential Rippers. Out goes the royal family and their adherents, Sir William Gull and J.K. Stephen. Out goes the artist Walter Sickert. Out goes the barrister and teacher Montague Druitt. Out goes Thomas Barnardo, Lewis Carroll, General Sam Browne and a host of upper and middle-class celebrities who had nothing in common with the down-and-outs of the East End – except, in Barnardo's case, trying to save them!

Research has also shown that a serial killer will strike in areas that are familiar to them. Because he eluded the increasing number of police patrols and dodged the vigilance committees, it is surely incontrovertible that the Ripper knew Whitechapel and Spitalfields like the back of his hand. Out go all the above – except, again, Barnardo, attached, as he was, to the London Hospital. Out go the various foreign sailors who were merely passing through the Port of London and did not know Whitechapel well enough. Out go longer visitors such as Dr Francis Tumblety and the Canadian G. Wentworth Bell Smith.

We also know that serial killers are creatures of habit. They find a certain type of victim and by and large stick to it – Bundy's girls with long, straight, dark hair for instance. They also choose a favourite method of murder and stick to that, too. The level of violence often increases, but the basic method and weapon do not change. So we can rule out Dr Neil Cream, who, though he targeted prostitutes, used poison. We can dismiss Severin Klosowski (George Chapman) who was not only a poisoner, but targeted his wives. Out goes the 'family annihilator' Frederick Deeming, whether he confessed to the last two Ripper murders or not.

So what are we left with? The Whitechapel murderer was a working-class man who lived and probably died in the area in which his crimes were committed. He was not a Jew because his victims were not (another serial killer pattern) and there is no evidence at all that only one of the victims was his real target, the rest being simply red herrings to confuse the police. I do not believe that he wrote 'taunting' letters and I believe that he was known to the police.

In 2008, my agent said to me, 'Can you find a new suspect for the Ripper murders?' This was a major challenge. Dozens of people had already been put forward, some preposterous, some plausible and a formidable amount of research had been carried out on all aspects of the case. I had even proposed my own 'spoof' suspect – the anti-drink campaigner, Nicholas Charrington – just to show how easy it is to put almost anybody alive in 1888 in the frame. The result of my own research was *Jack the Ripper: Quest for a Killer* published in 2009. That in turn was taken up by Atlantic Productions who produced a fifty-minute documentary *Jack the Ripper: Killer Revealed* for the Discovery Channel.

Sticking your head above the parapet with a new suspect is always risky. I deliberately kept away from the Ripper websites to avoid most of the flak, but even so, my suspect was branded a 'non-starter' by most Ripperologists. So, what was my starting point?

I read the remarkable attempt at psychological profiling by Dr Thomas Bond, police surgeon to A Division, who carried out the post mortem on Mary Kelly. It is perhaps unfortunate that Bond's first line in this context, that Mary was found naked, is wrong; she was actually wearing a chemise, but after that, his analysis is extraordinary and would not be bettered until the FBI's centenary analysis in 1988.

Bond believed that Jack had committed all five of the murders he was asked to examine: Mary Ann 'Polly' Nichols, Annie Chapman, Elizabeth 'Liz' Stride, Catherine 'Kate' Eddowes and Mary Kelly, based on the method of murder–cutting of the throat from left to right while the victim was lying down. The killer had struck with great speed from the right, giving the victim no chance of screaming. Because of the lack of space in the cramped room in Miller's Court, he had struck Mary Kelly from in front or the left. Contrary to what almost everyone else believed, Bond asserted that the killer would not be covered in blood but would certainly have blood spatters on parts of his clothing. The object of the killing, Bond wrote, was mutilation. The weapon was a sharp knife with a blade at least six inches long and perhaps an inch wide. The first two points of the criminal profile discuss the sort of man Jack was, but first I must point out one area where I disagree with Bond – as did most police surgeons at the time. His eighth point reads:

> 'In each case the mutilation was inflicted by a person who had no scientific nor anatomical knowledge. In my opinion,

> he does not even possess the technical knowledge of a butcher or horse slaughterer or any person accustomed to cut up dead animals.'

This is an extraordinary assumption referring to a killer who could remove Annie Chapman's uterus, Mary Kelly's heart and Kate Eddowes' kidney, the last 'operation' carried out in less than fifteen minutes in the dark! We have to remember that thousands of people following the Ripper murders in the press believed that Jack was a doctor and there were many in the medical profession who took offence at that and denied it vehemently.

Bond's tenth point says that the killer is strong, cool and daring. He worked alone, destroying the idea that the murders were carried out by a gang. Jack had periodic bouts of homicidal and erotic mania. Perhaps the cause of this was satyriasis, an obsession with sex, or religious mania, although Bond rejects both of these. The Whitechapel murderer would be a 'quiet, inoffensive-looking man', probably middle-aged and neatly dressed. He would need an overcoat to cover any bloodstains on his clothing. He would be a loner, perhaps eccentric in his habits and with no regular job. Perhaps he had a small income or pension. He was living with respectable people who would find his behaviour odd at times. They would not report him to the police 'for fear of trouble', although a reward might make them change their mind.

If we fast-forward to 1988, another 'Thomas Bond' produced a psychological profile. Special agent John E. Douglas of the Behavioural Science Unit of the FBI at Quantico, Virginia, came to various conclusions based on the evidence he had read. A considerable amount of research has been carried out since then, but the basic facts of the Ripper case remain unchanged. The killer, Douglas contended, was an 'asocial loner'. He was employed 'in positions where he could work alone and experience vicariously his destructive fantasies, perhaps as a butcher or hospital or mortuary attendant.' His dress would be 'neat and orderly'. His 'sexual relationships mostly with prostitutes' – and in Whitechapel and Spitalfields, Jack had plenty of choice. He 'may have contracted venereal disease.' This is hinted at in numerous letters to the police and forms the basis of a vague and early theory on identity of the killer, the un-attributable 'Dr Stanley', killing the victims out of revenge for his syphilitic son. Of the victims, only Liz Stride, as a professional

Swedish prostitute, had treatment for the disease, though it is possible that Mary Kelly's stay in a Cardiff infirmary was in connection with this. Douglas believed, based on long years of experience with American serial killers, that Jack was 'aged in his late twenties'. He was employed 'since the murders were mostly at weekends'. He was 'free from family accountability and so unlikely to be married.' He was 'not surgically skilled' – Douglas is following Bond's hypothesis here and as we have seen, it is flawed. He was 'probably in some form of trouble with the police before the first murder.' He 'lived or worked in the Whitechapel area and his first homicide would have been close to his home or place of work… . Undoubtedly, the police would have interviewed him.'

Douglas expanded on these ideas in 2000 in *The Cases That Haunt Us*. The attack on Polly Nichols showed a naivety – arguably, Jack's first kill. He was unsure of himself and struck in a 'blitz' attack because he could not 'get her where he wants her through any kind of verbal means'. Douglas found the attack on Annie Chapman showed 'a perverse anatomical curiosity'. Jack 'hates women and probably fears them.' Removing Annie's uterus effectively neuters her; she is no longer a woman. By 2000, Douglas had changed his mind about the killer's anatomical skill – Jack had some. He came from a dysfunctional family with an absent father and domineering mother.

Given this profile, back in 2008, was there anyone who fitted the pattern? We have to remember that psychological profiling is an imprecise science – there are always exceptions to the rule – and we are talking about a murder case that is now 130 years old.

The next modern technique I turned to for help was that of criminal geoprofiling or murder-mapping. The phrase was first coined in the late 1980s by Canadian police officer Kim Rossmo and is well-defined by behavioural psychologist Dr David Canter in the context of victimology – 'not who they are, but where they are'. Behavioural investigator Professor Laurence Alison explains: 'Today's geoprofilers would break down the sub-tasks the offender needed to accomplish in order to escape and examine the exit points from the scene of each attack.' This was particularly important in confined spaces, such as Dutfield's Yard, Mitre Square and Miller's Court. A serial killer is a hunter, along the lines of a big cat in the wild. He will not travel far from his lair in search of prey because he needs to get back to safety quickly; unlike a real big cat, he has an army of policemen on his tail.

If we take Sir Melville Macnaghten's (probably wrong) 'canonical five', Polly Nichols died closest to my suspect's home and 'lair'. Annie Chapman was next, in terms of chronology and distance. Liz Stride is further south, in Dutfield's Yard and Kate Eddowes further away still, the furthest from home. Given that the Mitre Square victim was a 'panic' situation in that Jack had been interrupted in Dutfield's Yard, this is hardly surprising. He wanted to get as far away as he could. In the murder of Mary Kelly, Jack was completing a circle once again, as he was when walking along Goulston Street after the murder of Kate Eddowes, on his way home.

Putting together the pattern created by murder-mapping and the pattern created by behavioural analysis, I focused on one man. John Douglas had pinpointed someone who 'could work alone and experience vicariously his destructive fantasies, perhaps as a butcher or hospital or mortuary attendant.' And the mortuary attendant who kept cropping up was Robert Mann. David Canter was writing about serial killer Jeffrey Dahmer when he wrote: 'He needed to enshrine his fascination with bodies, especially dead bodies… . When asked what the purpose of this display was, [Dahmer kept various body parts in his fridge] he replied that it was "a place where I could feel at home".'

For Robert Mann, the display area was his lair – the dilapidated mortuary of the Whitechapel Union Workhouse in Eagle Place, off Montague Street. It was not physically attached to the workhouse, which was in Baker's Row (now Vallance Road) three minutes' walk from Buck's Row, where Polly Nichols died. The building stood alone and it was the site of the post mortems carried out on Polly Nichols, Annie Chapman and Mary Kelly; post mortems which Robert Mann witnessed up close and personal, watching police surgeons dissect corpses in a way that had already given him the rough knowledge of anatomy that characterized the Ripper's work.

Who was Robert Mann? Like so many in the East End, he is anonymous and banal, exactly the kind of serial killer who literally gets away with murder. He was born in 1836 and the census of 1841 shows the Mann family living in Hope Street, Whitechapel, on the edge of what would become Jack's hunting ground. His father, also Robert, was a silk weaver, but the prosperous days of such people were gone. This was the 'hungry forties', with high unemployment and machinery fast taking over the old hand-loom methods of production. As a small boy, Robert junior would have worked with his father, developing, especially in his arms and wrists, the physical strength to which Dr Bond alludes in the killer's MO. Robert senior died in 1847 from the all-too-common typhus fever, by which time the family was in the newly established workhouse in Baker's Row. Robert junior appears in the workhouse lists in 1851, which would have been his last year in the boys' ward. From then on, he was with adult males – 'the broken workmen, the drunkards and dissolute, the inadequate and handicapped, the crippled and retarded'. There is no record of Robert's mother, the middle-aged Elizabeth, nor of his 17-year-old sister Amelia. Perhaps Elizabeth had remarried and taken her daughter with her into relative prosperity. Evidence from the time of the Whitechapel murders suggests that Robert Mann suffered from fits – was he having these already by 1851? And is that why Elizabeth left him behind? Look again at the ages of Jack's victims – only Mary Kelly was in her 20s. The others, factoring in, as I believe we must – Martha Tabram and Alice McKenzie, killed on either side of the 'canonical five' – were all middle-aged; the age at which Elizabeth Mann abandoned her inadequate son. 'Research has shown,' wrote Laurence Alison, 'that neglect and isolation are powerful disinhibitors to violence.' Mother-fixation and mother-murder are common themes in serial killer motivation. Subconsciously, Mann was killing his mother in an act of revenge.

At some point, Mann worked in the docks. This was casual labour, a few men being taken on a first-come-first-served daily basis, and at some point he was lodging in Wentworth Street, just around the corner from George Yard Buildings where Martha Tabram was murdered in August 1888. In terms of murder-mapping, this again follows the pattern – it was an area that Mann knew minutely.

By 1888, Mann seems to have been permanently living in the workhouse and had wangled the job as mortuary assistant. With this limited privilege, he was able to come and go, not exactly as he pleased, but certainly more than most inmates. There is a record, for example, that he was sent out onto the streets in 1884, to pick up the body of a little girl and bring it to the mortuary. Other evidence shows that the gate-keeping at the workhouse was very lax, so who knew where the mortuary attendant was at any given time? He almost certainly had a key to the mortuary and this gave him access to his 'lair' whenever he wanted it. Look again at the murder sites – Martha Tabram died on a small landing stairway in George Yard Buildings; Polly Nichols outside the locked gates of the small Brown's Stable Yard; Annie Chapman was murdered in the cramped back yard of 29 Hanbury Street; Liz Stride in the narrow entranceway to Dutfield's Yard; Kate Eddowes was butchered in the darkest corner of Mitre Square; Mary Kelly was dissected in a twelve by ten-foot room in Miller's Court. Mann was trying, consciously or otherwise, to recreate the confines of his lair, the mortuary where he was, for hours, alone with the dead. Some serial killers return to the murder sites, revisiting the corpses; in the most extreme cases, such as Ted Bundy, having sex with them.

How much of the Bond/Douglas profiling fits Robert Mann? We have already noted the likelihood of physical strength. A weaver and dock labourer was used to man-handling heavy machinery and a mortuary attendant regularly moved dead bodies. He was cool and daring – clearly the murderer was, but we have no way of knowing this aspect of Mann's personality because we know so little about him. 'Quiet, inoffensive, neatly dressed.' No one comments on Mann's loudness. In fact, his performance at inquests was poor – we shall look at this later. His workhouse garb, complete with overcoat, fits the bill exactly. 'Solitary and eccentric'; Mann worked with an assistant, James Hatfield, in the mortuary, but there is no reason to suppose this was always the case and there is no mention of other friends or acquaintances. His inquest appearance was certainly odd enough to be deemed eccentric. 'He had no occupation, but a small income or pension.' His occupation was sporadic, in that he was not always called upon to assist in the mortuary unless there was a death. Apart from that, as a pauper, he received full board and lodging so the income or pension becomes irrelevant.

'He is possibly living among respectable persons…who may have grounds for suspicion that he is not quite right in his mind at times.' It is doubtful that many Victorians would have regarded workhouse inmates as respectable, although they generally received more sympathy than animosity. The staff were undoubtedly respectable. If Mann's behaviour at the inquest is anything to go by, not being 'quite right in his mind' would certainly have been a viable viewpoint. He could and did work alone in the Eagle Place mortuary where he could 'experience vicariously his destructive fantasies.' We know nothing about his sex life or whether he had a sexually transmitted disease. That he was afraid of women may be evidenced by the incident when nurses came to wash Annie Chapman's body; Mann left the mortuary, perhaps outraged by women invading what he saw as his personal space. 'Unlikely to have been married' – Robert Mann remained a bachelor all his life. We know that he was born and died in Whitechapel (in 1896, from phthisis, a pulmonary disease) which fits the pattern of geoprofiling. I believe that this illness, which takes years to kill anyone suffering from it, explains his half-hearted attack on Alice Mackenzie. Experts at the time were unsure whether this was a Ripper killing because of the slight mutilations. If Mann was physically ill, coughing up blood and feeling weak, this would explain the lack of wounds. He picked up enough medical expertise to carry out his mutilations on the other victims from watching police surgeons at work and had access to the knives they routinely used, most of which were of the dimensions described by Dr Bond. 'Undoubtedly the police would have interviewed him.' They did not, directly, but were with him when all three victims were delivered to the mortuary.

What about Mann's appearance at inquests? In September, he appeared as a witness in the case of Polly Nichols. Inspector Joseph Helson of J Division had told him specifically not to touch the body but Mann denied under oath that he had given him such an order. In fact, he could not recall having seen Helson, despite the inspector's evidence to the contrary. He remembered Polly's clothes were not cut (presumably because he had not cut them) but could not remember anything about blood patterns. It was James Hatfield, Mann said, who had removed Polly's clothes. No sooner had Mann answered these questions from the coroner, Wynn Baxter, and a juryman than Baxter dropped a bombshell: 'It appears the mortuary keeper is subject to fits and neither his memory nor statements are reliable.' Journalists reporting this inquest followed the coroner's lead, calling Mann 'poor old keeper' and from that we have the image of a shambling geriatric barely capable of walking and chewing gum. In the world of today's Ripper mythology, he is portrayed in the hugely influential graphic novel *From Hell* as an octogenarian who has a falling down fit in the course of the storyboarding.

In fact, Mann was 53 and it is more than possible that journalists confused him with James Hatfield, who was 62. Consistently throughout his testimony, Mann mentioned Hatfield as 'his mate', shifting attention to him. Hatfield does not mention Mann at all. We do not know where Baxter's information came from about Mann's unreliability, but in that one casual sentence he had effectively eliminated him from any police inquiry. He was subject to fits and his memory was poor. In other words, Robert Mann could say anything and he would be ignored. We cannot be sure of the origin of the fits he suffered, but if they were symptomatic of temporal lobe epilepsy, that condition is shared by over seventy per cent of known serial killers. When expert David Canter summed up on serial killer Fred West in the 1980s he posed a question: 'How could he have killed so many people without being noticed? This poorly educated, intellectually dull man… . People thought he was harmless.'

They were wrong about Fred West. And I believe they were wrong about Robert Mann too.

M.J. Trow has written highly praised historical biographies as well as studies of true crime. He is also a very successful novelist. Among his recent publications are the lives of Boudicca, Vlad the Impaler, Kit Marlowe, the hero of the Charge of the Light Brigade, Captain William Morris as well as the books War Crimes: Underworld Britain in the Second World War *and* Foul Deeds and Suspicious Deaths in the Isle of Wight. *He has produced several best-selling accounts of criminal cases, in particular volumes on Derek Bentley,* The Wigwam Murder, *and* Jack the Ripper – Quest for a Killer. *But he is perhaps best known for his many novels which include the* Lestrade *and* Maxwell *series.*

Chapter 12

Francis Tumblety – The Man in the Slouch Hat

By Michael Hawley

Francis Tumblety was first mentioned as a Jack the Ripper suspect by Detective Chief Inspector John Littlechild of the Metropolitan Police in a letter to journalist and author George R. Sims, dated 23 September 1913. This letter was discovered by crime historian Stewart P. Evans for sale in an antiquarian bookshop in Richmond-upon-Thames. It pointed to the very real possibility that the Ripper crimes came to a stop because the killer had fled to America soon after the murders.

Francis Tumblety met young Richard S. Norris in New Orleans during intermission at the St Charles Theatre in 1881. According to *The Daily Picayune*, 25 March 1881, Tumblety arrived in New Orleans on Friday, 25 February 1881, and remained in New Orleans for an extended period of time. After the performance, Tumblety invited Norris for dinner then asked if he would come up to his room at the St Charles Hotel to write a letter for him. Norris agreed. While under oath, Norris stated to Judge Gabriel Fernandez in a lawsuit case on 12 May 1905, that Tumblety then opened up his travel trunk and showed him a few items: 'He [Tumblety] told me they [gold medals] were awarded to him by the English Government. Then there was a sort of tray in the trunk, and there were all sorts of large knives in there, surgical instruments.'

Note that Tumblety owned the very same type of knives that most experts agree Jack the Ripper used on his victims. Also, he had possession of these in the 1880s and in his travel trunk, the same trunk he likely used on his yearly trips to London.

Norris stated to Judge Fernandez that the St Charles Hotel room event occurred before Tumblety had been arrested in a 'sort of put up job', which occurred on 24 March, 1881. Norris continued:

> 'There were large knives in the trunk; and then he came over to me, and felt my pulse, and felt my legs. I was smoking a cigarette at the time, and he said, "Throw that away", and he handed me a cigar, saying it was bad to smoke cigarettes. He said the trouble with young men are those cigarettes, and those **confounded street walkers. He said, if he had his way they would all be disembowelled**.' [author's emphasis]

Although at the time of his deposition Norris was a veteran telegraph operator for the New Orleans Police Department, he admitted that in his teenage days he would prostitute himself for men on occasion in order to make money, and it was apparent to him that Tumblety had a sexual attraction to him. Norris stated that in their first few meetings in 1881, Tumblety did not attempt anything sexual and added that Tumblety curiously moved from the St Charles Hotel to 109 Canal Street. Norris then stated, 'One night he took me to his room, and he locked the door on me.' Norris explained how Tumblety threatened him with one of the knives and sexually abused him. Tumblety then asked Norris to have sex, but he refused unless he was paid. Under cross-examination, the attorney asked Norris when this occurred. Norris replied, 'This happened in 1880 or 1881.' Since Francis Tumblety was in Europe during the entire 1880 Mardi Gras season, their first meetings would have been in 1881, which conforms to Tumblety's arrest on 24 March 1881. Note that the sexual abuse occurred after the comments about street walkers being disembowelled.

During cross-examination, Norris explained that these events occurred over twenty years ago, meaning before the Whitechapel murders. How many other suspects are known to not only have possessed the same weapons likely used by Jack the Ripper but have also made such a Ripper-like threat to prostitutes before the murders even occurred?

The possibility that Norris merely lied actually conflicts with numerous points. Norris was married with children at the time of his deposition and worked for the New Orleans Police Department. Admitting under oath that he illegally engaged in male prostitution as a teenager would likely not go down well with his wife or with the police department. Records indicate that Norris had an excellent reputation at the New Orleans Police Department, was promoted to head a department that handled sensitive information, and even retired with multiple awards. Further reinforcing the veracity of his story are the numerous Tumblety mannerisms and characteristics Norris accurately revealed, indicating first-hand knowledge. Norris would not have known about Tumblety's passion for theatre, nor that he often asked young men to write his letters. Norris casually mentioned Tumblety changing hotel rooms. Only recently has it been discovered that Tumblety was in the habit of changing hotel rooms on a monthly basis. Norris also commented upon Tumblety's intersex condition, formerly known as hermaphroditism, which could only have come from first-hand knowledge.

A number of Jack the Ripper candidates have been taken seriously by modern researchers because they were suspected by an important Scotland Yard official involved in the Whitechapel murders investigation. Tumblety fits into this category, and was actually mentioned by no less than three Scotland Yard officials. In late November 1888, Assistant Commissioner Robert Anderson requested all information on Tumblety from Brooklyn's chief of police specific to the Whitechapel murders. In December 1888, a *Toronto Mail* reporter asked First Class Inspector Walter Andrews, a detective named as working on the Whitechapel murders case by Scotland Yard detective Walter Dew, if he knew Francis Tumblety and his connection to the murders. Lastly, Chief Inspector Littlechild, head of Special Branch at the time of the murders, stated in his 1913 private letter to British journalist, George R. Sims, that 'amongst the suspects', Tumblety was 'a very likely one'.

If Assistant Commissioner Anderson had taken Tumblety seriously why did he, along with his dedicated subordinate, Chief Inspector Donald Swanson, not mention Tumblety later on in life? At the time, most in Scotland Yard believed the post-Mary Kelly victim Alice Mackenzie, murdered on July 17 1889, was a Ripper victim, and since Tumblety was in New York, he could not have been the killer. It was only years later that Chief Constable Melville Macnaghten concluded that Mary Kelly was the last Ripper victim. If Anderson had inquired for information out of New Orleans, as he did in other US cities, he may very well have heard about Norris' account of Tumblety carrying around surgical knives in his travel trunk and commenting upon how all street walkers should be disembowelled. Norris said he informed the New Orleans chief of police in 1888. Anderson, as well as Macnaghten, likely had no knowledge of Norris' experience with Tumblety, and formed their opinions without this information.

Using hindsight, police officials involved in the case gave their professional opinions on the identity of the killer. Many decided upon a particular suspect because an eyewitness account matched their favoured suspect's physical description. There are a number of inherent problems with using a person's memory as the determining factor. First, in this case, no one saw the murders, thus it is only an assumption that the eyewitness described the offender. Second, even if they did, their recollections may have been in error. Recently, a compelling study by the Innocence Project at the School of Law at Yeshiva University demonstrated the weakness of eyewitness testimony. It studied 239 cases where the determining factor for conviction was eyewitness testimony. Shockingly, seventy-three per cent of these convictions were overturned by DNA testing. Additionally, surveys taken reveal that most jurors place heavy emphasis upon eyewitness testimony, believing human memory is accurate and unalterable. Psychologists explain that false memory is a reality, produced by a process called memory reconstruction. With valuable kinds of evidence not available in 1888, such as fingerprinting, DNA evidence and fibre analysis, Scotland Yard detectives were forced to place heavy emphasis upon eyewitness testimony. When nearly three quarters of the convictions in one study today are overturned by DNA evidence, it would be interesting to discover how many in the nineteenth century were falsely convicted. In view of this, it seems prudent to be less emboldened about a favoured suspect – to the exclusion of all others – just because a particular Scotland Yard official was convinced.

The very first time the public knew of the notorious Dr Francis Tumblety being arrested on suspicion for the Whitechapel crimes was in major US newspapers on 19 November 1888, after the reporters received the information from the office of New York City's detective department, which was headed by Thomas F. Byrnes. Coincidentally, it was at this time Assistant Commissioner Anderson had contacted chiefs of police from two other US cities about Tumblety.

One day earlier, *The New York World* and partnering newspapers, such as *The Boston Globe* and *Chicago Daily Tribune*, published a 17 November 1888 *New York World* newscable telegraphed from London stating: 'Another arrest was a man who gave the name "Dr. Kumblety of New York".' The reporter who broke the story was *New York World* London Chief Correspondent E. Tracy Greaves. Not only was he ignorant of who 'Kumblety' was but he had no idea that the New York doctor had posted bail the day before. Tumblety was arrested on suspicion for the Whitechapel crimes prior to 7 November 1888. The November and December Central Criminal Court calendars state that Tumblety was initially taken into custody on 7 November but this was for the case in front of Central Criminal Court, the gross indecency and indecent assault charges. Greaves received information that 'Kumblety' was first arrested on suspicion, but was later 'committed for trial in the Central Criminal Court under a special law passed soon after the modern Babylon exposures.' Greaves never met Tumblety at this time, as evidenced by him incorrectly reporting, in the 21 November issue of the *New York World* evening edition, that Tumblety was still in custody. In view of this, Tumblety could not have initiated his connection with the Whitechapel crimes.

Tumblety stated to a *New York World* reporter in late January 1889 that he was slumming in Whitechapel at the time of the murders and had dressed down; a nightly activity he was obsessed with for the rest of his life. Tumblety then explained that the reason he was arrested on suspicion was because of his American slouch hat: 'Now, I happened to have on a slouch hat, and this, together with the fact that I was an American, was enough for the police. It established my guilt beyond any question.' Under sworn testimony in a court case in 1905, Daniel O'Donovan recalled seeing Tumblety in Baltimore in 1901 wearing a slouch hat, stating: 'On two or three occasions during the period of time that I saw him last, he wore a slouch hat, and on one particular occasion I remember he wore a pair of cutting shoes; both the slouch hat and the cutting shoes seemed to brace up his appearance considerably.'

The five stories Greaves released in the newscable on 17 November were all breaking stories on the Whitechapel investigation and never made the London newspapers. In fact, the headliner, the Sir George Arthur story, stated that Scotland Yard was successful in keeping the event out of the British papers. While foreign correspondents, including Greaves, made it a habit of reprinting newsworthy stories from the London dailies, these breaking stories had to have come from a different London source. Greaves admitted in two earlier newscables released on

6 and 9 October 1888, that he had a 'Scotland Yard informant' and since the material was inside information on the case, the 'Kumblety' story clearly came from his informant. Still, Scotland Yard never publicly admitted these stories, including the arrest of 'Kumblety'. This should not be a surprise, since the police were under orders not to discuss the details of the case with the press. This also disproves the claim that Scotland Yard used the murders to mask a different reason for arresting Tumblety–a Fenian connection.

Tumblety had a remand hearing in front of the police magistrate within twenty-four hours of his 7 November arrest, which set his committal hearing for 14 November. Since the magistrate allowed bail at his committal hearing, he likely allowed bail at his earlier remand hearing. There has been confusion by some as to why Scotland Yard would have permitted Tumblety to be released on bail if they were so convinced he was Jack the Ripper. It is unlikely that police officials were convinced, beyond question, that Tumblety was the killer, but they did indeed take seriously this possibility. Also, the writ of *habeas corpus* was in effect in 1888 as it is today, meaning when Tumblety was arrested on suspicion, the police were bound by British law and could only hold him for twenty-four hours once arrested and identified. They then had to either release him or charge him and present him to the police magistrate. Evidence that Scotland Yard took Tumblety seriously is the fact that they committed him to trial for the winnable misdemeanour case in order to get him off the streets. Instead of illegally holding him against his will and losing a lawsuit, they opted to accomplish this legally. However, they underestimated his skill at vanishing; a skill he perfected years earlier.

After the committal hearing Tumblety was remanded to Holloway Prison, but posted bail two days later. The grand jury returned a 'true bill' on 19 November, meaning there was enough evidence to convict at Central Criminal Court, scheduled for the following day. This is when Tumblety knew his fate was prison. His attorney successfully had his court case postponed to 10 December but Tumblety absconded, being spotted in France no later than 23 November. It was not until Tumblety missed his 10 December court case that a warrant was issued for his arrest. Even so, Scotland Yard spotted him in France a full two weeks earlier at a time he was legally out of custody, demonstrating their interest in him was something other than the charge in front of the courts. Note that Tumblety did not escape from England because he was suspected of the murders but due to the realization he would be imprisoned on the misdemeanour case.

Much has been written on Tumblety in the last twenty years, causing entrenched and divergent opinions about him, but the evidence was unduly incomplete. The wealth of new evidence collected recently paints a clearer picture, which includes over forty sworn testimonies of individuals who knew Tumblety during the Whitechapel murders and up to the time of his death in 1903. Francis Tumblety was born in 1830 in rural Ireland with a sexual dysfunction called hermaphroditism and was raised in Ireland during hard times. He arrived in Rochester, New York, at the age of 17, escaping the ravages of the 1847 Great Irish Famine. A resident of Rochester, boat captain William Streeter, recalled young Frank Tumblety and said he was a loner. Numerous eyewitness accounts of people who knew Tumblety at different times in his life corroborate his antisocial personality characteristics and reveal that he never associated with anyone except for the young men he would dominate.

In 1856, 26-year-old Tumblety began his lifelong profession as a travelling, newspaper-advertising 'cure-all' quack doctor. Within three years he had acquired such wealth that he would be considered a millionaire today. It was a life of exploitation focusing upon the upper class; his botanical medicine never actually curing major diseases, but certainly making patients feel improvement for a short period of time. If his quackery was publicly revealed to the extent that he was not making money, he simply left town and exploited another city. He left Toronto a wealthy man, now able to control his future. At the outset, his hatred of women revealed itself. Shortly after Tumblety opened up his very first office in London, Ontario, as a fully fledged Indian herb doctor, the mayor fined him £5 for insulting a local female resident under his care, a Mrs Carden. By 1860, Tumblety had temporarily opened up offices across Canada, ending up at the Atlantic coastal town of Saint John, New Brunswick. His poor treatment of certain women followed as this extract from the 25 November edition of the *Boston Herald* shows:

> 'Dr. Tumblety made his appearance at St. John, N.B... . After a while the more intelligent people got their eyes open to the fact that he was a charlatan, and pretty soon afterward stories began to go round about his indecorus [*sic*] treatment of some of his lady patients.'

There is corroborating evidence of his indecorous treatment of women in Saint John in Tumblety's first autobiography, printed in 1866. He published a poem written about him in a local Saint John newspaper, The *Albion*, and in it we see a statement about his relationship with the area's single women:

> 'Tumblety had a killing air,
> Though curing was his professional trade,
> Rosy of cheek, and glossy of hair,
> Dangerous man to widow or maid.'

This poem also reveals that Tumblety did not hate all women, only single women. The reason for his hatred of 'widow or maid' is also the reason why he had such a hatred of prostitutes; they lured impressionable young men away from a life of homosexuality. Note what he stated in a private letter to young Thomas Henry Hall Caine, his love interest in 1875, about Chinese women used as prostitutes:

> 'In morals and obscenity they are far below those of our most degraded prostitutes. Their women are bought and sold, for the usual purposes and they are used to decoy youths of the most tender age, into these dens, for the purpose of exhibiting their nude and disgusting person to the hitherto innocent youths of the cities.'

This Scotland Yard suspect who owned surgical knives in the 1880s, who had an unusual hatred of seductive women, and who was quoted saying all street walkers should be disembowelled, was even reported to have owned a collection of uterus specimens. While this fact has been known since the 1990s, the evidence confirming this has only recently been discovered. When it was reported in the New York newspapers on 19 November 1888, that Tumblety had stayed at posh hotels along Broadway Avenue in Manhattan, a *New York World* reporter visited these hotels and collected eyewitness accounts, publishing them one week later. The reporter then sought out law firms on Broadway the following day stating: 'In this city he had a little experience with the law, and this enabled the lawyers to worm out something of his.' He first spoke with New York City real estate attorney William P. Burr at 320 Broadway, but then curiously left Manhattan for New Jersey and spoke with fellow New York City real estate attorney Charles Dunham. Since Dunham's office was at 335 Broadway in the 1880s, it is clear the reporter sought out Dunham, as opposed to Dunham initiating a conversation with the *New York World*. Since both Burr and Dunham were New York City real estate lawyers having neighbouring offices, it is highly likely they were daily acquaintances of each other and the reporter heard about Dunham having a Tumblety story from Burr.

Dunham recalled first meeting Tumblety in Washington DC just after the first Battle of Bull Run in July 1861. Dunham claimed to be a colonel in the Army in 1861, and since reports record Dunham as a colonel attempting to stand up a battalion, albeit unsuccessfully, he would have indeed walked around the capital in a colonel's uniform in July 1861. Dunham spoke to the reporter about when Tumblety invited him, as well as other officers under General McClellan, to a dinner, symposium and illustrated medical lecture on H Street. General McClellan's residence was also on H Street. This was printed in the *New York World* on 1 December:

> 'At length it was whispered about that he [Tumblety] was an adventurer. One day my Lieutenant-Colonel and myself accepted the "doctor's" invitation to a late dinner-symposium, he called it – at his rooms. He had very cosy and tastefully furnished quarters in, I believe, H street… . Then he invited us into his office where he illustrated his lecture, so to speak.'

Dunham then commented upon Tumblety's uterus collection:

> 'When the doors were opened quite a museum was revealed – tiers of shelves with glass jars and cases, some round and others square, filled with all sorts of anatomical specimens. The "doctor" placed on a table a dozen or more jars containing, he said, the matrices of every class of woman. Nearly a half of one of these cases was occupied exclusively with these specimens.'

A number of researchers have claimed Dunham lied, since he was a reptile journalist during the Civil War and was known to give deceptive stories to the newspaper. The argument claims Dunham's motivation was vindictiveness and/or an attempt to earn money for his story. According to foremost Dunham expert, Carman Cumming, the evidence shows that during the Civil War, Dunham was a spy for someone in Washington DC, thus his job was to lie. Dunham's expertise was to bait adversaries with false stories. In the 1870s and 1880s though, Dunham was a family man earning an income as an attorney in real estate and his reptile journalism days ended with the war. It is the very reason why Cumming stated that his 1 December interview about Tumblety was 'strange' as it was out of character. We actually have corroboration that Tumblety gave illustrated medical lectures in the early 1860s *and* had a keen interest in anatomical specimens. The *Buffalo Courier*, 31 May 1914, commented upon Tumblety being in Buffalo, New York, in July 1863 selling cure-alls and 'giving lectures with Thespian emphasis.' In *Vanity Fair*, 31 August 1861, a reporter complained about Tumblety's exhibition of anatomical pictures hanging outside his New York office:

> 'In a central part of Broadway – we forget the exact Spot, there are so many there to confuse the eye – the passers by are daily outraged by the exhibition of certain anatomical pictures, which look as if they might once have formed part of the collection of a lunatic confined in a leper hospital.'

Tumblety had every reason to give a medical lecture to General McClellan's officers; a common practice for surgeons in the nineteenth century. Tumblety did not have a medical diploma and he was attempting to convince the general to take him on as a staff surgeon. Being accepted as a military surgeon would have been a medical coup; effectively allowing him to bypass medical school but still gain credentials. His goal was to be accepted by the medical community as a credible, fully fledged surgeon. This is confirmed in his autobiographies, *A Few Passages In the Life of Dr. Francis Tumblety* and *A Narrative of Dr. Tumblety*. Even though the general rejected Tumblety, he claimed that he 'offered' his services as a staff surgeon. Tumblety then claimed to have received credentials for his medical services to France's military ambulance 'during the war' in 1870 and 1871, fulfilling his ambition to gain credibility as a surgeon through military service.

We have corroborating and credible evidence that Tumblety owned the very kind of female internal organ that Jack the Ripper took from two of his victims. In preparation for possibly meeting General McClellan's staff surgeons, it stands to reason Tumblety would have studied anatomical images similar to those he possessed in New York. Dunham stated that Tumblety housed his anatomical collection in travel trunks, so where did he get them? Personally harvesting these organs from cadavers would have given Tumblety the confidence to face military surgeons and improve his anatomical knowledge.

Tumblety's relentless personal drive up until the late 1870s was making money through his quack doctor business. However, the year 1880 saw a significant change in Tumblety's behaviour, most notably in his business practices and his travel. Although he continued to travel to England once or twice a year beginning in 1873, he no longer opened up offices in the US, and began to travel to Hot Springs, Arkansas, Saratoga Springs, New York, New Orleans, Louisiana, and St Louis, Missouri. Tumblety shifted from a life of making money to a life of improving health. He wrote about the benefits of 'hydrotherapy' offered at Hot Springs and Saratoga Springs.

His heart and kidney troubles now dominated his life, and in January 1888 he told a *Toronto Mail* reporter that he was in constant fear of sudden death because of his kidney and heart disease. Here is a man who claimed to be able to cure all disease, yet he could not cure himself. There are numerous accounts of Tumblety claiming women were the curse of the land. Case in point, according to his young male assistant and likely sex interest, Martin McGarry, in 1882 who told the *New York World* on 5 Dec 1888:

> 'He always disliked women very much. He used to say to me: "Martin, no women for me." He could not bear to have them near him. He thought all women were impostors, and he often said that all the trouble in this world was caused by women.'

Note how in the very same year of the murders, Tumblety, a man who was reported to have an anatomical collection with particular interest in his uterus specimens, was in fear of his life due to his heart and kidney disease. How curious that these were the three organs taken by Jack the Ripper.

If Jack the Ripper was a sadistic sexual serial killer, Whitechapel murders suspect Dr Francis Tumblety was not the offender. However, forensic scientist and criminal profiler Dr Brent Turvey PhD and forensic pathologist Dr William Eckert MD, independently studied the Whitechapel murders, specifically the crime scene reports from Polly Nichols to Mary Kelly. They interpreted the offender's behaviour as non-sadistic, observing a lack of sexual assault to the victims, a lack of torture while alive, post-mortem humiliation through mutilation, and display behaviour. Turvey observed experimental behaviour, as opposed to ritualistic, and a need to instil fear or terror in the public. Turvey states: 'They [offender behaviour] describe an offender who evidences both anger-retaliatory and reassurance-oriented behaviors.' Specific to anger-retaliatory behaviours, the offender attacked the very identity of a woman, indicative of misogyny. Reassurance-oriented behaviours come from a feeling of personal inadequacy and are intended to restore self-confidence and self-worth. Collecting souvenirs, such as the organs or Chapman's rings, is a 'token of remembrance' commonly associated with reassurance-oriented needs.

Both anger-retaliatory and reassurance-oriented behaviours fit Francis Tumblety remarkably well. Chief Inspector Littlechild, head of Scotland Yard's Special Branch division at the time of the murders, said that it was 'very likely [the suspect's] feelings toward women were remarkable and bitter in the extreme, a fact on record.' While Scotland Yard's 'record' or file no longer exists, there is an official file in the State of Missouri Circuit Court archives that records numerous accounts of Tumblety's bitter hatred of women, including prostitutes. Tumblety's Baltimore attorney, Frank Widner, stated under oath that in 1902 Tumblety would cover his face with his newspaper when a woman walked by him. Widner recalled an incident when a woman felt so threatened by him that she refused to be in the same room with him. Richard S. Norris stated under oath that he told a number of prostitutes at a brothel, called a sporting house, that Tumblety 'hated your kind of people – your class of people.'

With respect to reassurance-oriented behaviours and deep-seated feelings of inadequacy, Tumblety's New Orleans attorney stated under oath that Tumblety would ask him to read and re-read portions of his braggadocious autobiography to him, specifically, the sections discussing his close friendship with royalty and famous people. Specific to reassurance-oriented behaviour is the practice of collecting trophies. Tumblety had a reason to collect the kidney, heart, and uterus but only one inanimate object was taken from the Ripper victims – Annie Chapman's wedding ring and keeper ring set. Few have a credible reason to explain why Jack the Ripper stole only these items, but if Tumblety was the killer, it is obvious. The only items on any of the victims that represented the male-female emotional bond were these rings, and Tumblety, a homosexual and misogynist, hated this. How intriguing that amongst all of the precious jewellery in his possession at the time of his death, he also carried with him 'two imitation set rings'.

Approximately one month prior to Tumblety's death on 2 May 1903, he entered St John's, a Catholic hospital, for the purpose of dying. He checked in under the alias Frank Townsend, to ensure family members did not know. Curiously, the only other time Tumblety was known to have used this alias was when he left England just after the murders. By 16 May 1903, Tumblety had written out his last will and testament. The attorney, T.D. Cannon, curiously omitted the phrase 'revoking all other wills made by me'. Tumblety died on 28 May 1903, and soon after, Cannon submitted the will to probate. Family members who were ignored by Tumblety contested the will claiming he was not of sound mind and body, therefore the will should be deemed null and void. It was then discovered Tumblety wrote out an earlier will and testament in Baltimore in 1901. It is normal procedure to submit earlier wills to probate in the chance the last will and testament is rejected. Additionally, the executor of the 1901 will, Joseph R. Kemp, petitioned the St Louis Probate Court to accept the 1901 will in conjunction with the 1903 will on grounds that earlier wills were not revoked and it did not conflict with the 1903 will. In so doing, Tumblety's wishes would be fulfilled. The court did not reject the 1901 will but merely concluded that the 1903 will was 'complete'. The 1901 will was simply ignored. Challenging the veracity of the 1901 will was never an issue.

The significance of the 1901 will is to whom he bequeathed a large amount of money. Tumblety gave it to the Home for Fallen Women, the very women he hated most and the same women who were murdered by Jack the Ripper. Why? It was not because he felt guilty, but Tumblety, a devout Catholic who knew full well he was about to meet his maker, was attempting to atone for his sins; in other words, make amends for wrongs in his past.

Michael Hawley is the author of The Ripper's Haunts *and the highly acclaimed* Jack the Ripper Suspect Dr. Francis Tumblety. *He is also the author of a series of three fiction novels,* Curse of the Bayou Beast, Jack's Lantern *and* The Ripper's Hellbroth. *He is a commander and naval aviator in the US Navy (retired), and is currently enjoying a career as a secondary Earth, Science and Chemistry teacher at Tonawanda City High School. He resides with his wife and six children in Greater Buffalo, New York.*

Chapter 13

Person(s) Unknown

By Katherine Ramsland, PhD

A key issue with the Ripper case is that proposing a theory means making a leap over one type of information gap or another. There is much we don't know, and many of the facts can fit several scenarios. Probability analysis helps to choose the most likely, but each speculation has a margin of error. Some theorists assume that investigators in 1888 could correctly link cases, while others claim that Jack the Ripper (JtR) wrote letters or the Goulston Street message. Some accept stereotypes about serial killers and others think that logic turns belief into fact. I address these items as I provide a context for generating a profile of the type of person who would commit the JtR crimes.

Although several approaches to profiling exist, the FBI's criminal investigative analysis is the most familiar, so I use this frame. I've worked in some capacity with several FBI supervisory Special Agents who were members of the Behavioral Science Unit (formerly BSU and now the Behavioral Analysis Unit, or BAU). I co-authored Gregg McCrary's casebook *The Unknown Darkness* and assisted with research on John Douglas' book *The Cases that Haunt Us*, in which he took on JtR. Although profiling has its problems, as a method of linkage analysis it offers a systematic approach.

Mind the Gap

For criminal profiling, behaviour observed at crime scenes is interpreted with probability analysis to derive likely offender traits. For example, based on an analysis of MO, ritual and victimology in many other cases, it's likely that JtR was male. Yet even the most methodical work harbours two types of potential error:

1. Rejecting a true claim as false
2. Accepting a false claim as true

If I say it's false that JtR wrote the letter to George Lusk, but he did, I make the first type. If I say JtR wrote this letter, but he didn't, I make the second. Reducing the odds for one type increases the odds of the other. The ideal is to find the middle ground.

Statistical analysis improves our chances, but this requires representative sampling and reliable measures. In this regard, profiling has been negligent, especially in its fledgling days. No study as yet establishes the method as scientific. It remains an interpretive art, improved with the centralized database and honed with experience. Thus, profiling is vulnerable to not just methodological errors but also cognitive errors.

Criminologist Kim Rossmo has examined the influence on investigation of perceptual sets, or the readiness to perceive something in accordance with one's expectations. Investigators arrive at scenes with a mental frame based on training and experience, which directs their attention. Often it's effective, but it can also cause threshold diagnosis and selective attention. They can miss important clues and misconstrue others.

This occurs because the human brain relies on amodal completion. When we see only parts of a physical structure, our brain automatically fills in gaps to help us make sense of what we're looking at. This also happens with informational gaps. Lacking a complete set of facts, we use plausible assumptions to complete the narrative. However, 'plausible' is subjective and is not necessarily 'true'. Past experience, cultural tales and our knowledge base set us up to see what we expect to see. For example, those theorists who hope to prove that JtR killed within a geometric pattern for an occult purpose will organize the data through this perceptual lens. Facts that don't fit might be distorted, minimized or discarded. This is easy to do when we don't know which facts are most germane to the case.

Additionally, we're prone to information persistence. That is, we often remember something as true even after we know it's been disproven. In 2008, the FBI's National Center for the Analysis of Violent Crime (NCAVC) issued *Serial Murder: Multi-Disciplinary Perspectives for Investigators*. In it, they listed outdated notions about serial killers from the 1980s that they hoped to dispel. There is no profile of a serial killer, they insisted, and it's wrong to think that they're all dysfunctional, sexually motivated white male loners who cannot stop and who want to get caught. Early BSU member Robert Ressler said that for every attempt to state a 'truth' about serial killers, there are counterexamples. Some killers have a victim preference, for example, but many do not. Even those with a preference don't always adhere to it. Still, the earlier notions persist in various media.

When we speculate, we tend to impose our expectations onto the facts rather than using the facts to form testable hypotheses. This is especially true for those who select a suspect and work toward the victims. To best understand who might commit these crimes, we start with the victims.

Victimology

Victimology is the comprehensive study of victim details, including a timeline of their known movements prior to the crime. The goal is to evaluate personal and situational details to accurately place victims along a risk continuum from low to high, and to calculate who they might have encountered, and how. With the victims at the centre, says former FBI profiler Gregg McCrary, we work outward in concentric spheres. Investigators should eliminate those closest to the victims, especially anyone harbouring a motive to harm. The first sphere includes immediate family members, intimate partners etc. The next sphere includes friends, associates, co-workers, neighbours, customers, and distant relatives. The least likely scenario, on the outside circle, is a stranger homicide.

These factors are integrated with the forensic and behavioural evidence to generate likely motives and opportunities. The crime locations help to establish the degree of risk, as do the victims' ages and occupations. Low-risk victims tend to live normal lives. High-risk victims include those engaged in marginal behaviour, such as prostitution, walking at night in a high-crime area, and a desperate need for money.

Unique details can affect how certain factors are weighted. For example, if the car of a missing person is found backed into a parking spot, this might not seem important. However, if someone who knows the person insists that she hated to back her car up, the car's position would suggest that someone else manoeuvered it or forced her to. Her idiosyncrasy gives this factor more significance.

In the JtR case, several things complicate victimology. One is a blind acceptance of investigative theories in 1888. Another is the acceptance of stereotypes about serial killers. A third is the lack of reliable records. We work with what we have, aware of the potential for errors.

Not everyone agrees on when the Ripper murders began, but 'canonically' it was when Mary Ann Nichols, an alcoholic prostitute, went out on 31 August 1888 near to 1am to earn money for lodging. She got drunk. She was vulnerable. At 3.45am her body was found with a deeply slit throat and severe cuts into her abdomen and genitals. The killer had controlled this 5ft 2in 43 year old with a blitz attack, grabbing her around the neck.

The next three attacks during the early morning hours of 8 September and 30 September also involved inebriated, dark-haired prostitutes around 5ft tall, and in their 40s. None was sexually assaulted but all had facial bruising. Annie Chapman's throat was cut from the left, her gut was cut open and her intestines were draped over her right shoulder. Her legs were drawn up and spread outward. Several cheap rings were missing and coins and an envelope had been placed around her. Also missing were her bladder, half of her vagina, and her uterus. Elizabeth Stride died from a deep slash to her throat before the disembowelled body of Catherine Eddowes turned up forty-five minutes later. Her intestines had been pulled out and placed over the right shoulder, and her uterus and a kidney had been sliced out and taken. Her throat was deeply cut to the vertebrae and her face was oddly mutilated. Three metal buttons and a thimble lay next to her and part of her apron was missing (and was found on another street).

On 8 November, Mary Jane Kelly, a blonde (or ginger), 5ft 7in 24 or 25-year-old prostitute, invited a man into her rented room. He slashed open her throat, mutilated her face, and ripped open her lower torso, pulling out her internal organs. He cut a chunk of flesh from her thigh and placed it on the table with the tips of her nose and ears. He also removed her heart and emptied her abdomen, spreading its contents around the room. The uterus and kidneys were placed with one breast under her head and the other breast near her right foot. There were gashes to her arms and legs. Doctors estimated that this frenzy had endured for two hours.

Many Ripperologists accept that the murder spree began in 1888. Maybe it ceased in November or maybe it continued for several more years, and possibly in other locations. We really don't know how many victims can be attributed to JtR, or even if the canonical five should all be included. Distinct differences with Stride and Kelly raise questions. (John Douglas notes that the knife used on Stride was different from the one used on Eddowes. He speculates that it's more likely that the killer had two knives than two lust killers were operating on the same night. Still…he's assuming, based on his perceptual set.)

Later victims have also been suggested, but none was treated like Kelly. Rose Mylett appeared to have been strangled with a cord. Alice McKenzie, a 40ish prostitute, had stab wounds and superficial cuts, along with a slit throat, cuts in the pubic area, and an incision from chest to belly. Francis Coles, a 5ft, 31-year-old prostitute had two cuts to her neck.

So, how do we decide who's on the list? Former homicide detective Robert Keppel, the Seattle-based investigator who'd hunted and interviewed Ted Bundy, took a unique approach to JtR's victimology. To minimize subjective bias, he used the Homicide Investigation Tracking System (HITS) database, a programme within the Attorney General's office that tracks and investigates murders. He entered data about eleven murdered prostitutes in Whitechapel between 1888 and 1891 who've been 'commonly recognized' as possible Ripper victims. After analysis, he found that just six (the canonical five plus 39-year-old prostitute Martha Tabram) were linked according to a distinct behavioural signature that included piquerism (sexual arousal from pricking or cutting the skin), positioning, overkill, display, planning, mutilation, organ harvesting, incapacitation, domination and control. Keppel compared these six to a cohort of 3,359 victims of homicide in Washington State from 1981 to 1995 (one third of them females). From this, he found that the signature characteristics of the JtR victims were rare: 'There were only six records of female victims, one a prostitute, with probed, explored, or mutilated body cavities.'

Recognizing that his cohort has key differences from those in 1888 London, he nevertheless states that this comparison supports the notion that these six victims qualify as being linked to a single offender who was committing sexualized violence. Because it is unlikely to have two such offenders operating in a single geographical location at the same time, the indoor assault on Kelly was the result of an opportunity not offered in the other cases. Blitzing the first four versus accompanying Kelly did not seem to Keppel a disqualifying deviation.

In *Jack the Ripper Suspects*, Paul Williams defines viable suspects from among 333 identified as those accused of one or more of nine murders in the Whitechapel area from 1888 to 1891. He offers Keppel's candidates plus Emma Smith, Alice McKenzie, and Frances Coles. (Smith was killed before Tabram.)

To address our primary question – who would do this? – we must start somewhere. Only Keppel went to the trouble of making a database comparison, so his work offers a platform to create a profile that can also serve those who extend the victim range. The six he identified were white prostitutes with a history of drinking. Five were around 5ft tall with dark hair. They were easily accessible and in need of money, willing to be out at night even in dangerous conditions. At least four, possibly five, were attacked from behind. He considered the stabbing in these cases to be a secondary sexualized mechanism for penetrating and exerting power.

The Method

More than 300 people have been accused of being JtR. The authorities knew of some suspects and researchers have added more. Yet no matter how many coincidences one can muster for weaving a 'totality of the circumstances' case, no narrative has yet closed the case. This doesn't prove that any given suspect is innocent, but a case built primarily on logic and interpretation doesn't prove guilt either. Plenty of cases made on a totality of circumstances that seemed highly plausible have turned out to be wrong.

Let's look first at the profiling method. Howard Teten founded the FBI's Behavioral Science Unit (BSU) during the 1970s in response to increased stranger crimes and cases of serial murder. Prior to Teten's stint with the FBI, he'd developed a way to make homicide investigation more systematic. To learn behavioural analysis, he read Thomas Bond's writing about JtR, along with theories from contemporary criminologists. Then he collected crime scene data from local police agencies. For each case, he prepared a description of the kind of person he thought was responsible. When satisfied, he checked his accuracy against the facts about the convicted offender. The more he practised, the better he got.

Upon joining the FBI, Teten teamed up with Patrick Mullany to teach his behavioural analysis method. Eventually, they offered profiling to local law enforcement. Other agents were picked for training. This became the BSU.

Profiling is part of the broader programme of criminal investigative analysis, which unfolds in stages:

1. Has a crime been committed?
2. What kind of crime?
3. Will the investigation benefit from behavioural analysis?

If so, they develop a retrospective behavioural profile from the case details. They examine key items such as MO, physical evidence, geographical associations, crime scenes and behaviour that can link incidents to one another and ultimately to an offender. The purpose is to focus the potential suspect pool and identify areas for investigative advice. Profiling is educated speculation about the type of person who might have committed the crime(s) in question.

The analysis involves data from police and autopsy reports, including photographs, witness statements, location maps, body position, patterns of evidence, and whether or not a weapon was picked up, or left, at the scene. Wound analysis involves knowing wound types and a reconstruction of how they occurred. Significant factors include the approximate time of the incident, its endurance, whether the offender arrived prepared, the weather conditions at the time (if outside), the crime scene environment and details about if and how a body was moved. Certain factors help to clarify how offenders think – how they entered, why they chose that specific time or location, and who they targeted.

Behavioural analysts must decide which factors are most significant and they rate their confidence about the accuracy of each item. With several cases that appear similar, they perform a linkage analysis, which is the process of identifying distinct associations from the forensic evidence and behavioural attributes. This involves knowledge of rituals, in which the core behaviours are relatively stable. Rituals can reveal an offender's age and experience. Obvious psychopathology and sexual deviance give profiles their most unique detail. When similar aberrant acts show up in several cases, such as biting, dismembering, or distinct cutting patterns, they form a 'signature'.

Richard Cottingham presents a good example. In 1979, he left two nude, beheaded prostitutes in a New Jersey motel room, taking their heads and hands to thwart identification. Both had been extensively bitten, raped, tortured and set on fire. He treated three more prostitutes in this manner, removing the breasts of one. In 1980, one victim screamed loud enough to draw help and Cottingham was caught. This separated father-of-three was a computer programmer for an insurance company. In his home was a trophy room where he'd kept items from his victims. His distinct signature was to incapacitate with a chemical restraint, bind and gag with physical restraints, batter or burn in vulnerable areas, and cut or gouge with sharp implements. The bodies of each victim revealed methodical, prolonged, ritualistic torture. Deviations were related to his attempts to prevent identification, add shock value, or change his MO. His approach to torture and mutilation made it easy to link his victims.

The Profile

From scene elements, profilers deduce such aspects of offender behaviour as whether they have a routine, a vehicle, and steady employment. They look for indicators of how the offender approached and controlled victims, and whether victims were kept alive for a while or killed quickly. Profiling offers basic facts: the offender's age range, racial identity, MO, current living situation, education level, possible military experience, travel patterns, self-image, manner of dress, likelihood of a criminal or psychiatric record, and psychological traits. A profiler might also speculate on a fantasy scenario that compels the offender or estimate the likelihood and location of future attacks.

In 1980, agents John Douglas and Roy Hazelwood added the behavioural continuum between being 'organized' and 'disorganized'. From a small database, they provided a basic guideline: organized offenders tend to be educated, intelligent, personable, aware of law enforcement, narcissistic, and prepared. They clean up potential evidence and often hide a victim's body. They might take a trophy. Yet, with addiction, they tend to grow more disorganized. On this end of the behavioural continuum, offenders tend to suffer from a mental illness – especially psychosis – or be criminally inexperienced. They use weapons found at the scene and fail to notice evidence that can identify them. They often pose or mutilate bodies post-mortem.

However, in a 2014 monograph, BAU agents state that this description has limited use in serial murder investigations: 'The NCAVC has not embraced the organized/disorganized dichotomy for over ten years and does not currently utilize the dichotomy when reviewing cases.' Thus, ideas from past decades about JtR being disorganized might no longer apply. Let's look at a case.

In Florida during the 1980s, Bobby Joe Long was an organized killer. He trolled around with a murder kit and picked up prostitutes, exotic dancers and drug addicts from an area where women desperate for money hung out. No one ever saw him pick up a woman who went missing, so he was careful. He'd beat, dominate, rape, strangle and stab them or slit their throats. Yet, he also did things that might make profilers think he was disorganized. After death, he'd often leave the bodies where he killed them and would pose them for effect. He even broke the hips of one. He committed his crimes in locations where he felt comfortable. Although he was a careful predator, he sometimes acted on opportunity. He would be a mixed type, which is to say that the dichotomy doesn't offer much help. JtR might just as easily be an organized offender (as Keppel suggests) who sometimes behaved like a disorganized one.

Sometimes, serial offenders commit their crimes in a tight area, which draws on geographic profiling. Kim Rossmo directs the Center for Geospatial Intelligence and Investigation, where he applies criminal geographic targeting software to crimes to acquire geographical markers. He generates a 3-D image that exposes the offender's zone of familiarity. From this, Rossmo can interpret the offender's mental map, or perception of the crime area, as well as his likely place of residence or work.

Rossmo once applied his programme to the JtR canonical five. The murders were within a mile of one another and the total hunting ground was about half a square mile. Rossmo pinpointed an area for JtR's residence between Commercial Street and Brick Lane, just north of Whitechapel Road. Because this area had a high concentration of lodging houses, filled with transients, it was difficult to be specific. Examining where the fourth victim's apron was dropped relative to her body suggested a route to the killer's home. JtR, Rossmo thought, was a single white male who lived alone in the general Whitechapel area. He probably drank and ate in the same pubs as his victims and might have known them.

Research reveals quite a few different motives for serial murder. From lust to anger, to greed, offenders kill repeatedly for a variety of reasons. The most familiar type is the lust murderer. In this category we have

Ted Bundy, John Wayne Gacy, Jeffrey Dahmer, Dennis Rader, Richard Cottingham and Ed Kemper. They are generally calculating, prepared and predatory. Lust murder, a sexualized attack driven by a need for power and control, often involves a deviance that becomes addictive, triggering escalation.

Who Would Do This?

Based on probability analysis and revised notions, we can describe the kind of person or people who might do this. From among the more than 300 suspects, we have a range of possibilities, including lone males, lone females, gangs and groups. The degree of mutilation in the treatment of victims, however, significantly reduces the list. Even as 'collateral damage' for proposed political groups, this treatment is extreme. Gangs don't tend to carve out body cavities (although one gang – the Chicago Rippers – did remove breasts).

From the assumed victimology, the assault on sexual areas suggests a male lust killer. Although we've seen a few female lust killers, they don't (yet) assault their victims with knives. A punitive mission killer cannot be ruled out, but lust killers can also be mission killers. They can have an obsessive vendetta and might rationalize their attacks as permissible. Some even think they're heroes or doing God's work. From 1982 to 1984, numerous female victims (mostly prostitutes) were found strangled or stabbed around the Green River in Washington State. In 2001, DNA linked Gary Ridgway to several victims. Under arrest, he showed authorities more graves until his toll reached forty-eight, but he was sure there were more than eighty. He told the police that he was their 'helper' in ridding the world of prostitutes.

Since serial killers generally kill within their racial group, we can narrow the suspect pool to a Caucasian member of one of the prominent ethnic groups in the East End, as JtR did not stand out in a memorable way. People would have seen him walking the streets, but they didn't recall him as distinct. The theory involving a geometric pattern for an occult ritual makes the victims random (wrong place, wrong time), as do the political theories and the lack of evidence for any victims being stalked. These women were readily available. Perhaps JtR chose them over others, but we have no evidence of this.

The killer probably kept to himself and would seem tense and rigid, possibly angry. He knew how to approach and control the victims long enough to kill them in a quick blitz, but he could not or did not want to try to charm them. (Some might argue that Stride's and Kelly's companions, if either was JtR, did address them.) Killing in the open, with a regular police presence, suggests narcissistic immunity, which is typical of organized offenders; they believe they're superior and therefore untouchable. The stealthy blitz approach could also suggest military experience. He was not seeking a sexual encounter, so something else aroused him, possibly the achievement of domination. Since he seemed to want specific organs, he had some anatomical knowledge. His aim was to kill and sometimes to mutilate but not to rob (although one victim was missing her rings). The considerable risk he took suggests that he either knew the timing of police patrols or was repeatedly lucky. If the former (more likely, given the increased police presence), then he was organized enough to avoid witnesses or to avoid behaviour that might inspire concern. (There are witness reports, including from some who were vigilant about the danger, but none was clearly linked to the killer.) If JtR killed according to a geometric pattern, this too suggests an organized offender.

Although early behavioural profiling identified post-mortem mutilation as the act of a disorganized offender, we do see it in some organized offenders. Motive seems to carry more weight for a killer's post-mortem treatment than the degree of organization. Rodney Alcala often posed his victims. When he picked up a prostitute in 1977, for example, he twisted her body into a tight ball on the side of the road. The legs were awkwardly bent to cause the buttocks to spread apart. The top of the head touched the ground between the knees. The right arm was folded under the body, and the right hand was under the vaginal area, with blood-drenched fingers curled upward. This is elaborate post-mortem posing, yet given his high IQ, manipulative charm, and ability to avoid leaving evidence, Alcala is on the organized end.

Likewise, JtR showed disdain for the victims, leaving many posed in a degrading manner. To associates, he would have expressed scorn for women or for prostitutes. He would own knives and practise with them, probably on animals. He would not tolerate being crossed by anyone he considered inferior, especially females.

Whether JtR would communicate with police, journalists or vigilante groups poses a difficult question, if we look at other lust or mission killers. Dennis Rader, the 'BTK' killer, sent notes, poems, and other items in order to achieve fame and a sense of power. Gary Ridgway, a mission killer, sent an odd letter, 'whatyouneedtonoaboutthegreenriverman' to the local newspaper. However, Ted Bundy stayed under the radar. So did Jeffrey Dahmer, Bobby Joe Long, Richard Cottingham, and any number of other such killers. In the case of the Yorkshire Ripper, a recording was sent purporting to be from the killer, but it was from an imposter. Sustained authentic communication is rare.

Victims' ages often help to estimate an offender's age, but only if there appears to be a distinct victim type or tight age range. JtR assaulted on opportunity rather than selection by age or appearance. If he approached from behind, he might not have known the age. There's disagreement on how skilled he was with butchery, but he was probably older than mid-20s. It's possible that this spate of crimes was not his first. (Bobby Joe Long was a prolific rapist before becoming a serial killer.) He'd developed a lifetime of rage against either women or prostitutes. He was most likely a loner, but even if he had relationships or a social group, he'd still spend time alone to indulge in his fantasies and learn his routes. He probably drank to reduce inhibitions (like Gacy, Dahmer and Bundy). He knew how to hide blood on his clothing or he lived close enough to believe he could quickly escape. Even if he knew his victims, he'd feel no remorse for his treatment of them. If he was a mission killer, he'd experience satisfaction with each successful strike.

The last two victims in the canonical series were the most mutilated, indicating an increased need to strike out at women (or prostitutes), dehumanize them, and reduce them to something barely recognizable as human. Even if we eliminated Kelly, the violations to Eddowes attest to an escalated need to mutilate based in anger and desecration. It's likely that JtR did not think of his victims as people. Like other lust killers, he would view them only as a means to his ends. Dennis Rader called them 'projects'. Bundy and Ridgway viewed them as possessions.

As Rossmo states, JtR probably lived in or close to Whitechapel, although since the murders occurred on weekends, it's possible that he used his free days to travel from another area. In that case, he'd still need a place to which to return to clean up and lie low.

Can lust killers stop? It seems that they can, without dying or being arrested. Dennis 'BTK' Rader went for long periods without killing (although he kept stalking) and Ed Kemper turned himself in. So did long-haul trucker Wayne Adam Ford. In 1998, he carried a severed female breast into a police department in California. He admitted to killing three prostitutes and a hitchhiker. He'd dismembered two, keeping pieces in his freezer. From one, he'd removed the head, arms, and legs, and from another the breast he carried. If JtR did stop, it's not because he was sated. He did so for practical reasons. But if he continued, he would not necessarily keep trying to better himself. Bundy treated some early victims more elaborately than later ones. Rader hanged and stabbed some early victims but decided to stick with strangulation. Mission killer Herbert Mullen dissected his second victim but no other.

Since life trajectories for lust killers can differ significantly, I will not speculate on JtR's childhood circumstances. His anger is the result of a rigid temperament plus his reaction to something that happened to him. We can't say what it was, since some people perceive humiliation or neglect with the same reactive anger as others do to physical or sexual abuse. JtR had an active fantasy about assault or murder that made him feel powerful and gave him scenarios for acting out. He could control himself when necessary, but the need to act would be intense. There would be times when he failed because the moment – or potential victim – was not right.

Summary

A good hypothesis fits the facts; it doesn't force, neglect or distort them. Many theorists equate probability or firm belief with the truth, over-emphasizing similarities and/or minimizing items that fail to support their position. Yet, until we know who JtR was, we must speculate. We cannot be certain why he wasn't identified, how many victims he had, whether he wrote letters or whether he moved on, killed himself or was institutionalized.

However, we know about other killers who behaved like him. Lust killers tend to be predatory and prepared. Killers who prepare are generally not impulsive, although they might act on opportunity. JtR's aim was to degrade and mutilate, showing anger and possibly some sense of mission. He knew how to slip away, undetected. Satisfaction lay in domination not in fame.

Dr Katherine Ramsland is an international expert on serial murder and a professor of forensic psychology at DeSales University in the US, where she teaches about death investigation, extreme offenders, profiling, and behavioural criminology. A frequent commentator on true crime documentaries, she consults on equivocal deaths and teaches seminars to attorneys, law enforcement, and writers. The author of sixty-three books and over 1,000 articles, she used Ripper lore in her paranormal novels, The Ripper Letter *and* Track the Ripper *and her extensive work with Dennis Rader* became Confession of a Serial Killer: The Untold Story of Dennis Rader, the BTK Killer. *She has yet to be challenged on her claim to be the Ripperologist of the Lehigh Valley.*

Bibliography

Alison, L., Eyre, M. (2009). *Killer in the Shadows*. Pennant Books.

Andersen, D. (2014). *Blood Harvest – My Hunt for Jack the Ripper*. David Andersen.

Anderson, R. (1910). *The Lighter Side of My Official Life*. Hodder & Stoughton.

Arkowitz, H., Lilienfeld, S. (2010) Why Science Tells Us Not to Rely on Eyewitness Accounts, *Scientific American Mind* scientificamerican.com/article/do-the-eyes-have-it/

Beadle B. (1995). *Jack the Ripper: Anatomy of a Myth*. Wat Tyler Books.

Beadle, B. (2009). *Jack the Ripper: Unmasked*. John Blake Publishing.

Begg, P. (2004). *Jack the Ripper: The Facts*. Robson Books.

Circuit Court Archives. (1904-1908). City of St Louis, State of Missouri, Case Number 31430, Series A.

Cobb, R.C. (2017). *The Diary of Jack the Ripper Research & Conclusion*. Secret Chamber Publishing.

Cumming, C. (2004). *Devil's Game: The Civil War Intrigues of Charles A. Dunham*. University of Illinois.

Dew, W. (1938). *I Caught Crippen*. Blackie & Son.

Douglas, J., Hazelwood, R.R. (1980). The Lust Murderer. *FBI Law Enforcement Bulletin*. *49*, pp. 18-20.

Douglas, J., Olshaker, M. (1995). *Mindhunter: Inside the FBI's Elite Serial Crime Unit.* Scribner.

Douglas, J., Olshaker, M. (2000). *The Cases that Haunt Us*. Scribner.

Eckert, W.G. (1989). The Ripper Project: Modern Science Solving Mysteries of History. *American Journal of Forensic Medicine and Pathology*. 10(2), pp. 164-171.

Evans, S.P., Rumbelow, D. (2006). *Jack the Ripper: Scotland Yard Investigates*. The History Press.

Fido, M. (1986). *Murder Guide to London*. Littlehampton Book Services.

Fido, M. (1987). *The Crimes, Detection and Death of Jack the Ripper*. Weidenfeld & Nicolson.

Fleet, H.L (1922). *My Life and a Few Yarns*. George Allen and Unwin.

Hawley, M.L. (2016). *The Ripper's Haunts*. Sunbury Press.

Hawley, M.L. (2018). *Jack the Ripper Suspect Dr. Francis Tumblety*. Sunbury Press.

Hinton, B. (1998). *From Hell – The Jack the Ripper Mystery*. Bakehouse Publications.

I'anson, N., I'anson T. (2012). *Ripperologist* 124 ripperologist.co.uk. Mango Books.

Keppel, R.D., Birnes.W.J. (1997). *Signature Killers: Interpreting the Calling Card of the Serial Murderer.* Pocket Books.

Keppel, R.D (2000). Investigation of the Serial Offender: Linking Cases through Modus Operandi and Signature in *Serial Offenders: Current Thoughts, Recent Findings,* edited by Schlesinger, L. CRC Press.

Keppel, R.D., Birnes, W.J. (2003). *The Psychology of Serial Killer Investigations*. Academic Press.

Marshall, P., Phillips, C. (2012). *Ripperologist* 128 ripperologist.co.uk. Mango Books.

Matters, L. (1929). *The Mystery of Jack the Ripper*. W.H. Allen.

McCrary, G.O with Ramsland, K. (2003). *The Unknown Darkness: Profiling the Predators Among Us*. William Morrow.

Morton, R.J., Hilts, M.A. (2008). Serial Murder: *Multi-Disciplinary Perspectives For Investigators*. Fbi.gov.

Morton R.J., Tillman, J.M., Gaines, S.J. (2014). *Serial Murder: Pathways For Investigations*. Fbi.gov.

Priestley, M.P. (2016). *Jack the Ripper: One Autumn in Whitechapel*. Secret Chamber Publishing.

Ramsland, K. (2005). *The Human Predator: A Historical Chronicle of Serial Murder and Forensic Investigation.* Berkley.

Ramsland, K. (2017). *The Psychology of Death Investigations: Behavioral Analysis for Psychological Autopsy and Criminal Profiling.* CRC Press.

Rossmo, D.K. (2000). *Geographic profiling*. CRC Press.

Rossmo, D.K. (2008). *Criminal Investigative Failures*. CRC Press.

Rumbelow, D. (1975) *The Complete Jack the Ripper*. NY Graphic Society.

Rumbelow, D. (1988). *Jack the Ripper: The Complete Casebook.* Contemporary Books.

Ryder, S. (ed) *Casebook: Jack the Ripper*. Casebook.org.

Sims, G.R. (1901). *Living London.* Cassell.

Storey, N.R. (2012). *The Dracula Secrets: Jack the Ripper and the Darkest Sources of Bram Stoker*. The History Press.

Sugden, P. (1994). *The Complete History of Jack the Ripper*. Robinson.

Trow, M.J. (2009). *Jack the Ripper: Quest for a Killer*. Wharncliffe Books.

Tumblety, F. (1866). *A Few Passages in the Life of Dr. Francis Tumblety.* Originally self-published in Cincinnati and reproduced at Casebook.org.

Tumblety, F. (2013). *Narrative of Dr. Tumblety*. Originally published at Russells' American Steam Printing House, New York 1872. Createspace.

Turvey, B. (2009). *Forensic Victimology*. Academic Press.

Turvey, B. (2012). *Criminal Profiling: An Introduction to Behavioral Evidence Analysis*. Academic Press.

Williams, P. (2018). *Jack the Ripper Suspects: The Definitive Guide and Encyclopedia*. RJ Parker Publishing.

Index